ISBN: 9781290812269

Published by:
HardPress Publishing
8345 NW 66TH ST #2561
MIAMI FL 33166-2626

Email: info@hardpress.net
Web: http://www.hardpress.net

FIDELITY

GIFT

Printers

S. J. Parkhill & Co., Boston U.S.A.

TO
LUCY HUFFAKER

FIDELITY

CHAPTER ONE

It was hard to get back into the easy current of everyday talk. Cora Albright's question had too rudely pulled them out of it, disturbing the quiet flow of inconsequential things. Even when they had recovered and were safely flowing along on the fact that the new hotel was to cost two hundred thousand dollars, after they had moved with apparent serenity to lamentation over a neighbor who was sick in bed and without a cook, it was as if they were making a display of the ease with which they could move on those commonplace things, as if thus to deny the consciousness of whirlpools near by.

So they seemed to Dr. Deane Franklin, who, secured by the shadow of the porch vine, could smile to himself at the way he saw through them. Though Deane Franklin's smile for seeing through people was not so much a smile as a queer little twist of the left side of his face, a screwing up of it that half shut one eye and pulled his mouth out of shape, the same twist that used to make people call him a homely youngster. He was thinking

1

that Cora's question, or at any rate her manner in asking it, would itself have told that she had lived away from Freeport for a number of years. She did not know that they did not talk about Ruth Holland any more, that certainly they did not speak of her in the tone of everyday things.

And yet, looking at it in any but the Freeport way, it was the most natural thing in the world that Cora should have asked what she did. Mrs. Lawrence had asked if Mr. Holland—he was Ruth's father—was getting any better, and then Cora had turned to him with the inquiry: "Do you ever hear from Ruth?"

It was queer how it arrested them all. He saw Mrs. Lawrence's start and her quick look over to her daughter—now Edith Lawrence Blair, the Edith Lawrence who had been Ruth's dearest friend. It was Edith herself who had most interested him. She had been leaning to the far side of her big chair in order to escape the shaft of light from the porch lamp. But at Cora's question she made a quick turn that brought her directly into the light. It gave her startled face, so suddenly and sharply revealed, an unmasked aspect as she turned from Cora to him. And when he quietly answered: "Yes, I had a letter from Ruth this morning," her look of amazement, of sudden feeling, seemed for the instant caught there in the light. He got her quick look over to Amy—his bride, and then her conscious leaning back from the disclosing shaft into the shadow.

He himself had become suddenly conscious of Amy. They had been in California for their honeymoon, and had just returned to Freeport. Amy was not a Freeport girl, and was new to his old crowd, which the visit of Cora Albright was bringing together in various little reunions. She had been sitting over at the far side of the group, talking with Will Blair, Edith's husband. Now they too had stopped talking.

"She wanted to know about her father," he added.

No one said anything. That irritated him. It seemed that Edith or her mother, now that Cora had opened it up, might make some little attempt at the common decencies of such a situation, might ask if Ruth would come home if her father died, speak of her as if she were a human being.

Cora did not appear to get from their silence that she was violating Freeport custom. "Her mother died just about a year after Ruth—left, didn't she?" she pursued.

"About that," he tersely answered.

"Died of a broken heart," murmured Mrs. Lawrence.

"She died of pneumonia," was his retort, a little sharp for a young man to an older woman.

Her slight wordless murmur seemed to comment on his failure to see. She turned to Cora with a tolerant, gently-spoken, "I think Deane would have to admit that there was little force left for fighting pneumonia. Certainly it was a broken life!''— that last was less gently said.

Exasperation showed in his shifting of position. ''It needn't have been,'' he muttered stubbornly.

''Deane—Deane!'' she murmured, as if in reproach for something of long standing. There was a silence in which the whole thing was alive there for those of them who knew. Cora and Edith, sitting close together, did not turn to one another. He wondered if they were thinking of the countless times Ruth had been on that porch with them in the years they were all growing up together. Edith's face was turned away from the light now. Suddenly Cora demanded: ''Well, there's no prospect at all of a divorce?''.

Mrs. Lawrence rose and went over to Amy and opened a lively conversation as to whether she found her new maid satisfactory. It left him and Edith and Cora to themselves.

''No,'' he answered her question, ''I guess not. Not that I know of.''

''How terrible it all is!'' Cora exclaimed, not without feeling; and then, following a pause, she and Edith were speaking of how unbecoming the new hats were, talking of the tea one of their old friends was giving for Cora next day.

He sat there thinking how it was usually those little things that closed in over Ruth. When the thought of her, feeling about her, broke through, it was soon covered over with—oh, discussion of how some one was wearing her hair, the health of some one's baby or merits of some one's cook.

He listened to their talk about the changes there had been in Freeport in the last ten or twelve years. They spoke of deaths, of marriages, of births; of people who had prospered and people who had gone to pieces; of the growth of the town, of new people, of people who had moved away. In a word, they spoke of change. Edith would refer things to him and he occasionally joined in the talk, but he was thinking less of the incidents they spoke of than of how it was change they were talking about. This enumeration of changes gave him a sense of life as a continuous moving on, as a thing going swiftly by. Life had changed for all those people they were telling Cora about. It had changed for themselves too. He had continued to think of Edith and the others as girls. But they had moved on from that; they were moving on all the time. Why, they were over thirty! As a matter of fact they were women near the middle thirties. People talked so lightly of change, and yet change meant that life was swiftly sweeping one on.

He turned from that too somber thinking to Amy, watched her as she talked with Mrs. Lawrence. They too were talking of Freeport people and affairs, the older woman bringing Amy into the current of life there. His heart warmed a little to Edith's mother for being so gracious to Amy, though that did not keep him from marveling at how she could be both so warm and so hard —so loving within the circle of her approval, so unrelenting out beyond it.

Amy would make friends, he was thinking, lovingly proud. How could it be otherwise when she was so lovely and so charming? She looked so slim, so very young, in that white dress she was wearing. Well, and she was young, little older now than these girls had been when they really were "the girls." That bleak sense of life as going by fell away; here *was* life—the beautiful life he was to have with Amy. He watched the breeze play with her hair and his whole heart warmed to her in the thought of the happiness she brought him, in his gratitude for what love made of life. He forgot his resentment about Ruth, forgot the old bitterness and old hurt that had just been newly stirred in him. Life had been a lonely thing for a number of years after Ruth went away. He had Amy now—all was to be different.

They all stood at the head of the steps for a moment as he and Amy were bidding the others good-night. They talked of the tea Edith was to give for Amy the following week—what Amy would wear—how many people there would be. "And let me pick you up and take you to the tea to-morrow," Edith was saying. "It will be small and informal—just Cora's old friends—and then you won't have so many strangers to meet next week.''

He glowed with new liking of Edith, felt anew that sweetness in her nature that, after her turning from Ruth, had not been there for him. Looking at her through this new friendliness he was thinking how beautifully she had developed. Edith was a mother now, she had two lovely children. She was larger than in her girlhood; she had indeed flowered, ripened. Edith was a sweet woman, he was thinking.

"I do think they're the kindest, most beautiful people!" Amy exclaimed warmly as they started slowly homeward through the fragrant softness of the May night.

CHAPTER TWO ·

He had known that Amy would ask, and wondered a little at her waiting so long. It was an hour later, as she sat before her dressing-table brushing her hair that she turned to him with a little laugh and asked: "Who is this mysterious Ruth?"

He sighed; he was tired and telling about Ruth seemed a large undertaking.

Amy colored and turned from him and picked up her brush. "Don't tell me if you don't want to," she said formally.

His hand went round her bared shoulder. "Dearest! Why, I want to, of course. It's just that it's a long story, and tonight I'm a little tired." As she did not respond to that he added: "This was a hard day at the office."

Amy went on brushing her hair; she did not suggest that he let it go until another time so he began, "Ruth was a girl who used to live here."

"I gathered that," she replied quietly.

Her tone made no opening for him. "I thought a great deal of her," he said after a moment.

"Yes, I gathered that too." She said it dryly, and smiled just a little. He was more conscious than ever of being tired, of its being hard to tell about Ruth.

8

"I gathered," said Amy, still faintly smiling, though her voice went a trifle higher, "that you thought more of her—" she hesitated, then amended—"think more of her—than the rest of them do."

He answered simply: "Yes, I believe that's so. Though Edith used to care a great deal for Ruth," he added meditatively.

"Well, what did she do?" Amy demanded impatiently. "What *is* it?"

For a moment his cheek went down to her soft hair that was all around her, in a surge of love for its softness, a swift, deep gratitude for her loveliness. He wanted to rest there, letting that, for the time, shut out all else, secure in new happiness and forgetting old hurts.

But he felt her waiting for what she wanted to know and so with an effort he began: "Why, you see, dear, Ruth—it was pretty tough for Ruth. Things didn't go right for her—not as they did for Cora and Edith and the girls of her crowd. She—" Something in the calm of Amy's waiting made it curiously hard to say, "Ruth couldn't marry the man she cared for."

"Why not?" she asked dispassionately.

"Why, because it wasn't possible," he answered a little sharply. "She couldn't marry him because he wasn't divorced," he said bluntly then.

Amy's deep gray eyes, they had seemed so unperturbed, so unsympathetically calm, were upon him now in a queer, steady way. He felt himself flushing. "Wasn't divorced?" she said with a little laugh. "Is that a way of saying he was married?"

He nodded.

"She cared for a man who was married to someone else?" she asked with rising voice.

Again he only nodded, feeling incapable, when Amy looked at him like that, of saying the things he would like to be saying for Ruth.

Abruptly she drew her hair away. "And you can sympathize with—*like*—a person who would do that?"

"I certainly both sympathize with and like Ruth."

That had come quick and sharp, and then suddenly he felt it all wrong that a thing which had gone so deep into his own life should be coming to Amy like this, that she should be taking the attitude of the town against his friend, against his own feeling. He blamed his way of putting it, telling himself it was absurd to expect her to understand a bald statement like that. At that moment he realized it was very important she should understand; not only Ruth, but something in himself—something counting for much in himself would be shut out if she did not understand.

It made his voice gentle as he began: "Amy, don't you know that just to be told of a thing may

make it seem very different from what the thing
really was? Seeing a thing from the outside is
so different from living through it. Won't you
reserve judgment about Ruth—she is my friend
and I hate to see her unfairly judged—until some
time when I can tell it better?"

"Why have *you* so much to do with it? Why
is it so important I do not—judge her?" Amy's
sweetness, that soft quality that had been dear
to him seemed to have tightened into a hard
shrewdness as she asked: "How did *you* happen
to know it all from within?"

He pushed his chair back from her and settled
into it wearily. "Why, because she was my
friend, dear. I was in her confidence."

"I don't think I'd be very proud of being in
the confidence of a woman who ran away with
another woman's husband!"

Her hostile voice fanned the old anger that had
so many times flamed when people were speaking hostilely of Ruth. But he managed to say
quietly: "But you see you don't know much
about it yet, Amy."

He was facing her mirror and what he saw in
it made him lean forward, his arms about her,
with an impulsive: "Sweetheart, we're not going
to quarrel, are we?"

But after his kisses she asked, as if she had
only been biding her time through the interruption: "*Did* she run away with him?"

His arm dropped from her shoulder. "They left together," he answered shortly.

"Are they married now?"

"No."

Amy, who had resumed the brushing of her hair, held the brush suspended. "*Living* together —all this time—and *not* married?"

"They are not married," was his heated response, "because the man's wife has not divorced him." He added, not without satisfaction: "She's that kind of a person."

Amy turned and her eyes met his. "What kind of a person?" she said challengingly. "I presume," she added coolly, "that she does not believe in divorce."

"I take it that she does not," was his dry answer.

She flushed, and exclaimed a little tremulously: "Well, really, Deane, you needn't be so disagreeable about it!"

Quickly he turned to her, glad to think that he had been disagreeable; that was so much easier than what he had been trying to keep from thinking.

"I didn't mean to be disagreeable, Amy dear. I suppose I've got in the habit of being disagreeable about Ruth: people here have been so hard about her; I've resented their attitude so."

"But why should you *care?* Why is it such a personal matter to you?"

He was about to say, "She was my friend," but remembering he had said that before, he had anew a sense of helplessness. He did not want to talk about it any more. He had become tired out with thinking about it, with the long grieving for Ruth and the sorrowing with her. When he found Amy their love had seemed to free him from old hurts and to bring him out from loneliness. Wonderful as the ecstasy of fresh love was he had thought even more of the exquisite peace that rests in love. Amy had seemed to be bringing him to that; and now it seemed that Ruth was still there holding him away from it. The thought brushed his mind, his face softening for the instant with it, that Ruth would be so sorry to have that true.

Amy had braided her hair; the long fair braid hung over her shoulder, beautifully framing her face as she turned to him. "Had you supposed, when you all knew her, when she was in your crowd, that she was—that kind of a person?"

His blood quickened in the old anger for Ruth; but there was something worse than that—a sick feeling, a feeling in which there was disappointment and into which there crept something that was like shame.

The telephone rang before he need reply. When he turned from it, it was to say hurriedly, "I'll have to go to the hospital, Amy. Sorry—that woman I operated on yesterday—" He was in the next room, gathering together his things before he had finished it.

Amy followed him in. "Why, I'm so sorry, dear. It's too bad—when you're so tired."

He turned and caught her in his arms and held her there close in a passion of relief at the gentleness and love of her voice that swept away those things about her he had tried to think were not in his mind. Amy was so sweet!—so beautiful, so tender. Why of course she wouldn't understand about Ruth! How absurd to expect her to understand, he thought, when he had blurted things out like that, giving her no satisfaction about it. He was touchy on the subject, he gladly told himself, as he held her close in all the thankfulness of regaining her. And when, after he had kissed her good-by she lifted her face and kissed him again his rush of love for her had power to sweep all else away.

CHAPTER THREE

It was in that mood of passionate tenderness for Amy, a glow of gratitude for love, that he sent his car swiftly toward the hospital. His feeling diffused warmth for the town through which he drove, the little city that had so many times tightened him up in bitterness. People were kind, after all; how kind they were being to Amy, he thought, eager to receive her and make her feel at home, anxious that she be happy among them. The picture of Edith as she stood at the head of the steps making plans for Amy warmed his heart to her. Perhaps he had been unfair to Edith; in that one thing, certainly, she had failed as a friend, but perhaps it was impossible for women to go that far in friendship, impossible for them to be themselves on the outer side of the door of their approval. Even Amy. . . . That showed, of course, how hard it was for women whose experiences had all fallen within the circle of things as they should be to understand a thing that was —disrupting. It was as if their kindly impulses, sympathy, tenderness, were circumscribed by that circle. Little as he liked that, his own mood of the moment, his unrecognized efforts at holding it, kept him within that sphere where good feeling lived. In it were happy anticipations of the life he and Amy would have in Freeport. He had long been out of humor with his town, scornful. He told himself now that that was a wrong attitude. There was a new feeling for the homes he was passing, for the people in those homes. He had a home there, too; it seemed to make him one with all those people. There was warmth in that feeling of being one with others.

He told himself that it was absurd to expect Amy to adjust herself all in a minute to a thing he had known about for years, had all the time known from within. He would make Amy understand; if Ruth came, Amy would be good to her. At heart she was not like those others, and happiness would make her want to be kind.

He saw her face lifted for that second goodby kiss—and quickened his speed. He hoped he would not have to be long at the hospital, hoped Amy would not be asleep when he got back home. He lingered happily around the thought of there being a home to go back to, of how Amy would be there when he got back.

But it was at a slower speed that, an hour later, he traveled those same streets. He had lost his patient. It was no failure of the operator, but one of those cases where the particular human body is not equal to the demand made upon it, where there was no reaction. He got no satisfaction in telling himself that the woman could not have lived long without the operation; she had not lived with it—that was the only side it turned to him. The surgery was all right enough, but life had ebbed away. It brought a sense of who was master.

He had been practising for twelve years, but death always cut deep into his spirit. It was more than chagrin, more than the disheartenment of the workman at failure, when he lost a patient. It was a real sense of death, and with that a feeling of man's final powerlessness.

That made it a different town through which he drove upon his return; a town where people cut their way ruthlessly through life—and to what end? They might be a little kinder to each other along the way, it would seem, when this was what it came to for them all. They were kind enough about death—not so kind about the mean twists in life.

That feeling was all wrapped up with Ruth Holland; it brought Ruth to him. He thought of the many times they had traveled that road together, times when he would take her where she could meet Stuart Williams, then pick her up again and bring her home, her family thinking she had been with him. How would he ever make Amy understand about that? It seemed now that it could not be done, that it would be something they did not share, perhaps something lying hostilely between them. He wondered why it had not seemed to him the shameful thing it would appear to anyone he told of it. Was that something twisted in him, or was it just that utter difference between knowing things from within and judging from without? To himself, it was never in the form of argument he defended Ruth. It was the memory of her face at those times when he had seen what she was feeling.

He was about to pass the Hollands'—her old home. He slackened the car to its slowest. It had seemed a gloomy place in recent years. The big square house in the middle of the big yard of oak trees used to be one of the most friendly-looking places of the town. But after Ruth went away and the family drew within themselves, as they did, the hospitable spaciousness seemed to become bleakness, as if the· place itself changed with the change of spirit. People began to speak of it as gloomy; now they said it looked forsaken. Certainly it was in need of painting—new sidewalks, general repairs. Mr. Holland had seemed to cease caring how the place looked. There weren't flowers any more.

In the upper hall he saw the dim light that burns through the night in a house of sickness. He had been there early in the evening; if he thought the nurse was up he would like to stop again.. But he considered that it must be almost one—too late for disturbing them. He hoped Mr. Holland was having a good night; he would not have many more nights to get through.

He wished there was some one of them to whom he could talk about sending for Ruth. They had not sent for her when her mother died, but that was sudden, everyone was panic-stricken. And that was only two years after Ruth's going away; time had not worked much then on their feeling against her. He would have to answer her letter and tell her that her father could not live. He wanted to have the authority to tell her to come home. Anything else seemed fairly indecent in its lack of feeling. Eleven years—and Ruth had never been home; and she loved her father— though of course no one in the town would believe *that*.

His car had slowed almost to a stop; there was a low whistle from the porch and someone was coming down the steps. It was Ted Holland— Ruth's younger brother.

"Hello, Deane," he said, coming out to him; "thinking of coming in?"

"No, I guess not; it's pretty late. I was just passing, and wondering about your father."

"He went to sleep; seems quiet, and about the same."

"That's good; hope it will keep up through the night."

The young fellow did not reply. The doctor was thinking that it must be lonely for him—all alone on the porch after midnight, his father dying upstairs, no member of the immediate family in the house.

"Sent for Cy, Ted?" he asked. Cyrus was the older brother, older than both Ted and Ruth. It was he who had been most bitter against Ruth. Deane had always believed that if it had not been for Cyrus the rest of them would not have hardened into their pain and humiliation like that.

Ted nodded. "I had written, and today, after you said what you did, I wired. I had an answer tonight. He has to finish up a deal that will take him a few days, but I am to keep him informed— I told him you said it might be a couple of weeks —and he'll come the first minute he can."

There was a pause. Deane wanted to say: "And Ruth?" but that was a hard thing to say to one of the Hollands.

But Ted himself mentioned her. "Tell you what I'm worrying about, Deane," he blurted out, "and that's Ruth!"

Deane nodded appreciatively. He had always liked this young Ted, but there was a new outgoing to him for this.

"Father asked for her this afternoon. I don't care whether he was just right in his mind or not—it shows she's *on* his mind. 'Hasn't Ruth come in yet?' he asked, several times."

"You send for her, Ted," commanded the doctor. "You ought to. I'll back you up if Cy's disagreeable."

"He'll be disagreeable all right," muttered the younger brother.

"Well, what about Harriett?" impatiently demanded Deane. "Doesn't she see that Ruth ought to be here?" Harriett was Ruth's sister and the eldest of the four children.

"Harriett would be all right," said Ted, "if it weren't for that bunch of piety she's married to!"

Deane laughed. "Not keen for your brother-in-law, Ted?"

"Oh, I'll tell you, Deane," the boy burst out, "for a long time I haven't felt just like the rest of the family have about Ruth. It was an awful thing—I know that, but just the same it was pretty tough on *Ruth*. I'll bet she's been up against it, good and plenty, and all we've seemed to think about is the way it put us in bad. Not mother —Cy never did really get mother, you know, but father would have softened if it hadn't been for Cy's everlasting keeping him nagged up to the fact that he'd been wronged! Even Harriett would have been human if it hadn't been for Cy —and that upright husband she's got!"

The boy's face was flushed; he ran his hand back through his hair in an agitated way; it was evident that his heart was hot with feeling about it all. "I don't know whether you know, Deane," he said in a lowered voice, "that mother's last words were for Ruth. They can't deny it, for I was standing nearest her. 'Where's Ruth?' she said; and then at the very last—'Ruth?' ''

His voice went unsteady as he repeated it. Deane, nodding, was looking straight down the street.

"Well," said Ted, after a minute, "I'm not going to have *that* happen again. I've been thinking about it. I did write Ruth a week ago. Now I shall write to her before I go to bed to-night and tell her to come home."

"You do that, Ted," said the doctor with gruff warmth. "You do that. I'll write her too. Ruth wrote to me."

"Did she?" Ted quickly replied. "Well"—he hesitated, then threw out in defiant manner and wistful voice, "well, I guess Ruth'll find she's got one friend when she comes back to her old town."

"You bet she will," snapped Deane, adding in another voice: "She knows that."

"And as for the family," Ted went on, "there are four of us, and I don't know why Ruth and I aren't half of that four. Cy and Harriett haven't got it all to say."

He said it so hotly that Deane conciliated: "Try not to have any split up, Ted. That would just make it harder for Ruth, you know."

"There'll not be any split up if Cy will just act like a human being," said the boy darkly.

"Tell him your father was asking for Ruth and

that I told you you must send for her. See Harriett first and get her in line.''

''Harriett would be all right,'' muttered Ted, ''if let alone. Lots of people would be all right if other people didn't keep nagging at them about what they ought to be.''

Deane gave him a quick, queer look. ''You're right there, my son,'' he laughed shortly.

There was a moment's intimate pause. There seemed not a sound on the whole street save the subdued chug-chug of Deane's waiting machine. The only light in the big house back in the shadowy yard was the dim light that burned because a man was dying. Deane's hand went out to his steering wheel. ''Well, so long, Ted,'' he said in a voice curiously gentle.

'' 'By, Deane,'' said the boy.

He drove on through the silent town in another mood. This boy's feeling had touched something in his heart that was softening. He had always been attracted to Ted Holland—his frank hazel eyes, something that seemed so square and so pleasant in the clear, straight features of his freckled face. He had been only a youngster of about thirteen when Ruth went away. She had adored him; ''my good-looking baby brother,'' was her affectionate way of speaking of him. He was thinking what it would mean to Ruth to come home and find this warmth in Ted. Why, it might

make all the difference in the world, he was gratefully considering.

When he came into the room where Amy was
sleeping she awoke and sat up in bed, rubbing
sleepy eyes blinded by the light. "Poor dear,"
she murmured at sight of his face, "so tired?"

He sat down on the bed; now that he was home,
too tired to move. "Pretty tired. Woman
died."

"Oh, Deane!" she cried. "Deane, I'm *so*
sorry."

She reached over and put her arms around him.
"You couldn't help it, dear," she comforted.
"You couldn't help it."

Her sympathy was very sweet to him; as said
by her, the fact that he couldn't help it did make
some difference.

"And you had to be there such a long time.
Why it must be most morning."

"Hardly that. I've been at the Hollands' too
—talking to Ted. Poor kid—it's lonesome for
him."

"Who is he?" asked Amy.

"Why—" and then he remembered. "Why,
Ruth Holland's brother," he said, trying not to
speak consciously. "The father's very sick, you
know."

"Oh," said Amy. She moved over to the other
side of her bed.

"They're going to send for Ruth."

Amy made no reply.

He was too utterly tired to think much about it—too worn for acute sensibilities. He sat there yawning. "I really ought to write to Ruth myself tonight," he said, sleepily thinking out loud, "but I'm too all in." He wanted her to take the letter off his conscience for him. "I think I'd better come to bed, don't you, honey?"

"I should think you would need rest," was her answer.

She had turned the other way and seemed to be going to sleep again. Somehow he felt newly tired but was too exhausted to think it out. He told himself that Amy had just roused for the minute and was too sleepy to keep awake. People were that way when waked out of a sound sleep.

CHAPTER FOUR

The next evening Dr. Franklin got home for dinner before his wife had returned from her tea. "Mrs. Franklin not home yet?" he asked of Doris, their maid; he still said Mrs. Franklin a little consciously and liked saying it. She told him, rather fluttered with the splendor of it—Doris being as new to her profession as he to matrimony—that Mrs. Blair had come for Mrs. Franklin in her "electric" and they had gone to a tea and had not yet returned.

He went out into the yard and busied himself about the place while waiting: trained a vine on a trellis, moved a garden-seat; then he walked about the house surveying it, after the fashion of the happy householder, as if for the first time. The house was new; he had built it for them. From the first moment of his thinking of it it had been designed for Amy. That made it much more than mere house. He was thinking that it showed up pretty well with the houses of most of their friends; Amy needn't be ashamed of it, anyhow, and it would look better in a couple of seasons, after things had grown up around it a little more. There would be plenty of seasons for them to grow in, he thought, whistling.

Then he got the gentle sound of Edith's pretty little brougham and went down to meet them. She and Amy looked charming in there—light dresses and big hats.

He made a gallant remark and then a teasing one. "Been tea-tattling all this time?"

"No," smiled Edith; "we took a ride."

"Such a beautiful ride," cried Amy. "Way up the river."

He had helped her out and Edith was leaning out talking to her. "I think I'd better come for you about one," she was saying. He thought with loving pride of how quickly Amy had swung into the life of the town.

During dinner he sat there adoring her: she was so fair, so beautifully formed, so poised. She was lovely in that filmy dress of cloudy blue. Amy's eyes were gray, but the darkness of her long lashes gave an impression of darkness. Her skin was smooth and fair and the chiseling of her features clean and strong. She held herself proudly; her fair hair was braided around a well-poised head. She always appeared composed; there never seemed any frittering or disorganizing of herself in trivial feeling or movement. One out of love with her might find her rather too self-possessed a young person.

So engaged was Deane in admiring her that it was not until they were about to leave the table that he was conscious of something unusual about her; even then he did not make out the excitement just beneath her collected manner.

He wanted to show her what he had done to the vines and they went out in the yard. Presently they sat down on the garden-seat which he had moved a little while before. He had grown puzzled now by Amy's manner.

' She was smoothing out the sash of her dress. She sang a little under her breath. Then she said, with apparent carelessness: "Mrs. Williams was at the tea today."

He knit his brows. "Mrs.—?" Then, understanding, his face tightened. "Was she?" was his only reply.

Amy sang a little more. "It's her husband that your friend is living with, isn't it?" she asked, and the suppressed excitement came nearer to the surface though her voice remained indifferent.

He said "Yes" shortly and volunteered nothing. His face had not relaxed.

"What a sad face she has," Amy murmured.

"Think so?" He reached over and picked up a twig and flipped a piece of it off his finger. "Oh, I don't know. I call it cold rather than sad."

"Oh, well, of course," cried Amy, "*your* sympathies are all on the other side!"

He did not reply. He would try to say as little as possible.

"I must say," she resumed excitedly, then drew herself back. "Mrs. Blair was telling me the whole story this afternoon," she said quietly, but with challenge.

The blood came to his face. He cleared his throat and impatiently threw away the twig he had been playing with. "Well, Edith didn't lose much time, did she?" he said coldly; then added with a rather hard laugh: "That was the reason for the long ride, I suppose."

"I don't know that it is so remarkable," Amy began with quivering dignity, "that she should tell me something of the affairs of the town." After an instant she added, "I am a stranger here."

He caught the different note and turned quickly to her. "Dearest, there's nothing about the 'affairs of the town' I won't tell you." He put his arm around the back of the seat, the hand resting on her shoulder. "And I must say I don't think you're much of a stranger here. Look at the friends you've made already. I never saw anything like it."

"Mrs. Blair does seem to like me," she answered with composure. Then added: "Mrs. Williams was very nice to me too."

His hand on her shoulder drew away a little and he snapped his fingers. Then the hand went back to her shoulder. "Well, that's very nice," he said quietly.

"She's coming to see me. I'm sure I found her anything but cold and hard!"

"I don't think that a woman—" he began hotly, but checked himself.

But all the feeling that had been alive there just beneath Amy's cool exterior flamed through. "Well, how you can stand up for a woman who did what *that* woman did—!"

Her cheeks were flaming now, her nostrils quivered. "I guess you're the only person in town that does stand up for her! But of course you're right—and the rest of them—" She broke off with a tumultuous little laugh and abruptly got up and went into the house.

He sat there for a time alone, sick at heart. He told himself he had bungled the whole thing. Why hadn't he told Amy all about Ruth, putting it in a way that would get her sympathies. Surely he could have done that had he told her the story as he knew it, made her feel what Ruth had suffered, how tormented and bewildered and desperate she had been. Now she had the town's side and naturally resented his championing of what was presented as so outrageous a thing. He went over the story as Edith would give it. That was enough to vindicate Amy.

He rose and followed her into the house. She was fingering some music on the piano. He saw how flushed her face was, how high she carried her head and how quick her breathing.

He went and put his arms around her. "Sweetheart," he said very simply and gently, "I love you. You know that, don't you?"

An instant she held back in conflict. Then she hid her face against him and sobbed. He held her close and murmured soothing little things.

She was saying something. "I was so happy," he made out the smothered words. "It was all so—beautiful."

"But you're happy *now*," he insisted. "It's beautiful *now*."

"I feel as if my marriage was being—spoiled," she choked.

He shook her, playfully, but his voice as he spoke was not playful. "Look here, Amy, don't say such a thing. Don't let such a thing get into your head for an instant! Our happiness isn't a thing to talk like that about."

"I feel as if—*that woman*—was standing between us!"

He raised her face and made her look into his own, at once stern and very tender. "Amy love, we've got to stop this right *now*. A long time ago—more than ten years ago—there was a girl here who had an awfully hard time. I was sorry for her. I'm sorry for her now. Life's hit her good and hard. We're among the fortunate people things go right for. We can be together —happy, having friends, everybody approving, everybody good to us. We're mighty lucky that it is that way. And isn't our own happiness going to make us a little sorry for people who are outside all this?'' He kissed her. ''Come now, sweetheart, you're not going to harden up like that. Why, that wouldn't be *you* at all!''

She was quiet; after a little she smiled up at him, the sweet, reminiscently plaintive little smile of one just comforted. For the moment, at least, love had won her. ''Sometime I'll tell you anything about it you want to know,'' he said, holding her tenderly and smoothing her hair. ''Meanwhile—let's forget it. Come on now, honey, change your dress—get into something warmer and go for a ride with me. I've got to make a couple of calls, and I want you along.''

''You know,'' he was saying as he unfastened her dress for her, ''after I knew I was going to have you, and before I got you here, I used to think so much about this very thing—the fun of having you going around with me—doing things together. Now it seems—'' He did not finish, for he was passionately kissing the white shoulder which the unfastened dress had bared. ''Amy, dear,''—his voice choked—''oh, *doesn't* it seem too good to be true?''

His feeling for her had chased the other things away. She softened to happiness, then grew gay. They were merry and happy again. All seemed well with them. But when, on his rounds, they passed the Hollands' and Ted waved from the porch he had an anxious moment of fearing she would ask who that was and their crust of happiness would let them through. He quickly began a spirited account of an amusing thing that had happened in the office that day. His dream had been of a happiness into which he could sink, not ground on the surface that must be fought for and held by effort; but he did not let himself consider that then.

CHAPTER FIVE

The train for Chicago was several hours out from Denver when the man who had decided that it was an uninteresting car began watching the woman who was facing him from several seats away. He was one of those persons with a drab exterior but not a similarly colored imagination, and he was always striving to defeat the meager life his exterior consigned him to by projecting himself into the possible experiences of people he watched on the trains.

Afterwards he wondered that he should at first have passed this woman by with the mere impression of a nice-looking woman who seemed tired. It was when he chanced to look at her as she was looking from the window that she arrested him. Her sweet face had steeled itself to something, she was as if looking out at a thing that hurt her, but looking with the courage to bear that hurt. He turned and looked from the window in the direction of her intense gaze and then smiled at himself as he turned back from the far-reaching monotonous plain of Eastern Colorado; he might have known that what she was looking at was not spread out there for anyone else to see.

She interested him all through the two days. She puzzled him. He relieved the tedium of the journey with speculations on what sort of thing it was she was thinking about, going over. He would arrive at a conclusion in which he felt considerable satisfaction only to steal another look at her and find that she did not look at all like the woman he had made up his mind she was. What held him was the way feeling shaped her. She had a delicate, sweet face, but there were times when it was almost repellent in its somberness, when it hardened in a way that puzzled him. She would sit looking from the window and it was as if a dense sadness had settled down upon her; then her face would light with a certain sad tenderness, and once he had the fancy of her lifting her head out of gloom to listen to a beautiful, far-away call. There were long meditations, far steady looks out at something, little reminiscent smiles that lingered about her sensitive mouth after her eyes had gone sad again. She would grow tired of thinking and close her eyes and seem to try to rest. Her face, at those times, showed the wear of hard years, laying bare lines that one took no count of when her eyes were lighted and her mouth sensitive. Frequently she would turn from herself and smile at the baby across the aisle; but once, when the baby was crowing and laughing she abruptly turned away. He tried to construct "a life" for her, but she did not stay in

any life he carefully arranged. There were times
when he impatiently wondered why he should be
wondering so much about her; those were the
times when she seemed to have let it all go, was
inert. But though he did not succeed in getting
a "life" for her, she gave him a freshened sense
of life as immensely interesting, as charged with
pain and sweetness.

It was over the pain and the sweetness of life
that this woman—Ruth Holland—brooded during
the two days that carried her back to the home of
her girlhood. She seemed to be going back over
a long bridge. That part of her life had been
cut away from her. With most lives the past
grew into the future; it was as a growth that
spread, the present but the extent of the growth
at the moment. With her there had been the
sharp cut; not a cut, but a tear, a tear that left
bleeding ends. Back there lay the past, a separated thing. During the eleven years since her
life had been torn from that past she had seen it
not only as a separate thing but a thing that had
no reach into the future. The very number of
miles between, the fact that she made no journeys
back home, contributed to that sense of the cleav-
age, the remoteness, the finality. Those she had
left back there remained real and warm in her
memory, but her part with them was a thing
finished. It was as if only shoots of pain could
for the minute unite them.

Turning her face back toward home turned her back to herself there. She dwelt upon home as she had left it, then formed the picture of what she would find now. Her mother and her grandfather would not be there. The father she had left would not be there. A dying man would be there. Ted would be grown up. She wondered if anyone had taken care of the flowers. Would there be any roses? She and her mother had always taken care of them. Edith—? Would Terror be there? He was only about three when she left; dogs did live as long as that. She had named him Terror because of his puppy pranks. But there would be no puppy pranks now. It would be a sedate old dog she would find. He would not know her—she who had cared for him and romped with him through his puppyhood. But they had not shared experiences.

On the train carrying her back home her own story opened freshly to her. Again and again she would be caught into it. . . .

Ruth Holland—the girl of twenty—was waiting for Deane Franklin to come and take her to the dance at the Country Club. She was dressed and wandering restlessly about the house, looking in mirrors as she passed them, pleased with herself in her new white dress. There was an excitement in the fact that she had not seen Deane for almost a year; he had been away, studying medicine at Johns Hopkins. She wondered if he would seem any different; wondered—really more interested in this than in the other—if she would seem any different to him.

She did not think of Deane "that way" she had told Edith Lawrence, her bosom friend from childhood, when Edith that afternoon had hinted at romantic possibilities. Edith was in romantic mood because she and Will Blair were in the happy state of getting over a quarrel. For a month Ruth had listened to explosions against Will Blair. Now it was made up and Edith was in sweetly chastened spirit. She explained to Ruth at great length and with much earnestness that she had not understood Will, that she had done him a great injustice; and she was going to the party with him that night. Edith and Will and Deane and Ruth were going together.

They were singularly unmatured for girls of twenty. Their experiences had not taken them outside the social life of the town, and within it they had found too easy, pre-prepared sailing for any real finding or tests of themselves. They were daughters of two of the town's most important families; they were two of the town's most attractive girls. That fixed their place in a round of things not deepening, not individualizing. It was pleasant, rather characterless living on a limited little part of the surface of life. They went to "the parties," occupied with that social round that is as definite a thing in a town of forty thousand as in a metropolis. Their emotional experiences had been little more than part of their social life—within it and of the character of it. Attractive, popular, of uncontested place in the society in which they found themselves, they had not known the strivings and the heart-aches that can intensify life within those social boundaries. They were always invited. When they sat out dances it was because they wanted to. Life had dealt too favoringly and too uneventfully with them to find out what stuff was really in them. They were almost always spoken of together— Edith Lawrence and Ruth Holland—Ruth and Edith. That was of long standing; they had gone to primary school together, to Sunday-school, through the high-school. They told each other things; they even hinted at emotions concealed within their breasts, of dissatisfactions and longings there were no words for. Once Ruth confided that sometimes she wept and could not have said why, and great seemed the marvel when Edith confessed to similar experiences. They never suspected that girlhood was like that; they were like that, and set apart and united in being so.

But those spiritual indulgences were rare; for

the most part they were what would be called two wholesome, happy girls, girls whose lot had fallen in pleasant places.

Ruth wanted to go to college, but her father had kept her from it. Women should marry and settle down and have families was the belief of Cyrus Holland. Going to college put foolish notions in their heads. Not being able to go had been Ruth's first big disappointment. Edith had gone East to a girls' school. At the last minute, realizing how lonely she would be at home without her chum, Ruth had begged to go with her. Her mother had urged it for her. But it was an expensive school to which Edith was going, and when he found what it would cost Ruth's father refused, saying he could not afford it, and that it was nonsense, anyway. Ruth had then put in a final plea for the State University, which would not cost half as much as Edith's school. Seeing that it meant more to her than he had known, and having a particular affection for this younger daughter of his, Mr. Holland was on the point of giving in when the newspapers came out with a scandal that centered about the suicide of a girl student at the university. That settled it; Ruth would stay home with her mother. She could go on with music, and study literature with Miss Collins. Miss Collins stood for polite learning in the town. There was not the remotest danger of an education received through her unfeminizing a girl. But Ruth soon abandoned Miss Collins, scornfully informing her parent that she would as soon study literature with a mummy.

With Ruth, the desire to go to college had been less a definite craving for knowledge than a diffused longing for an enlarged experience. She wanted something different, was impatient for something new, something more. She had more curiosity about the life outside their allotted place than her friend Edith Lawrence had. She wanted to go to college because that would open out from what she had. Ruth would have found small satisfaction in that girls' school of Edith's had her father consented to her going. It was little more than the polite learning of Miss Collins fashionably re-dressed. Edith, however, came home with a new grace and poise, an added gift of living charmingly on the surface of life, and held that school was lovely.

During that year her friend was away—Ruth was nineteen then—she was not so much unhappy as she was growingly impatient for something more, and expectant of it. She was always thinking that something was going to happen—that was why things did not go dead for her. The year was intensifying to her; she missed her friend; she had been baffled in something she wanted. It made her conscious of wanting more than she had. Her energies having been shut off from the way they had wanted to go, she was all the more zest-

ful for new things from life. There was much
in her that her life did not engage.

She loved dancing. She was happily excited
that night because they were going to a dance.
Waiting for Deane, she wondered if he had danced
any during the year, hoping that he had, and was
a little better dancer than of old. Dear Deane!
She always had that "Dear Deane!" feeling after
she had been critical about him.

She wished she did think of Deane "that way"
—the way she had told Edith she did not think of
him. But "that way" drew her from thoughts
of Deane. She had stopped before her dressing-
table and was toying with her manicure things.
She looked at herself in the glass and saw the color
coming to her cheeks. She sat there dreaming—
such dreams as float through girlhood.

Her mother came in to see how she looked.
Mrs. Holland was a small, frail-looking woman.
Ruth resembled her, but with much added.
Things caught into Ruth were not in her mother.
They resembled each other in certain definite
things, but there was something that flushed Ruth
to life—transforming her—that did not live in
her mother. They were alike as a beautiful shell
enclosing a light may be like one that is not lighted.
Mrs. Holland was much occupied with the social
life of her town. She was light-hearted, well-
liked. She went to the teas and card parties
which abounded there and accepted that as life

with no dissatisfaction beyond a mild desire for more money.

She also enjoyed the social life of her daughter; where Ruth was to go and what she would wear were matters of interest and importance. Indeed life was compounded of matters concerning where one would go and what one would wear.

"Well, Sally Gordon certainly did well with that dress," was her verdict. "Some think she's falling off. Now do try and not get it spoiled the first thing, Ruth. Dancing is so hard on your clothes."

She surveyed her daughter with satisfaction. Ruth was a daughter a mother would survey with satisfaction. The strong life there was in her was delicately and subtly suggested. She did not have what are thought to be the easily distinguishable marks of intense feeling. She suggested fine things—a rare, high quality. She was not out-and-out beautiful; her beauty lurked within her feeling. It was her fluidity that made her lovely. Her hazel eyes were ever changing with light and feeling, eyes that could wonderfully darken, that glowed in a rush of feeling and shone in expectancy or delight,—eyes that the spirit made. She had a lovely brow, a sensitive, beautiful mouth. But it needed the light within to find her beauty. Without it she was only a sweet-looking, delicately fashioned girl.

"That's Deane," said Ruth, as the bell rang.

"I want to see him too," said Mrs. Holland, "and so will your father."

Ruth met him in the hall, holding out both hands with, "Deane, I'm *so* glad to see you!"

He was not an expressive youth. As he shook Ruth's hands with vigor, he exclaimed, "Same here! Same here!" and straightway he seemed just the Deane of old and in the girl's heart was a faint disappointment.

As a little boy people had called Deane Franklin a homely youngster. His thick, sandyish hair used to stand up in an amazing manner. He moved in a peculiarly awkward way, as if the jointing of him had not been perfectly accomplished. He had a wide generous mouth that was attractive when it was not screwed out of shape. His keen blue eyes had a nice twinkle. His abrupt, hearty manner seemed very much his own. He was better dressed than when Ruth had last seen him. She was thinking that Deane could actually be called attractive in his own homely, awkward way. And yet, as he kept shaking her hands up and down, broadly·grinning, nodding his head,—"tickled to death to be back," she felt anew that she could not think of Deane "that way." Perhaps she had known him too long. She remembered just how absurd he had looked in his first long trousers—and those silly little caps he had worn perched way back on his head! Yet she really loved Deane, in a way; she felt a great deal nearer to him than to her own brother Cyrus.

They had gone into the living-room. Mrs. Holland thought he had grown—grown broader, anyway; Mr. Holland wanted to know about the medical school, and would he practice in Freeport? Ted wanted to know if Johns Hopkins had a good team.

"That's Will, I guess," he said, turning to Ruth as the bell rang.

"Oh, Will," cried Mrs. Holland, "do ask Edith to come in and show us her dress! She won't muss it if she's careful. Her mother told me it was the sweetest dress Edith ever had."

Edith entered in her bright, charming way, exhibiting her pretty pink dress with a pleasure that was winning. She had more of definite beauty than Ruth—golden hair, really sunny hair, it was, and big, deep blue eyes and fresh, even skin. Ruth often complained that Edith had something to count on; she could tell how she was going to look, while with her—Ruth—there was never any knowing. Some of the times when she was most anxious to look her best, she was, as she bewailed it, a fright. Edith was larger than Ruth, she had more of a woman's development.

Mrs. Holland followed them out to the carriage. "Now don't stay until *all* hours," was her parting admonition, in a tone of comfortable resignation to the fact that that was exactly what they would do.

"Well," said Mr. Holland, who had gone as far as the door, "I don't know what young folks are coming to. After nine o'clock now!"

"That must be a punk school Deane goes to," said Ted, his mind not yet pried from the football talk.

CHAPTER SIX

"Our dance."

With a swift little movement the girl turned a glowing face to the man standing before her. Flushed with dancing, keyed high in the pleasure and triumphs of the evening, she turned the same radiant face to Stuart Williams as he claimed their dance that she would have turned to almost anyone claiming a dance. It was something that came to life in the man's eyes as he looked down into her flushed face, meeting her happy, shining eyes, that arrested the flashing, impersonal smile of an instant before and underneath that impersonal gladness of youth there was a faint flutter of self.

He was of the "older crowd;" it happened that she had never danced with him before. He was a better dancer than the boys of her own set, but somehow that old impersonal joy in dancing was a lesser thing now than the sense of dancing with this man.

"That was worth coming for," he said quietly, when the dance and the encore to it were over and they found themselves by one of the doors opening out on the balcony.

She looked up with a smile. It was a smile

47

curiously touched with shyness. He saw the color
wavering in her sensitive, delicate face. Then he
asked lightly: "Shall we see what's being dis-
pensed from this punch-bowl?"

With their ice, they stood looking out into the
moonlight over a wide stretch of meadow to far
hills. "A fine night to ride over the hills and far
away," he laughed at last, his voice lingering a
little on the fancy.

She only laughed a little in reply, looking off
there toward over the hills and far away. Watching her, he wondered why he had never thought
anything much about her before. He would have
said that Ruth Holland was one of the nice attractive girls of the town, and beyond that could
have said little about her. He watched the flow
of her slender neck into her firm delicate little
chin, the lovely corners of her mouth where feeling lurked. The fancy came to him that she had
not settled into flesh the way most people did,
that she was not fixed by it. He puzzled for the
word he wanted for her, then got it—luminous
was what she was; he felt a considerable satisfaction in having found that word.

"Seems to me you and Edith Lawrence grew
up in a terrible hurry," he began in a slow, teasing manner. "Just a day or two ago you were
youngsters racing around with flying pigtails, and
now here you are—all these poor young chaps—
and all us poor old ones——fighting for dances

with you. What made you hurry so?" he laughed.

The coquette in most normal girls of twenty rose like a little imp up through her dreaming of over the hills and far away. "Why, I don't know," she said, demurely; "perhaps I was hurrying to catch up with someone."

His older to younger person manner fell away, leaving the man delighting in the girl, a delightfully daring girl it seemed she was, for all that look of fine things he had felt in her just a moment before. He grew newly puzzled about her, and interested in the puzzle. "Would you like to have that someone stand still long enough to give you a good start?" he asked, zestful for following.

But she could not go on with it. She was not used to saying daring things to "older men." She was a little appalled at what she had done— saying a thing like that to a man who was married; and yet just a little triumphant in her own audacity, and the way she had been able to make him feel she was something a long way removed from a little girl with flying pigtails.

"I really have been grown up for quite a while," she said, suddenly grave.

He did not try to bring her back to the other mood,—that astonishing little flare of audacity; he was watching her changing face, like her voice it was sweetly grave.

The music had begun again—this time a waltz.

A light hand upon her arm, he directed her back towards the dancing floor.

"I have this taken," she objected hesitatingly.

"This is an extra," he said.

She felt sure that it was not; she knew she ought to object, that it was not right to be treating one of the boys of her own crowd that way. But that consciousness of what she ought to be doing fell back—pale, impotent—before the thing she wanted to do. . . .

They were silent for a little time after; without commenting on doing so, they returned to their place outside. "See?" she said presently, "the moon has found another hill. That wasn't there when we were here before."

"And beyond that are more hills," he said, "that we don't see even yet."

"I suppose," she laughed, "that it's not knowing where we would get makes over the hills and far away—fun."

"Well, anything rather than standing still." He said it under his breath, more to himself than to her. But it was to her he added, teasingly and a little lingeringly: "Unless, of course, one were waiting for someone to catch up with one."

She smiled without turning to him; watching her, the thought found its way up through the proprieties of his mind that it would be worth waiting a long time if, after the wait, one could go over the hills and far away with a girl through whom life glowed as he could see it glowed in this girl; no, not with a girl like this—boldly, humorously and a little tenderly he amended in his mind —but with *this* girl.

She wheeled about. "I must go back," she said abruptly. "This dance is with Will Blair—I must go back. I'll have a hard enough time," she laughed, a little nervously, "making it right with Louis Stephens."

"I'll tell him I heard it was an extra," he said.

She halted, looking up at him. "Did you hear that?" she demanded.

He seemed about to say some light thing, but that died away. "I wanted the dance," was his quiet reply.

CHAPTER SEVEN

It was a June evening a year later that Stuart Williams sat on the steps of the porch that ran round the side of his house, humoring the fox terrier who thought human beings existed to throw sticks for dogs. After a while the man grew tired of that theory of human existence, and bade the panting Fritz lie down on the step below him. From there Fritz would look up to his master appealingly, eyes and tail saying, "Now let's begin again." But he got no response, so, in philosophic dog fashion, soon stretched out for a snooze.

The man was less philosophic: he had not that gift of turning from what he wanted to what he could have.

A little later he would go to the rehearsal of the out-of-door play the Country Club was getting ready to give. Ruth Holland would be there: she too was in the play. Probably he would take her home, for they lived in the same neighborhood and a little apart from the others. It was Mrs. Lawrence who, the night of the first rehearsal, commented with relief for one more thing smoothly arranged upon their going the same way.

For five weeks now they had been going the

same way; their talk on those homeward walks had been the lightest of talk, for the most part a laughing over things that had happened during the rehearsal. And yet the whole world had become newly alive, until tonight it seemed a tremulous, waiting world. That light talk had been little more than a pulling back from the pauses, little more than retreat, safeguard. It was the pauses that lived on with him, creating his dreams; her face as she turned it to him after a silence would sometimes be as if she had been caught into that world touched to new life—world that waited. They would renew the light talk as if coming back from something.

He let himself slip into dreaming now; he had told himself that that, at least, could work no one harm, and in quiet hours, when he smoked, relaxed, he was now always drawn over where he knew he must not let himself go. It was as if something stronger than he was all around him. One drooping hand caressed his dog; he drew in the fragrance from a rose trellis near by; the leaves of the big tree moved with a gentle little sound, a sound like the whisper of sweet things; a bird note—goodnight—floated through the dusk. He was a man whom those things reached. And in the last year, particularly in those last weeks, it had come to be that all those things were one with Ruth Holland; to open to them meant being drawn to her.

He would tell himself that that was wrong, mad; nothing he could tell himself seemed to have any check on that pull there was on him in the thought of her. He and his wife were only keeping up the appearance of marriage. For two years he had not had love. He was not a man who could learn to live without it. And now all the desirableness of life, hunger for love, the whole of earth's lure seemed to break in through the feeling for this girl—that wrong, wonderful feeling that had of itself flushed his heart to new life.

Sharply he pulled himself about, shifting position as if to affirm his change of thinking. It turned him from the outer world to his house; he saw Marion sitting in there at her desk writing a letter. He watched her, thinking about her, about their lives. She was so poised, so cool; it would seem, so satisfied. Was she satisfied? Did denial of life leave nothing to be desired? If there were stirrings for living things they did not appear to disturb her calm surface. He wondered if a night like this never touched old things in her, if there were no frettings for what she had put out of her life.

He watched her small, beautifully shaped dark head, the fine smooth hair that fell over the little ear he had loved to kiss! She was beautiful; it was her beauty that had drawn him to her. She was more beautiful than Ruth Holland, through whom it seemed all the beauty of the world reached him. Marion's beauty was a definite separate thing; his face went tender as he thought how Ruth Holland only grew beautiful in beauty, as if it broke through her, making her.

Once more he moved sharply, disturbing the little dog at his feet; he realized where his thoughts had again gone, how looking at his wife it was to this other girl he was drawn, she seeming near him and Marion apart. He grew miserable in a growing feeling of helplessness, in a sense of waiting disaster. It was as if the whole power of life was drawing him on to disaster. Again that bird call floated through the dusk; the gentle breeze stirred the fragrance of flowers; it came to seem that the world was beautiful that it might ensnare him, as if the whole power of the sweetness of life was trying to pull him over where he must not go. He grew afraid. He got the feeling that he must do something—that he must do it at once. After he had sat there brooding for half an hour he abruptly got up and walked in where his wife was sitting.

"Marion," he began brusquely, "I should like to speak to you."

She had been sitting with her back to the door; at his strange address of her she turned round in surprise; she looked startled when she saw his strained face.

"We've been married about six years, isn't it?"

He had come a little nearer, but remained standing. He still spoke in that rough way. She did not reply but nodded slightly, flushing.

"And now for two years we—haven't been married?"

She stiffened and there was a slight movement as if drawing back. She did not answer.

"I'm thirty-four and you're a little less than that." He paused and it was more quietly, though none the less tensely that he asked: "Is it your idea that we go through life like this?"

She was gathering together the sheets of paper on her desk. She did not speak.

"You were angry at me—disappointed. I grant you, as I did at the time, that it was a silly affair, not—not creditable. I tried to show you how little it meant, how it had—just happened. Two years have passed; we are still young people. I want to know—do you intend this to go on? Are our whole lives to be spoiled by a mere silly episode?"

She spoke then. "Mere silly episode," she said with a high little laugh, "seems rather a slight way to dispose of the fact that you were untrue to me." She folded her letter and was putting it in the envelope. It would not go in and she refolded it with hands not steady.

He did not speak until she had sealed the letter and was sitting there looking down at her hands, rubbing them a little, as if her interest was in them. "Marion," he asked, and his voice shook now, "doesn't it ever seem to you that life is too

valuable to throw away like this?'' She made no
reply and angered by her unresponsiveness he added sharply: ''It's rather dangerous, you know.''

She looked up at him then. ''Is this a threat?''
she asked with a faint, mocking smile.

He moved angrily, starting to leave the room.
''Have you no feeling?'' he broke out at her. ''Is
this all you *want* from life?''

She colored and retorted: ''It was not the way
I expected to live when I married you.''

He stood there doggedly for a moment, his face
working with nervousness. ''I think then,'' he
said roughly, ''that we'd better be decent enough
to get a divorce!'' At what he saw in her face
he cried passionately: ''Oh no, you don't believe
in divorce—but you believe in *this!*''

''Was it *I* who brought it about?'' she cried,
stung to anger.

She had risen and for an instant they stood
there facing each other. ''Haven't you any humanity?'' he shot rudely at her. ''Don't you ever
feel?''

She colored but drew back, in command of herself again. ''I do not desecrate my feelings,''
she said with composure; ''I don't degrade my
humanity.''

''Feeling—humanity!'' he sneered, and wheeled
about and left the room.

He started at once for his rehearsal. He was
trembling with anger and yet underneath that pas-

sion was an unacknowledged feeling of relief. It had seemed that he had to do something; now he told himself that he had done what he could. He walked slowly through the soft night, seeking control. He was very bitter toward Marion, and yet in his heart he knew that he had asked for what he no longer wanted. He quickened his step toward the Lawrences', where they were to hold the rehearsal, where he would find Ruth Holland.

CHAPTER EIGHT

After the maelstrom of passion had thrown her out where life left her time to think about what she had felt, Ruth Holland would wonder whether there was something in her that made her different from the good people of the world. Through it all she did not have the feeling that it would seem she would have; what she did did not make her feel as she knew, when she came to think it out, she would be supposed to feel about such a thing. In hours that would be most condemned she had had a simple feeling of life as noble. What would be called the basest things she had done had seemed to free something within her that made her more kind, more generous, more tender, made her as a singing part of a fine, beautiful world. Her degradation had seemed to burn away all that was not pure, giving her a sense of being lifted up; it was as if through this illicit love a spiritual fount was unsealed that made her consciously one with life at its highest. Afterwards she wondered about it, wondered whether she was indeed different from people who were good, or whether it could be that hearts had been shown, not as they were, but as it was deemed meet they should be shown.

When she and Deane, with Edith and Will Blair, went home from the dance that night, something new breathed through the night. It was hard to join in the talk; she wanted to be alone, alone with that new stir. She was gentle with Deane as they stood for a moment at the door. She felt tender toward him. A little throb of excitement in her voice, the way her eyes shone, made him linger there with her a moment or two. It was as if he wanted to say something but the timid, clumsy words he spoke just before leaving were, ''That sure is a peach of a dress. You had them all beat tonight, Ruth,'' and Ruth went into the house knowing now for sure how impossible it would be ever to think of Deane ''that way.'' In the hour before she went to sleep what she meant by ''that way'' was a more living thing than it had ever been before.

The year which followed was not a happy one; it was a disturbed, a fretted year; girlhood was too ruffled for contentment in the old things, and yet she was not swept on. The social life of the town brought her and Stuart Williams together from time to time. They always had several dances together at the parties. It was those dances that made the party for her. If he were not there, the evening was a dead thing. When he was, something came to life in her that made everything different. She would be excited; she had color; her eyes shone. It made her gay, as an intoxicant may make one gay. Though when she danced with him she went curiously silent; that stilled her. After going home she would lie awake for hours, live over every slightest thing he had said, each glance and move. It was an unreal world of a new reality—quickened, heightened, delirious, promising.

In that first year she sometimes wondered if it was what would be called a flirtation. It did not seem so to her, and it was true that after that first night at the Country Club the quality of flirtation somehow fell away. Afterwards, when it became the thing that made her life, she looked back in wonderment to the light little way it had begun. That too did not seem as it should be—that a thing of such tremendous and ruthless power, a thing that swept her whole life on at its will, should come into life in a way so slight, so light, so much of chance. At first it was just the faintest little breath; but it stirred something, it grew, it became a great wind that there was no force anywhere to combat. In that first year there was between them, unspoken of, a consciousness of feeling touched in the other, a sense of the disturbance, the pull. It seemed very wonderful to her that just his presence in the room could make her feel alive in a way she had never felt alive before. And it was sweet almost beyond belief, it was intoxicating, to come to know that her presence was that same strange wine to him. She had seen his eyes anxiously rove a crowded room and stop with her, his face lighting. She loved remembering his face once at a card party of the older crowd where she had been tardily summoned by a disappointed hostess. He had been in the room several minutes, she watching him unseen. He was not looking anxiously about this time, as she had seen him do at the dancing parties. She thought he looked tired as he and his wife came in, not as if anticipating pleasure. Then he saw her and she never forgot that leap of glad surprise in his eyes, the quick change in him, the new buoyancy.

She would have supposed, thinking back to it afterward, that she would have drawn back; that before feeling really broke through, a girl such as she, reared as she had been, a part of such a society, a girl, as they afterward said, who should have known right from wrong would, in that time of its gathering, have drawn back from so shameful a thing as love with another woman's husband. It was as mystifying to her that she did not fight against it as it was that it should have come. She did not understand the one nor the other. Certainly it was not as she would have supposed it would be had she heard of such a thing. Something seemed to have caught her up, to have taken her. She was appalled at times, but the truth was that she was carried along almost without resistance; ideas of resistance were there, but they were pale things, not charged with power. She would suppose, had she known the story only through hearing it, that she would have thought intensely and become wretched in the thought of Mrs. Williams. Perhaps if Mrs. Williams had been a plain little woman, or a sad looking one, that would have come home to her harder. But one would not readily pity Marion Williams, or get the feeling of wronging her. As Marion Averley she had been the reigning girl of the town. Ruth, ten years younger, had not come far enough out from her little girl's awe of Marion Averley, the young lady, to be quick in getting the feeling of wronging Marion Williams, the wife. Perhaps one would be more slow in getting a feeling of wronging the most smartly dressed woman in the room than would be the case with the wife dowdy or drab. Mrs. Williams, while not radiating happiness, seemed somehow impervious to unhappiness, and certainly to any hurt another woman could bring her. She had an atmosphere of high self-valuation. While she never appeared to be having an especially good time she gave a sense of being perfectly able to command a better one had it pleased her to do so.

People had supposed that Marion Averley would make a brilliant marriage. Her grandfather had made his money in lumber, in those early days of lumber kings on the Mississippi. Locally they were looked upon as rich people. Marion had gone to a fashionable school, to Europe. People of the town said there was nothing "local" about her. Other girls had been as much away and yet would return seeming just a part of the town. That was why everyone was surprised when the Averleys announced Marion's engagement to Stuart Williams. He was distinctly local and his people were less important than hers. He had come home from college and gone into business. His father had a small canning factory, an industry that for years had not grown much, remaining one of the small concerns in a town of rapidly growing manufactories. Stuart went into business with his father and very soon there were expansions, new methods; he brought imagination to bear upon it, and a big fund of young man's energy, until it rapidly came up from a "nice little business" to one of the things that counted in the town. He had a talent for business; his imagination worked that way and he was what they called a hustler. He soon became a part of a number of things, both personal affairs and matters of public concern. He came to be alluded to as one of the prominent young business men. Even before Marion Averley married him people were saying that he would make money.

They liked her for marrying him. They said it showed that there was more to her than they had supposed, that there was warmth she did not show. For she must have married him for the

good old reason that she had fallen in love with
him. Their engagement brought Stuart Williams
into a new social conspicuousness, though he had
the qualities—in particular a certain easy, sunny
manner—that had made him popular all along.
During the engagement people spoke of the way
Marion seemed to thaw out; they liked her much
better than they had in the days of being awed
by her sophistication, her aloofness.

After their marriage the Williams' were leaders
of the young married set. Their house was the
gayest place in town; Stuart Williams had the
same talent in hospitality that he had for business—growing, perhaps, out of the same qualities.
He was very generally and really deeply liked;
they called him a good fellow, a lovable chap.
For about four years people spoke of it as a successful marriage, though there were no children.
And then, just what it was no one knew, but the
Williams' began to seem different, going to their
house became a different thing. The people who
knew Marion best had a feeling that she was not
the same after the visit of that gay little Southern
matron whom she had known in school at Wash-
ington. It was very gay at the Williams' through
that visit, and then Marion said she was tired out
and they were going to draw in for a little, and
somehow they just never seemed to emerge from
that drawing in. Her friends wondered; they
talked about how Stuart and this friend of

Marion's had certainly hit it off wonderfully; some of them suspected, but Marion gave no confidences. She seemed to carry her head higher than ever; in fact, in some curious way she seemed to become Marion Averley again while Stuart Williams concentrated more and more upon the various business affairs he was being drawn into. It came about that the Williams' were less and less mentioned when the subject of happy marriages was up, and when time had swung Ruth Holland and Edith Lawrence into the social life of the town it was the analytical rather than the romantically minded citizens who were talking about them.

Perhaps life would have been quite another thing for a number of people if the Country Club had not decided to replenish its treasury by giving a play. Mrs. Lawrence was chairman of the entertainment committee. That naturally brought Edith and Ruth into the play, and one night after one of those periods of distraction into which the organizer of amateur theatricals is swept it was Mrs. Lawrence who exclaimed, ''Stuart Williams! Why couldn't he do that part?''—and Stuart Williams, upon learning who was in the cast, said he would see what he could do with it.

Again, at the close of the first rehearsal, as they stood about in the hall at the Lawrences', laughing over mishaps, it was Mrs. Lawrence who said,

"You and Ruth go the same way, don't you, Stuart?"

Tonight they were going that way after the final rehearsal. It was later than usual; they went slowly, saying little. They had fallen silent as they neared Ruth's home; they walked slowly and in silence outside the fence; paused an instant at the gate, then, very slowly, started up the walk which led to the big white square house and came to a stop beneath the oak tree which was so near the house that its branches brushed the upper window panes.

They stood there silent; the man knew that he ought to go at once; that in that silence the feeling which words had so thinly covered would break through and take them. But knowing he should go seemed without power to make him go. He watched the girl's slightly averted face. He knew why it was averted. He felt sure that he was not alone in what he felt.

And so he stood there in the sweetness of that knowing, the sweetness of that understanding why she held herself almost rigid like that, feeling surging higher in him in the thought that she too was fighting feeling. The breeze moved the hair on her temples; he could see the throb in her uncovered throat, her thin white dress moving over her quick breathing. Life was in her, and the desire for life. She seemed so tender, so sensitive.

He moved a step nearer her, unable to deny himself the sweetness of confirming what it was so wonderful to think. "I won't be taking you home tomorrow night," he said.

She looked at him, then swiftly turned away, but not before he had seen her eyes.

"Shall you care?" he pressed it, unsteadily.

He knew by her high head, her tenseness, that she was fighting something back; and he saw the quivering of her tender mouth.

She cared! She *did* care. Here was a woman who cared; a woman who wanted love—his love; a woman for whom life counted, as it counted for him. After barren, baffled days, days of denial and humiliation, the sweetness of being desired possessed him overwhelmingly as they stood there in the still, fragrant night before the darkened house.

He knew that he must go; he *had* to go; it was go now, or—. But still he just stood there, unable to do what he knew he should do, reason trying to get hold of that moment of gathering passion, training striving to hold life.

It was she who brought them together. With a smothered passionate little sob she had swayed toward him, and then she was in his arms and he was kissing her wet eyes, that tender mouth, the slim throbbing throat.

CHAPTER NINE

There followed three years of happiness wrung from wretchedness, years in which the splendor of love would blaze through the shame of concealment, when joy was always breaking out through fear, when moments of beautiful peace trembled there in the ugly web of circumstance. Life was flooded with beauty by a thing called shameful.

Her affairs as a girl went on just the same; the life on the surface did not change. She continued as Ruth Holland—the girl who went to parties with the boys of her own set, one of her particular little circle of girls, the chum of Edith Lawrence, the girl Deane Franklin liked best. But a life grew underneath that—all the time growing, crowding. She appeared to remain a girl after passion had swept her over into womanhood. To be living through the most determining, most intensifying experience of life while she appeared only to be resting upon the surface was the harassing thing she went through in those years before reality came crashing through pretence and disgrace brought relief.

She talked to but one person in those years. That was Deane. The night he told her that he loved her she let him see.

That was more than a year after the night Stuart Williams took her home from that last rehearsal; Deane was through school now and had come home to practice medicine. She had felt all along that once he was at home for good she might have to tell Deane; not alone because he would interfere with her meetings with Stuart, but because it seemed she could not bear the further strain of pretending with him. And somehow she would particularly hate pretending with Deane. Though the night she did let him see it was not that there was any determination for doing so, but because things had become too tense that night and she had no power to go on dissembling.

It began in irritation at him, the vicious irritation that springs out against the person who upsets a plan he knows nothing about, and cannot be told of.

She had come in from an errand down town and was about to dress hurriedly to go over to Edith's for dinner. She was going to make some excuse for getting away from there early and would have an hour with Stuart, one of those stolen hours that often crowded, agitated, a number of the hours before it, one of those hours of happiness when fear always stood right there, but when joy had a marvellous power to glow in an atmosphere of ugly things. A few nights before she had tried to arrange one of those times, and just as she was about to leave the house, saying

some vague thing about running in somewhere—
there was no strict surveillance on members of
the Holland household—a friend who had been
very ill and was just beginning to go about had
come to see her and she had been obliged to sit
there through the hour she had been living for,
striving to crowd down what she was feeling and
appear delighted that her friend was able to be
about, chatting lightly of inconsequential things
while she could think of nothing but Stuart waiting for her, had had to smile while she wanted to
sob in the fury of disappointed passion.

The year had brought many disappointments
like that, disappointments which found their way
farther into the spirit because they dared not show
on the surface. Of late there had been so many
of them that it was growing hard to hold from her
manner her inner chafing against them. There
were times when all the people who loved her
seemed trying to throw things in her way, and it
was the more maddening because blindly done.
It was hurting her relations with people; she hated
them when they blunderingly stepped in the way
of the thing that had come to mean everything to
her.

She was particularly anxious about this night
for Stuart was going out of town on a business
trip and she would not see him again for more
than a week. It was her grandfather who made
the first difficulty; as she was going up the stairs

he called, "You going over to the Lawrences' tonight, Ruth?"

When she had answered yes he continued: "It wouldn't be much out of your way, would it, to run on over to the Allens'?"

She hesitated; anything her grandfather asked of her was hard to refuse, not only because she loved him and because he was old, but because it hurt her to see how he missed the visiting around among his old friends that his rheumatism had of late cut him off from.

"Why—no," she answered, wondering just how she could get it in, for it did take her out of her way, and old Mr. Allen would want to talk to her; it was going to be hard to get away from Edith's anyway, and the time would be so short, for Stuart would have to leave for his train at half past nine. She quickly decided that she would go over there before dinner, even though it made her a little late. Maybe she didn't need to comb her hair, after all.

She was starting up the stairs when her grandfather called: "Wait a minute. Come here, Ruth."

She came back, twirling the fingers of one hand nervously. Her grandfather was fumbling in the drawer of his secretary. "I want you to take this letter—tell him I got it yesterday—" He stopped, peering at the letter; Ruth stood there with hand clenched now, foot tapping. "Why no, that's not the one,'' he rambled on; ''I must have put it up above here. Or could it—''

''Oh, I'm in a hurry, grandfather!'' cried the girl.

He closed the drawer and limped over to his chair. ''Just let it go, then,'' he said in the hurt voice of one who has been refused a thing he cannot do for himself.

''Now, grandfather!'' Ruth cried, swiftly moving toward him. ''How can you be so *silly*— just because I'm a little nervous about being late!''

''Seems to me you're always a little nervous about something lately,'' he remarked, rising and resuming the leisurely search for the letter. ''You young folks make such hard work of your good times nowadays. Anybody'd think you had the world on your shoulders.''

Ruth made no reply, standing there as quietly as she could, waiting while her grandfather scanned a letter. ''Yes, this is the one,'' he finally said. ''You tell him—'' She had the letter and was starting for the stairs while listening to what she was to tell, considering at the same time how she'd take the short cut across the high-school ball park—she could make it all right by half past six. Feeling kindly toward her grandfather because it was going to be all right, after all, she called back brightly: ''Yes, grandfather, I'll get it to him; I'll run right over there with it first thing.''

"Oh, look here, Ruth!" he cried, hobbling out
to the hall. "Don't do that! I want you to go
in the evening. He'll not be home till eight
o'clock. He's going—"

"Yes, grandfather," she called from the head
of the stairs in a peculiarly quiet voice. "I see.
It's all right."

Then she could not find the things she wanted
to put on. There was a button off her dress and
her thread broke in sewing it. She was holding
herself very tight when her mother came leisurely
into the room and stood there commenting on the
way Ruth's hair was done, on the untidiness of
her dressing-table, mildly reproving her for a
growing carelessness. Then she wandered along
about something Ruth was to tell Edith's mother.
Ruth, her trembling fingers tangling her thread,
was thinking that she was always to tell somebody
something somebody else had said, take something
from one person to another. The way people were
all held together in trivial things, that thin, seemingly purposeless web lightly holding them together was eternally throwing threads around her,
keeping her from the one thing that counted.

"There!" escaped from her at last, breaking
the thread and throwing the dress over her head.
Her mother sauntered over to fasten it for her,
pausing to note how the dress was wearing out,
speaking of the new one Ruth must have soon,
and who should make it. "Oh, I'm in a *hurry,*

mother!'' Ruth finally cried when her mother
stopped to consider how the dress would have had
more style if, instead of buttoning down the back,
it had fastened under that fold.

''Really, my dear,'' Mrs. Holland remonstrated,
jerking the dress straight with a touch of vexation, ''I must say that you are getting positively
peevish!''

As Ruth did not reply, and the mother could
feel her body tightening, she went on, with a loving little pat as she fastened the dress over the
hip, ''And you used to be the most sweet-tempered
girl ever lived.''

Still Ruth made no answer. ''Your father was
saying the other night that he was sure you
couldn't be feeling well. You never used to be a
bit irritable, he said, and you nearly snapped his
head off when he wanted—just to save you—to
drive you over to Harriett's.''

Though the dress was all fastened now, Ruth
did not turn toward her mother. Mrs. Holland
added gently: ''Now that wasn't reasonable, was
it?''

The tear Ruth had been trying to hold back fell
to the handkerchief she was selecting. No, it
wouldn't seem reasonable, of course; her father
had wanted to help her, and she had been cross.
It was all because she couldn't tell him the truth
—which was that she hadn't told him the truth,
that she wasn't going to Harriett's for an hour,

that she was going to do something else first. There had been a moment of actually hating her father when, in wanting to help her, he stepped in the way of a thing he knew nothing about. That, it seemed, was what happened between people when things could not be told.

Mrs. Holland, seeing that Ruth's hand was unsteady, went on, in a voice meant to soothe: "Just take it a little easier, dear. What under the sun have you got to do but enjoy yourself? Don't get in such a flutter about it." She sighed and murmured, from the far ground of experience: "Wait till you have a real worry."

Ruth was pinning on her hat. She laughed in a jerky little way and said, in a light voice that was slightly tremulous: "I did get a little fussed, didn't I? But you see I wanted to get over to Edith's before dinner time. She wants to talk to me about her shower for Cora Albright."

"But you have all evening to talk that over, haven't you?" calmly admonished Mrs. Holland.

"Why, of course," Ruth answered, a little crisply, starting for the door.

"Your petticoat's showing," her mother called to her. "Here, I'll pin it up for you."

"Oh, let it *go!*" cried Ruth desperately. "I'll fix it at Edith's," she added hurriedly.

"Ruth, are you crazy?" her mother demanded. "Going through the streets with your petticoat showing! I guess you're in no such hurry as that.''

It was while she was pinning up the skirt that Mrs. Holland remarked: ''Oh, I very nearly forgot to tell you; Deane's going over there for you to-night.''

Then to the mother's utter bewilderment and consternation Ruth covered her face with her hands and burst into sobs.

''Why, my *dear*,'' she murmured; ''why, Ruth *dear*, what *is* the matter?''

Ruth sank down on the bed, leaning her head against the foot of it, shaking with sobs. Her mother stood over her murmuring, ''Why, my dear, what *is* the matter?''

Ruth, trying to stop crying, began to laugh. ''I didn't know he was coming! I was so surprised. We've quarrelled!'' she gulped out desperately.

''Why, he was just as natural and nice as could be over the 'phone,'' said Mrs. Holland, pouring some water in the bowl that Ruth might bathe her eyes. ''Really, my dear, it seems to me you make too much of things. He wanted to come here, and when I told him you were going to be at Edith's, he said he'd go there. I'm sure he was just as nice as could be.''

Ruth was bathing her eyes, her body still quivering a little. ''Yes, I know,'' she spluttered, her face in the water; "he is that way when—after we've quarrelled."

"I didn't know you and Deane ever did quarrel," ventured Mrs. Holland. "When you do, I'll warrant it's your fault." She added, significantly: "Deane's mighty good to you, Ruth." She had said several things like that of late.

"Oh, he's good enough," murmured Ruth from the folds of the towel.

"Now, powder up a little, dear. There! And now just take it a little easy. Why, it's not a bit like you to be so——touchy."

She followed Ruth downstairs. "Got that letter?" the grandfather called out from his room.

"I'll send Ted with it, father," Mrs. Holland said hastily, seeing Ruth's face.

A sudden surge of love for her mother almost swept away Ruth's self-command. It was wonderful that some one wanted to help her. It made her want to cry.

Her mother went with her to the porch. "You look so nice," she said soothingly. "Have a good time, dearie."

Ruth waved her hand without turning her face to her mother.

Tears were right there close all through that evening. The strain within was so great—(what *was* she going to do about Deane?)—that there was that impulse to cry at the slightest friendliness. She was flushed and tired when she reached

Edith's, and Mrs. Lawrence herself went out and got her a glass of water—a fan, drew up a comfortable chair. The whole house seemed so kindly, so favoring. Contrasted with her secret turmoil the reposefulness, friendliness of the place was so beautiful to her that taut emotions were ready to give. Yet all the while there was that inner distress about how to get away, what to say. The affectionate kindness of her friends, the appeal of their well-ordered lives as something in which to rest, simply had no reach into the thing that dominated her.

And now finally she had managed it; Deane had come before she could possibly get away but she had said she would have to go up to Harriett's, that she must not be too late about it. Edith had protested, disappointed at her leaving so early, wanting to know if she couldn't come back. That waved down, there had been a moment of fearing Edith was going to propose going with her; so she had quickly spoken of there being something Harriett wanted to talk to her about. She had a warm, gentle feeling for Edith when finally she saw the way clearing. That was the way it was, gratitude to one who had moved out of her way gave her so warm a feeling that often she would impulsively propose things letting her in for future complications.

As she was saying goodnight there was another moment of wanting terribly to cry. They were so good to her, so loving—and what would they think if they knew? Her voice was curiously gentle in taking leave of them; there was pain in that feeling of something that removed her from these friends who cared for her, who were so good to her.

She asked Deane if he hadn't something else to do for an hour, someone to run in and see while she visited with Harriett. When he readily fell in with that, saying he hadn't been to the Bennetts' since coming home and that it would be a good time to go there, she grew suddenly gay, joking with him in a half tender little way, a sort of affectionate bantering that was the closest they came to intimacy.

And then at the very last, after one thing and then another had been disposed of, and just as her whole being was fairly singing with relief and anticipation, the whole thing was threatened and there was another of those moments of actually hating one who was dear to her.

They had about reached the corner near Harriett's where she was going to insist Deane leave her for the Bennetts' when they came upon her brother Ted, slouching along, whistling, flipping in his hand the letter he was taking to his grandfather's old friend.

"Hello," he said, "where y' goin'?"

"Just walking," said Ruth, and able to say it with a carelessness that surprised her.

"Oh," said Ted, with a nonchalance that made her want to scream out some awful thing at him, "thought maybe you were making for Harriett's. She ain't home."

She would like to have pushed him away! She would have liked to push him way off somewhere! She dug her nails down into her palm; she could hardly control the violent, ugly feeling that wanted to leap out at him—at this "kid brother" whom she adored. Why need he have said just *that?*—that particular thing, of all things! But she was saying in calm elderly sister fashion, "Don't lose that letter, Ted," and to Deane, as they walked on, "Harriett's at a neighbor's; I'll run in for her; she's expecting me to."

But it left her weak; her legs were trembling, her heart pounding; there seemed no power left at the center of her for holding herself in one.

And now she was rid of Deane! She had shaken them all off; for that little time she was free! She hurried toward the narrow street that trailed off into the country. Stuart would be waiting for her there. Her joy in that, her eagerness, rushed past the dangers all around her, the thing that possessed her avoiding thought of the disastrous possibilities around her as a man in a boat on a narrow rushing river would keep clear of rocks jutting out on either side. Sometimes the feeling that swept her on did graze the risks so close about her and she shivered a little. Suppose Harriett were at the Bennetts' when Deane got there! Suppose Deane said something when they got home; suppose Ted said something that wouldn't fit in with what Deane said; suppose Deane got to Harriett's too soon—though she had told him not to be there till after half past nine. Hadn't Deane looked queer at the last? Wouldn't he suspect? Wouldn't everybody suspect, with her acting like this? And once there was the slightest suspecting. . . .

But she was hurrying on; none of those worries, fears, had power to lay any real hold on the thing that possessed her; faster and faster she hurried; she had turned into the little street, had passed the last house, turned the bend in the road, and yes! there was Stuart, waiting for her, coming to her. Everything else fell away. Nothing else in the world mattered.

CHAPTER TEN

Ten o'clock found Ruth sitting on the porch at home with her mother and father, her brother Cyrus and Deane. Her father was talking with Deane about the operation that had been performed on the book-keeper in Mr. Holland's bank; Cyrus talked of somebody's new touring car, the number of new machines there were in town that year; her mother wondered where some of the people who had them got the money for them. The talk moved placidly from one thing to another, Mr. Holland saying at intervals that he must be going to bed, his wife slapping at the mosquitoes and talking about going inside—both delaying, comfortably stupid.

Ruth was sitting on the top step leaning back against the porch pillar. She said little, she was very tired now. Something in this dragging talk soothed her. It seemed safe just because it was so commonplace; it was relaxing. She was glad to be back to it—to the world of it; in returning safely to it she felt a curiously tender feeling for it, a perhaps absurd sense of having come through something for it. She could rest in it while within herself she continued to live back in that hour with Stuart, that hour which struggle and fear and the passionate determination to have in spite of everything had made terribly intense. They had closed themselves in with that little while of love, holding it apart from everything else, and yet every minute of it was charged with the consciousness of what was all around them. They had clung to that hour with a desperate passion, the joy of the moment that was there always stabbed with pain for a moment passing. At the last they had clung to each other as if time too—time, over which they had no control—was going to beat them apart. So much had been hard that in returning she had a warm feeling of gratitude to all of them for not making it harder for her, not questioning, exposing her; relief was so great that they were all newly dear for thus letting her alone. She had managed all right with Deane, the clumsy arrangement she had been forced into appeared to have just that haphazardness which characterizes most of the arrangements of life. Her mother had merely asked what the Lawrence's had for dinner; her father joked about the way she had trained the roses in the back yard. Strangely enough instead of feeling she had outraged them, been unworthy this easy, affectionate intercourse, she had a sense, now that she had again come through a precarious thing safely, of having saved them from something they knew not of, a strange lifted-up feeling of bearing something for them. Certainly that would not seem the feeling she should be having, but there was the odd part of it: the feelings she had were so seldom those she would expect herself to have.

Her mother and father had gone indoors; Cyrus sat out there with her and Deane for a time. Ruth did not love Cyrus as she loved Ted; he had always had too superior a manner with her for her feeling to be more than the perfunctory thing which sometimes passes for personal affection in families. It was simply that she had never admitted, even to herself, that she did not love him. He belonged to the set just older than Ruth's, though she and Deane and their friends were arriving now at the time of ceasing to be a separate entity as the young crowd and were being merged in the group just above them. That contributed to Cyrus's condescension, he being tempered for condescension.

When she and Deane were alone the talk lagged, Ruth sitting there at the head of the steps leaning against the pillar, he a few steps below her, sprawled out in awkward boyish fashion, looking up at her from time to time as she said something. Her silence did not make him feel cut off from her; the things she said were gently said; her tired smile was sweet. He spoke several times of going, but lingered. He was held by something in Ruth; it stirred something in him, not knowing that he was drawn by what another man had brought into life. He drew himself up and stole timid glances at Ruth as she looked out into the night, feeling something new in her to-night, something that touched the feeling that had all the time been there in him, growing as he grew, of itself waiting for the future as simply and naturally as all maturing things wait for the future. Ruth was the girl he had all the time cared for; he was shy about emotional things—awkward; he had had almost no emotional life; he had all the time been diffident about what she made him feel and so they had just gone along for a little time longer than was usual as boy and girl. But something sweet, mysterious, exhaling from her tonight liberated the growing, waiting feeling in him. It took him as he had not been taken before; he watched Ruth and was stilled, moved, drawn.

Finally, as if suddenly conscious of a long silence, she turned to him with something about the plans for Cora Albright's wedding—she was to be a bridesmaid and he an usher. She went on talking of the man Cora was to marry, a man she met away from home and had fallen desperately in love with. He associated the light of her face, the sweetness of her voice, with the things of romance of which she talked. All in a moment his feeling for her, what her strange, softened mood touched in him, leaped up, surging through him, not to be stayed. He moved nearer her. "You know, Ruth," he said, in queer, jerky voice, "*I* love you."

She gave a start, drew a little back and looked at him with a certain startled fixity as if he had stopped all else in her. For the moment she just looked at him like that, startled, fixed.

"Could you care for me at all, Ruth?" he asked wistfully, and with a bated passionateness.

And then she moved, and it seemed that feeling, too, moved in her again; there was a flow of emotions as she sat looking at him now. And then her strangely shining eyes were misty; her face quivered a little and very slowly she shook her head.

"Don't do that, Ruth," he said quickly, in a voice sharp with pain. "Don't do that! You don't *know*—maybe you hadn't thought about it —maybe—" He broke off, reached out for her hands, and could only stammer, "Oh, Ruth!—I love you so!"

He had her hands; he was clutching them very tight; he looked up at her again, imploring. She started to shake her head again, but did not really do it. She seemed about to speak, but did not. What could she say to Deane—how make him understand?—unless she told him. She thought of the years she had known him, how much they had been together, how good he had been to her. Again her eyes were misty. It was all so tangled. There was so much pain.

Feeling her softening, her tenderness, he moved nearer, her two hands pressed together so tight in his that it hurt her. "It wouldn't be so bad, would it, Ruth?" he urged wistfully, with a little laugh that broke with emotion. "You and I— mightn't life go pretty well for us?"

She turned away, looking out into the night. Feeling something in her that he did not understand he let her hands go. She put one of them up, still further averting her face, lost to him in the picture forming itself before her of how life would be if love came right; what it would mean not to have to hide, but to have those who cared for her happy in her happiness; what it would mean to give herself to love without fear, to wear her joy proudly before the world, revealing her womanhood. She was not thinking of what life with Deane would be but of what love that could have its place would be: telling her mother and father and Edith, being able to show the pride of being loved, the triumph of loving. Sitting there, turning her face from this friend who loved her, she seemed to be turning it to the years awaiting her, years of desperately clutching at happiness in tension and fear, not understood because unable to show herself,—afraid, harrassed, perhaps disgraced. She wanted to take her place among women who loved and were loved! She did not want to be shut away from her friends, not seeming to understand what she understood so well. This picture of what life would be if love could have its place brought home to her what it meant to love and perpetually conceal, stealing one's happiness from the society in which one lived. Why could it not have gone right for her too, as it had for Cora and would for Edith? She too wanted a wedding, she too wanted rejoicing friends.

She hid her face in her hands. Her body was quivering.

The boy's arm stole round her shoulders. She was feeling—maybe she did care. "Ruth," he whispered, "love does mean something to you, doesn't it?"

She raised her head and looked at him. And that look was a thing Deane Franklin never forgot; all the years did not blur his memory of it —that flaming claim for love that transformed her face.

And then it was lost in contrition, for she saw what he had seen, and what he hoped from that; in her compunction for having let him see what was not for him, the tender, sorrowing look, the impulsive outreaching of her hand, there was the dawn of understanding.

At first he was too bewildered to find words. Then: "You care for some one else?" he groped unbelievingly.

She looked away, but nodded; her tears were falling.

He moved a little away and then sat there quite still. A breeze had come up and the vines beat against the porch, making a sound that like the flaming look of a moment ago he never forgot.

She knew that he must be wondering; he knew her life there, or what seemed her life. He must be wondering who it was she cared for like that.

She laid her hand upon his arm; and when he turned to her she did not say anything at all, but the appeal that looked through pain perhaps went where words could not have gone.

"But you're not happy!" he exclaimed, in a sort of harsh exulting in that.

She shook her head; her eyes were brimming over.

He looked away from her, his own hurt and surprise rousing a savage thing in him that did not want to do what the pleading pain of her eyes so eloquently asked of him. He had always thought that *he* was to have Ruth. Well, he was not to have her—there were ugly things which, in that first moment, surged into his disappointment. Some one else was to have her. But she was not happy! Defeated feeling wrenched its own sorry satisfaction from that.

"Why aren't you happy?" he asked of her abruptly, roughly.

She did not answer, and so he had to look at her. And when he saw Ruth's face his real love for her broke through the ugliness of thwarted passion. "Can't you tell me, Ruth?" he asked gently.

She shook her head, but the concern of his voice loosed feeling she was worn out with holding in. Her eyes were streaming now.

His arm went round her shoulder, gently, as if it would shield, help. His love for her wrenched itself free—for that moment, at least, —from his own hurt. "Maybe I can help you, Ruth," he was murmuring.

CHAPTER ELEVEN

He went away from there that night not knowing more than that; it was merely that she let him see. He knew now that there was some big thing in her life he had known nothing about; that he had not understood Ruth, though he had known her through all the years and had thought he knew her so well. He was bewildered, his pain was blunted in that bewilderment. There was a sick sense of life as all different, but he was too dazed then for the pain that came later with definite knowing. He went home that night and because he could not sleep tried to read a medical book; usually that took all his mind, for the time other things would not exist for him. But that was not true tonight; that world of facts could not get him; he lived right on in the world of his own feeling. He was not to have Ruth; he did not seem able to get a real sense of that either, there was just a sick feeling about it rather than actual realization, acceptance. And what did it mean? Surely he knew Ruth's life, the people she went with; it was always he, when he was at home, Ruth went about with. Someone away from home? But she had been very

little away from home. Who could it be? He
went over and over that. It came to seem unreal; as if there were some misunderstanding,
some mistake. And yet, that look. . . . His own
disappointment was at times caught up into
his marvel at her; that moment's revelation of
what her caring could be was so wonderful as to
bear him out of the fact that it was not for him
she cared. That was the way it was all through,
his love for her deepening with his marvel at her,
the revelation of what she felt for another man
claiming more and more of himself for her. It
was a thing he would have scoffed at if told of,
it was a thing he could not somehow justify even
to himself, but it was true that the more he saw
of what love meant to Ruth the more Ruth came
to mean to him.

In those next few months, the months before
he actually knew, there were times when he could
almost persuade himself that there was something unreal about it all, torturous wonderings
as to who the man could be trailing off into the
possibility of there being no man, because he knew
of none; sometimes he tried to persuade himself
that this passionate feeling he had glimpsed in
Ruth was a thing apart from any particular man
—for who *was* the man? Sometimes he could,
for a moment, let in the hope that since she could
care like that she would care for him. Though
he more than half knew he deluded himself in

that; there was, now that his eyes were opened, that in Ruth's manner to indicate something in her life which did not appear on the surface. He saw how nervous she was—how strained at times, how worried and cross, which was not like Ruth at all. There were times when her eyes were imploring, times when they were afraid, again there were moments of that lovely calm, when feeling deep and beautiful radiated from her, as it had that night they sat on the steps and, drawn by something in her, he had to tell her that he loved her. She did queer unreasonable things, would become exasperated at him for apparently nothing at all. Once when she had told him she was going somewhere with her mother he later saw her hurrying by alone; another time she told him she was going to Edith's, and when he called up there, wanting to take them both with him for a long trip he had to make into the country, Edith said Ruth had not been there. Thoughts that he did not like, that he could not believe, came into his mind. He was not only unhappy, but he grew more and more worried about Ruth.

That went on for several months, and then one day late that same summer she came to him with the truth. She came because she had to come. He was a doctor; he was her friend; she was in a girl's most desperate plight and she had no one else to turn to. It was in his office that she told

him, not looking at him, her face without color
and drawn out of shape, her voice quick, sharp,
hard, so unlike Ruth's sweet voice that without
seeing her he would not have known it. She
threw out the bare facts at him as she sat there
very straight, hands gripped. He was stupefied
at first, but it was fury which then broke through,
the fury of knowing it was *this*, that not only was
he not to have Ruth, but that another man *had*
her, the fury that rose out of the driving back of
all those loose ends of hope that had eased pain
a little. And *Ruth—this!* He little knew what
things he might not have said and done in those
first moments of failing her, turning on her because he himself was hurt beyond his power to
bear. And then Ruth spoke to him. "But I
thought you believed in love, Deane," she said,
quietly.

"*Love!*" he brutally flung back at her.

"Yes, Deane, love," she said, and the simplicity, the dignity of her quiet voice commanded him
and he had to turn from himself to her. She was
different now; she looked at him, steadily, proudly.
Out of the humiliation of her situation she raised
a proud face for love; love could bring her disgrace, it could not strip her of her own sense of
the dignity of loving. Her power was in that, in
that claim for love that pain and humiliation could
not beat back.

"I notice *he's* not here," he sneered, still too overwhelmed to be won from his own rage to her feeling.

"I thought it better for me to come," she said simply, and as she said it and he remembered her drawn, wretched face in telling him, he was quieted a little by a sense of what it had cost her to come. "Because," she added, "you're my friend, you know."

He did not say anything, miserably wondering what she now thought of him as her friend.

"Oh, Deane," she broke out, "don't be hard! If you could know what he's suffering! Being a man—being a little older—what's that? If you can understand me, Deane, you've got to understand him, too!"

He stood there in silence looking at Ruth as, looking away from him now, she brooded over that. In this hour of her own humiliation her appeal was for the man who had brought it upon her. "How you love him!" escaped from him, in bitterness, and yet marvelling.

She turned to him then in her swift way, again, as on that night of his first seeing, her face transformed by that flaming claim for love; it was as if life was shining triumphant through the cloud of misery it had brought down around her. He could not rage against that look; he had no scorn for it. It lighted a country between them which words could not have undarkened. They came together there in that common understanding of the power and beauty of love. He was suddenly ashamed, humbled, feeling in her love a quality upon which no shameful circumstance could encroach. And after that she found relief in words, the words she had had to deny herself so long. It was as if she found it wonderfully good to talk, in some little measure linking her love, as love wants to link itself, with the other people of the world, coming within the human unit. Things which circumstances had prisoned in her heart, too intensified by solitude, leaped out like winged things let loose. But in that hour of talking with him, though words served her well, it was that proud, flaming claim for love which again and again lighted her face that brought him into understanding, winning him for her against his own love of her.

In the year which followed, that last year before circumstances closed in too tight and they went away, it was he who made it possible for Ruth to move a little more freely in the trap in which she found herself. He helped her in deceiving her family and friends, aided them in the ugly work of stealing what happiness they could from the society in which they lived. He did not like doing it. Neither did he like attending the agonies of child-birth, or standing impotently at the bed of the dying. It might seem absurd, in trying to explain one's self, to claim for this love the inevitability of the beginning and the end of life, and yet, seeing it as he saw it he did think of it, not as a thing that should or should not be, but as a thing that was; not as life should or should not be lived, but as life. This much he knew: that whatever they might have been able to do at the first, it had them now. They were in too powerful a current to make a well considered retreat to shoals of safety. No matter what her mood might have been in the beginning, no matter what she could have done about it then, Ruth was mastered not master now. Love *had* her—he saw that too well to reason with her. What he saw of the way all other people mattered so much less than the passion which claimed her made him feel, not that Ruth was selfish, but that the passion was mastering; the way she deceived made him feel, not that she was deceitful, but that love like that was as unable to be held back in the thought of wrong to others as in the consideration of safety for one's self; the two were equally inadequate floodgates. Not that those other things did not matter—he knew how they did make her suffer—but that this one thing mattered overwhelmingly more was what he felt in Ruth in those days when she would be thought to be with him and would be with Stuart Williams.

For himself that was a year of misery. He saw Ruth in a peculiarly intimate way, taken as he was into the great intimacy of her life. His love for her deepened with his knowing of her; and anxiety about her preyed upon him all the time, passionate resentment that it should have gone like-that for her, life claiming her only, as it seemed, to destroy her.

He never admitted to himself how much he really came to like Stuart Williams. There seemed something quixotic in that; it did not seem natural he should have any sympathy with this man who not only had Ruth's love, but was endangering her whole life. Yet the truth was that as time went on he not only came to like him but to feel a growing concern for him.

For the man changed in that last year. It was not only that he looked older—harassed, had grown so much more silent, but Deane as a physician noticed that he was losing weight and there was a cough that often made him look at him sharply. A number of times Ruth said, "I don't think Stuart's well," but she looked so wretched in saying it that he always laughed at her. The Williams' were not patients of his, so he felt that professional hesitance, even though he thought it foolish professionalism, in himself approaching Stuart about his health. Once when he seemed particularly tired and nervous Deane did venture to suggest a little lay-off from work, a change, but Stuart had answered irritably that he couldn't stop work, and didn't want to go away, anyhow.

It was almost a year after the day Ruth came

to him steeled for telling what had to be told that
the man of whom she that day talked came to tell
him what he had been suspecting, that he had
tuberculosis and would have to take that lay-off
Deane had been hinting at. It seemed it was
either go away or die, probably, he added, with
an attempted laugh, it was go away and die, but
better go away, he thought, than stay there and
give his friends an exhibition in dying.

They talked along over the surface of it, as is
people's way, Deane speaking mildly of tuberculosis, how prevalent, how easily controlled, how
delightful Arizona was, the charms of living out-
of-doors, and all the time each of them knew that
the other was not thinking of that at all, but thinking of Ruth.

Finally, bracing himself as for a thing that was
all he could do, Stuart spoke of her. "Ruth said
she was coming in to see you about something this
afternoon. I thought I'd get in first and tell you.
I wondered what you'd think—what we'd better
do—"

His voice trailed off miserably. He turned a
little away and sat there in utter dejection.

And as he looked at him it came to Deane that
love could be the most ruthless, most terrible thing
in the world. People talked to him afterwards
about this man's selfishness in taking his own
pleasure, his own happiness, at the cost of everyone else. He said little, for how could he make

real to anyone else his own feeling about what he had seen of the man's suffering, utter misery, as he spoke of the girl to whom he must bring new pain. Some one spoke to him afterwards of this "light love" and he laughed in that person's face. He knew that it was love bathed in pain.

A new sense of just how hideous the whole thing was made him suddenly demand: "Can't you—*do* anything about it? Isn't there any *way?* —any way you can get a divorce?" he bluntly asked.

"Mrs. Williams does not believe in divorce," was the answer, spoken with more bitterness than Deane had ever heard in any voice before.

Deane turned away with a little exclamation of rage, rage that one person should have this clutch on the life of another, of two others—and one of them Ruth—sickened with a sense of the waste and the folly of it,—for what was *she* getting out of it? he savagely put to himself. How could one get anything from life simply by holding another from it?

"Does she know anything about Ruth?" he asked with an abrupt turn to Stuart.

"She has mentioned her name several times lately and looked at me in doing it. She isn't one to speak directly of things," he added with a more subtle bitterness than that of a moment before. They sat there for a couple of minutes in silence —a helpless, miserable silence.

When, after that, Deane stepped out into the waiting-room he found Ruth among those there; he only nodded to her and went back and told Stuart that she was there. "But it's only three," said he helplessly, "and she said she was coming at four."

"Well, I suppose she came earlier than she intended," Deane replied, about as helplessly, and went over and stood looking out the window. After a moment he turned. "Better get it over with, hadn't you? She's got to be told," he said, a little less brusquely, as he saw the man wince, —"better get it over with."

Stuart was silent, head down. After a moment he looked up at Deane. It was a look one would turn quickly away from. Again Deane stood looking from the window. He was considering something, considering a thing that would be very hard to do. After a moment he again abruptly turned around. "Well, shall I do it?" he asked quietly.

The man nodded in a wretched gratefulness that went to Deane's heart.

So he called Ruth in from the waiting-room. He always remembered just how Ruth looked that day; she had on a blue suit and a hat with flowers on it that was very becoming to her. She looked very girlish; he had a sudden sense of all the years he had known her.

The smile with which she greeted Deane changed

when she saw Stuart sitting there; the instant's pleased surprise went to apprehension at sight of his face. "What's the matter?" she asked sharply.

"Stuart's rather bummed up, Ruth," said Deane.

Swiftly she moved over to the man she loved. "What is it?" she demanded in quick, frightened voice.

"Oh, just a bad lung," Deane continued, not looking at them and speaking with that false cheerfulness so hard fought for and of so little worth. "Don't amount to much—happens often —but, well—well, you see, he has to go away— for awhile."

He was bending over his desk, fumbling among some papers. There was no sound in the room and at last he looked up. Stuart was not looking at Ruth and Ruth was standing there very still. When she spoke her voice was singularly quiet. "When shall we go?" she asked.

CHAPTER TWELVE

Everyone who talked about it—and that meant all who knew anything about it—blamed Deane Franklin for not stopping Ruth. Perhaps the reason he did not try to defend himself was simply that he could not hope to show how simple was his acceptance of the fact that it would have been impossible to stop her. To understand that, one would have to have seen. Oh, to be sure, he could have put obstacles in her way, tightened it around her, but anything he might have done would only have gone to making it harder for Ruth to get away; it would not have kept her from going. And after all, he himself saw it as, if not the thing she should do, the thing—it being what it was then—she could not help doing. But one would have to have seen Ruth's face, would need to have been with her in those days to understand that.

As to warning her family, as he was so blamed by them and by all the town for not doing, that would have seemed to him just one of those things he could have thrown in her way. He did feel that he must try to talk to her of what it was going to mean to her people; he saw that she saw, that it had cruel power to make her suffer

—and no power to stop her. Nothing could have stopped her; she was like a maddened thing—desperate, ruthless, indomitable. She would have fought the world; she would have let the whole world suffer. Love's fear possessed her utterly. He had had the feeling all along that it was rushing on to disaster. He stood back from it now with something like awe: a force not for him to control.

And he, with it from within, was the only one who did not condemn Stuart Williams for letting Ruth go. A man, and older than she, they scorned him for letting an infatuated girl throw her life away like that. And it was not only that he saw that the man was sick and broken; it was that he saw that Stuart, just as Ruth, had gone in love beyond his power to control love, that he was mastered, not master, now. And in those last days, at least, it was Ruth who dominated him. There was something terrible in the simplicity with which she saw that she had to go; she never once admitted it to the things that were to be argued about. He talked to her, they both tried to talk to her, about the danger of getting tuberculosis. When he began on that she laughed in his face—and he could not blame her. As if *that* could keep her! And as she laughed her tortured eyes seemed mockingly to put to him— "What difference would it make?"

When, after it all came out, he did not join the

outraged town in the outcry against Ruth, when it further transpired that he had known about her going and had not tried to stop it, he was so much blamed that it even hurt his practice. There were women who said they would not countenance a young physician who had the ideas of life he must have. His own people were incensed at what they called the shameful advantage Ruth had taken of him, holding that she, as an evil woman, had exerted an influence over him that made him do what was against his own nature. As to the Hollands, there had been a stormy hour with Mr. Holland and Cyrus, and a far worse half hour with Mrs. Holland, when her utterly stricken face seemed to stiffen in his throat the things he wanted to say for Ruth, things that might have helped Ruth's mother. And then he was told that the Hollands were through, not alone with Ruth, but with him.

But he was called there two years later when Mrs. Holland was dying. She had been begging for him. That moved him deeply because of what in itself it told of her long yearning for Ruth. After that there were a number of years when he was not inside that gate. Cyrus did not speak to him and the father might as well not have done so. He was amazed, then, when Mr. Holland finally came to him about his own health. "I've come to you, Deane," he said, "because I think you're the best doctor in town now—and I need help.'' And then he added, and after that first talk this was the closest to speaking of it they ever came: ''And I guess you didn't understand, Deane; didn't see it right. You were young— and you're a queer one, anyway.''

Perhaps the reason he was never able to do better in explaining himself, or in defending Ruth, was simply because in his own thinking about it there were never arguments, or thoughts upon conduct, but always just that memory of Ruth's face as he had seen it in revealing moments.

Everyone saw something that Ruth should have done differently. In the weeks they spent upon it they found, if not that they would be able to forgive her, at least that they could think of her with less horror had she done this, had she not done that. But Ruth lived through that week seeing little beyond the one thing that she must get through it. She was driven; she had to go ahead, bearing things somehow, getting through them. She had a strange power to steel herself, to keep things, for the most part, from really getting through to her. She could not go ahead if she began letting things in. She sealed herself over and drove ahead with the singleness of purpose, the exclusions, of any tormented thing. It was all terrible, but it was as if she were frozen at the heart to all save the one thing.

She stayed through the week because it was the time of Edith Lawrence's wedding and she was to be maid-of-honor. "I'll have to stay till after Edith's wedding," she said to Deane and Stuart. Then on her way home from Deane's office she saw that she could not go on with her part in Edith's wedding. That she could see clearly enough despite the thing driving her on past things she should be seeing. What would she say to Edith?—how get *that* over?

Someone was giving a party for Edith that night; every day now things were being given for her. She must not go to them. How could she go? It would be absurd to expect that of herself. She would have to tell Edith that she could not be her bridesmaid. What a terrible thing Edith would think that was! She would have to give a reason—a big reason. What would she tell her?—that she had been called away?—but where? Should she tell her the truth? Could she? Edith would find it almost unbelievable. It was almost unbelievable to herself that her life could be permeated by a thing Edith knew nothing about. It was another of the things she would have said, had she known her story only through hearing it, would not be possible. But it was with Edith as it was with her own family—simply that such a thing would never occur to her. She winced in thinking of it that way. A number of times she had been right on the edge of a thing it seemed would surely be disclosing, but it strangely happened she had never quite gone over that edge. For one thing, Edith had been away from Freeport a good deal in those three years. Mrs. Lawrence had opposed Edith's marrying so young, and had taken her to Europe for one year, and in the last year they had spent part of the time in California. In the last couple of months, since Edith's return from the West, she had spoken of Ruth's not seeming like herself, of fearing she was not well. She had several times hurt Edith's feelings by refusing, for no apparent reason, to do things with her. But she had always been able to make that up afterwards and in these plans for the wedding she and Edith had been drawn close again.

When she went over to the Lawrences' late that afternoon she had decided that she would tell Edith. It seemed she must. ＼She could not hope to tell it in a way that would make Edith sympathize. There was not time for that, and she dared not open herself to it. She would just say it briefly, without any attempts at justifying it. Something like: "Edith, there's been something you haven't known. I'm not like you. I'm not what you think I am. I love Stuart Williams. We've loved each other for a long time. He's sick. He's got to go away—and I'm going with him. Good-by, Edith,—and I hope the wedding goes just beautifully."

But that last got through—got down to the feeling she had been trying to keep closed, the feeling that had seemed to seal itself over the moment she saw that she must go with Stuart. "I hope the wedding goes just beautifully!" Somehow the stiff little phrase seemed to mean all the old things. There was a moment when she *knew:* knew that she was walking those familiar streets, that she would not be walking them any more; knew that she was going over to Edith's—that all her life she had been going over to Edith's—that she would not be going there any more; knew that she was going away from home, that she loved her father and mother—Ted—her grandfather— and Terror, her dog. Realization broke through and flooded her. She had to walk around a number of blocks before she dared go to Edith's.

Miss Edith was up in her room, Emma, the maid, said, taking it for granted that Ruth would go right up. Yes, she always did go right up, she was thinking. She had always been absolutely at home at the Lawrences'. They always wanted her; there were times of not wanting to see anyone else, but it seemed both Edith and her mother always wanted her. She paused an instant on the stairs, not able to push past that thought, not able to stay the loving rush of gatefulness that broke out of the thought of having always been wanted.

She had a confused sense of Edith as barricaded by her trousseau. She sat behind a great pile of white things; she had had them all out of her chest for showing to some of her mother's friends, she said, and her mother had not yet put them back. Ruth stood there fingering a wonderfully soft chemise. It had come to her that she was not provided with things like these. What would Edith think of her, going away without the things it seemed one should have? It seemed to mark the setting of her apart from Edith, though there was a wave of tenderness—she tried to hold it back but could not—for dear Edith because she did have so many things like this.

Edith was too deep in the occupation of getting married to mark an unusual absorption in her friend. She was full of talk about what her mother's friends had said of her things, the presents that were coming in, her dress for the party that night, the flowers for the wedding.

It made Edith seem very young to her. And in her negligee, her hair down, she looked childish. Her pleasure in the plans for her wedding seemed like a child's pleasure. It seemed that hurting her in it would be horribly like spoiling a child's party. Edith's flushed face, her sparkling eyes, her little excited, happy laugh made it impossible for Ruth to speak the words she had come to say.

For three days it went on like that: going ahead with the festivities, constantly thinking she would tell Edith as soon as they got home from this place or that, waiting until this or that person had gone, then dumb before the childish quality of Edith's excitement, deciding to wait until the next morning because Edith was either too happy or too tired to talk to her that night. That ingenuousness of her friend's pleasure in her wedding made Ruth feel, not only older, but removed from her by experience. Those days of her own frozen misery were days of tenderness for Edith, that tenderness which one well along the road of living feels for the one just setting feet upon the path.

She was never able to understand how she did get through those days. It was an almost unbelievable thing that, knowing, she was able, up to the very last, to go right on with the old things, was able to talk to people as if nothing were different, to laugh, to dance. There were times when something seemed frozen in her heart and she could go on doing the usual things mechanically, just because she knew so well how to do them; then there were other times when every smallest thing was stabbed through and through with the consciousness that she would not be doing it again. And yet even then, she could go on, could appear the same. They were days of a terrible power for bearing pain. When the people of the town looked back to it, recalling everything they could about Ruth Holland in those days, some of them, remembering a tenderness in her manner with Edith, talked of what a hypocrite she was, while others satisfied themselves of her utter heartlessness in remembering her gaiety.

It was two days before the wedding when she saw that she was not going to be able to tell Edith and got the idea of telling Edith's mother. Refusing to let herself consider what she would say when she began upon it, she went over there early that morning—Edith would not be up.

Mrs. Lawrence was at breakfast alone. Ruth kept herself hard against the welcoming smile, but it seemed she was surely going to cry when, with a look of concern, Mrs. Lawrence exclaimed: "Why, Ruth dear, how pale you are!"

She was telling Emma to bring Ruth a cup of coffee, talking of how absurd it was the way the girls were wearing themselves out, how, for that reason, she would be glad when it was all over. She spoke with anxiety of how nervous Edith had grown in the past week, how tired she was as a result of all the gaiety. "We'll have to be very careful of her, Ruth," she said. "Don't go to Edith with any worries, will you? Come to me. The slightest thing would upset Edith now."

Ruth only nodded; she did not know what to say to that; certainly, after that, she did not know how to say the things she had come to tell. For what in the world could upset Edith so much as to have her maid-of-honor, her life-long friend, the girl she cared for most, refuse, two days before her wedding, to take her part in it?

"And you can do more than anyone else, Ruth," Mrs. Lawrence urged. "You know Edith counts so on you," she added with an intimate little smile.

And again Ruth only nodded, and bent over her coffee. She had a feeling of having been caught, of being helpless.

Mrs. Lawrence was talking about the caterer for the wedding; she wished it were another kind of salad. Then she wanted Ruth to come up and look at her dress; she wasn't at all satisfied with the touch of velvet they had put on it. After that some one else came in and Mrs. Lawrence was called away. Ruth left without saying what she had come to say. She knew now that she would not say it.

She went home seeing that she must go through with the wedding. It was too late now to do anything else. Edith would break down—her pleasure in her wedding spoiled; no, Edith must be spared—helped. She must do this for Edith. No matter what people thought of her, no matter what Edith herself thought—though *wouldn't* she understand? Ruth considered with a tortured wistfulness—the thing to do now was to go through with it. Edith must look beautiful at her wedding; her happiness must be unmarred. Later, when she was away with Will—happy—she could bear it better. And she would understand that Ruth had wished to spare her; had done it to help her. She held that thought with her—and drove ahead.

There were moments in those last two days at home when it seemed that now her heart was indeed breaking: a kindly note in the voice of her father or mother—one of Ted's teasing jokes—little requests from her grandfather; then doing things she had done for years and knowing while doing them that she would not be doing them any more—the last time she cut the flowers, and then that last night when she went to bed in her own room, the room she had had ever since old enough to have a room of her own. She lay there that night and listened to the branches of the great oak tapping the house. She had heard that sound all her life; it was associated with all the things of her life; it seemed to be speaking for all those things—mourning for them. But the closest she came to actual breaking down was that last day when her dog, laying his head upon her knee, looked with trust and affection up into her eyes. As she laid her hand upon his head his eyes seemed to speak for all the love she had known through all the years. It seemed she could not bear it, that her heart could not bear it; that she would rather die. But she did bear it; she had that terrible power for bearing.

If only she had told her mother, they said over and over again. But if she told her mother she would not go—that was how she saw that; they would not let her; or rather, she would have no strength left to fight through their efforts to keep her. And then how could she tell her mother when her mother would never in the world understand? She did not believe that her mother could so much as comprehend that she could love where she should not, that a girl like Ruth—or rather, *Ruth*—could love a man it was not right she love. She had never talked with her mother of real things, had never talked with her of the things of her deepest feeling. She would not know how to do it now, even had she dared.

Her mother helped her dress for the wedding, talking all the while about plans for the evening —just who was going to the church, the details about serving. Ruth clung to the thought that those *were* the things her mother was interested in; they always had been, surely they would continue to be. In her desperation she tried to think that in those little things her mother cared so much about she would, after a time, find healing.

With that cruel power for bearing pain she got away from home without breaking down; she got through that last minute when she realized she would not see Ted or her grandfather again,— they would not be at the wedding and would be in bed when she returned from it, and she was to leave that night on the two o'clock train. It was unbelievable to her that she had borne it, but she had driven ahead through utter misery as they commented on her dress, praising her and joking with her. That was in the living-room and she never forgot just how they were grouped—her grandfather's newspaper across his knees; Mary, who had worked for them for years, standing at the door; her dog Terror under the reading table —Ted walking round and round her. Deane was talking with her father in the hall. Her voice was sharp as she went out and said: "We must hurry, Deane."

The wedding was unreal; it seemed that all those people were just making the movements of life; there were moments when she heard them from a long way off, saw them and was uncertain whether they were there. And yet she could go on and appear about the same; if she seemed a little queer she was sure it was attributed to natural feeling about her dearest friend's wedding —to emotion, excitement. There were moments when things suddenly became real: a moment alone with Edith in her room, just before they went to the church; a moment when Mrs. Lawrence broke down. Walking down the aisle, the words of the service—that was in a vague, blurred world; so was Edith's strained face as she turned away, and her own walking down the aisle with Deane, turning to him and smiling and saying something and feeling as if her lips were frozen. Yet for three hours she laughed and talked with people. Mrs. Williams was at the reception; several times they were in the same group. Oh, it was all unreal—terrible—just a thing to drive through. There was a moment at the last when Edith clung to her, and when it seemed that she could not do the terrible thing she was going to do, that she was *not* going to do it—that the whole thing was some hideous nightmare. She wanted to stay with Edith. She wanted to be like Edith. She felt like a little girl then, just a frightened little girl who did not want to go away by herself, away from everything she knew, from people who loved her. She did not want to do that awful thing! She tried to pretend for a moment she was not going to do it—just as sometimes she used to hide her face when afraid.

At last it was all over; she had gone to the train and seen Edith and Will off for the East. Edith's face was pressed against the window of the Pullman as the train pulled out. It was Ruth she was looking for; it was to Ruth her eyes clung until the train drew her from sight.

Ruth stood there looking after the train; the rest of their little group of intimate friends had turned away—laughing, chattering, getting back in the carriages. Deane finally touched Ruth's arm, for she was standing in that same place looking after the train which had now passed from sight. When he saw the woe of her wet face he said gruffly: "Hadn't we better walk home?" He looked down at her delicate slippers, but better walk in them than join the others looking like that. He supposed walking would not be good for that frail dress; and then it came to him, and stabbed him, that it didn't much matter. Probably Ruth would not wear that dress again.

She walked home without speaking to him, looking straight ahead in that manner she all along had of ruthlessly pressing on to something; her face now was as if it were frozen in suffering, as if it had somehow stiffened in that moment of woe when Edith's face was drawn from her sight. And she looked so tired!—so spent, so miserable; as if she ought to be cared for, comforted. He took her arm, protectingly, yearningly. He longed so in that moment to keep Ruth, and care for her! He wanted to say things, but he seemed to be struck dumb, appalled by what it was they were about to do. He held her arm close to him. She was going away! Now that the moment had come he did not know how he was going to let her go. And looking like this!—suffering like this—needing help.

But he must not fail her now at the last; he must not fail her now when she herself was so worn, so wretched, was bearing so much. As they turned in at the gate he fought with all his strength against the thought that they would not be turning in at that gate any more and spoke in matter of fact tones of where he would be waiting for her, what time she must be there. But when they reached the steps they stood there for a minute under the big tree, there where they had so many times stood through a number of years. As they stood there things crowded upon them hard; Ruth raised her face and looked at him and at the anguish of her swimming eyes his hands went out to her arms. "Don't go, Ruth!" he whispered brokenly. "Ruth!—*don't go!*"

But that made her instantly find herself, that found the fight in her, to strengthen herself, to resist him; she was at once erect, indomitable, the purpose that no misery could shake gleamed through her wet eyes. Then she turned and went into the house. Her mother called out to her, sleepily asking if she could get out of her dress by herself. She answered yes, and then Mrs. Holland asked another sleepy question about Edith. Then the house was still; she knew that they were all asleep. She got her dress off and hung it carefully in the closet. She had already put some things in her bag; she put in a few more now, all the while sobbing under her breath.

She took off her slippers. After she had done that she stood looking at her bed. She saw her nightgown hanging in the closet. She wanted to put on her nightgown and get into bed! She leaned against the bed, crying. She wanted to put on her nightgown and get into bed! She was so tired, so frightened, so worn with pain. Then she shook herself, steeled again, and began putting on her shoes; put on her suit, her hat, got out her gloves. And then at the very last she had to do what she had been trying to make herself do all that day, and had not dared begin to do. She went to her desk and holding herself tight, very rapidly, though with shaking hand, wrote this note:

"Dear Mother; I'm going away. I love Stuart Williams. I have for a long time. Oh, mother—I'm so sorry—but I can't help it. He's sick. He has to go away, so you see I have to go with him. It's terrible that it is like this. Mother, try to believe that I can't help it. After I get away I can write to you more about it. I can't now. It will be terrible for you—for you all. Mother, it's been terrible for me. Oh, try not to feel any worse than you can help. People won't blame *you*. I wish I could help it. I wish —Can't write more now. Write later. I'm so sorry—for everybody. So good to me always. I love all— Ruth."

She put her head down on the desk and cried. Finally she got up and blindly threw the note over on her bed; with difficulty, because of the shaking of her hands, put on her gloves, picked up her bag. And then she stood there for a moment before turning off the light; she saw her little chair, her dressing-table. She reached up and turned off the light and then for another moment stood there in the darkened room. She listened to the branches of the oak tree tapping against the house. Then she softly opened her bed-room door and carefully closed it behind her. She could hear her father's breathing; then Ted's, as she passed his door. On the stairs she stood still: she wanted to hear Ted's breathing again. But she had already gone where she could not hear Ted's breathing. Her hand on the door, she stood still. There was something so unreal about this, so preposterous—not a thing that really happened, that could happen to *her*. It seemed that in just a minute she would wake up and find herself safe in her bed. But in another minute she was leaning against the outside door of her home, crying. She seemed to have left the Ruth Holland she knew behind when she finally walked down the steps and around the corner where Deane was waiting for her.

They spoke scarcely a word until they saw the headlight of her train. And then she drew back, clinging to him. "Ruth!" he whispered, holding her, "don't!" But that seemed to make her know that she must; she straightened, steeled herself, and moved toward the train. A moment later she was on the platform, looking down at him. When she tried to smile good-by, he whirled and walked blindly away.

She did not look from the window as long as the lights of the town were to be seen. She sat there perfectly still, hands tight together, head down. For two hours she scarcely moved. Such strange things shot through her mind. Maybe her mother, thinking she was tired, would not go to her room until almost noon. At least she would have her coffee first. Had she remembered to put Edith's handkerchiefs in her bag? Had anyone else noticed that the hook at the waist of Edith's dress had come unfastened? Edith was on a train too—going the other way. How strange it all was! How terrible beyond belief! Just as she neared the junction where she would meet Stuart and from which they would take the train South together, the thought came to her that none of the rest of them might remember always to have water in Terror's drinking pan. When she stepped from the train she was crying—because Terror might want a drink and wonder why she was not there to give it to him. He would not understand—and oh, he would miss her so! Even when Stuart, stepping from the darkness to meet her, drew her to him, brokenly whispering passionate, grateful words, she could not stop crying —for Terror, who would not understand, and who would miss her so! He became the whole world she knew—loving, needing world, world that would not understand, and would miss her so!

The woman who, on that train from Denver, had been drawn into this story which she had once lived was coming now into familiar country. She would be home within an hour. She had sometimes ridden this far with Deane on his cases. Her heart began to beat fast. Why, there was the very grove in which they had that picnic! She could scarcely control the excitement she felt in beginning to find old things. There was something so strange in the old things having remained there just the same when she had passed so completely away from them. Seeing things she knew brought the past back with a shock. She could hardly get her breath when first she saw the town. And there was the Lawrences'! Somehow it was unbelievable. She did not hear the porter speaking to her about being brushed off; she was peering hungrily from the window, looking through tears at the town she had not seen since she left it that awful night eleven years before. She was trembling as she stood on the platform waiting for the slowing train to come to a stop. There was a moment of wanting to run back in the car, of feeling she could not get off.

The train had stopped; the porter took her by the arm, thinking by her faltering that she was slipping. She took her bag from him and stood there, turned a little away from the station crowd.

Ted Holland had been waiting for that train, he also with fast beating heart; he too was a lit-

tle tremulous as he hurried down to the car, far
in the rear, from which passengers were alighting
from the long train. He scanned the faces of the
people who began passing him. No, none of them
was Ruth. His picture of Ruth was clear, though
he had not seen her for eleven years. She would
be looking about in that eager way—that swift,
bright way; when she saw him there would be that
glad nodding of her head, her face all lighting up.
Though of course, he told himself, she would be
older, probably a little more—well, dignified.
The romance that secretly hung about Ruth for
him made him picture her as unlike other women;
there would be something different about her, he
felt.

The woman standing there half turned from
him was oddly familiar. She was someone he
knew, and somehow she agitated him. He did not
tell himself that that was Ruth—but after seeing
her he was not looking at anyone else for Ruth.
This woman was not "stylish looking." She did
not have the smart look of most of the girls of
Ruth's old crowd. He had told himself that Ruth
would be older—and yet it was not a woman he
had pictured, or rather, it was a woman who had
given all for love, not a woman who looked as if
she had done just the things of women. This
woman stooped a little; care, rather than romance,
had put its mark upon her; instead of the secretly
expected glamour of those years of love there had

been a certain settling of time. He knew before he acknowledged it that it was Ruth, knew it by the way this woman made him feel. He came nearer; she had timidly—not with the expected old swiftness—started in the direction he was coming. She saw him—knew him—and in that rush of feeling which transformed her anything of secret disappointment was swept from him.

He kissed her, as sheepishly as a brother would any sister, and was soon covering his emotion with a practical request for her trunk check. But as they walked away the boy's heart was strangely warmed. Ruth was back!

As to Ruth, she did not speak. She could not.

CHAPTER THIRTEEN

It was the afternoon of Ruth Holland's return to Freeport that Edith Lawrence—now Edith Lawrence Blair—was giving the tea for Deane Franklin's bride and for Cora Albright, introducing Amy to the society of the town and giving Cora another opportunity for meeting old friends. "You see Cora was of our old crowd," Edith was laughingly saying to one of the older women in introducing her two guests of honor, "and Amy has married into it." She turned to Amy with a warm little smile and nod, as if wanting to assure her again that they did look upon her as one of them.

They had indeed given her that sense of being made one of them. Their quick, warm acceptance of her made them seem a wonderfully kindly people. Her heart warmed to them because of this going out to her, a stranger. That informality and friendliness which in a society like theirs prevails well within the bounds made them seem to her a people of real warmth. She was pleased with the thought of living among them, being one of them; gratified, not only in the way they seemed to like her, but by the place they gave her. There were happy little anticipations of the life just opening up. She was flushed with pleasure and gratification.

She was seeing the society of the town at its best that afternoon; the women who constituted that society were there, and at their best. For some reason they always were at their best at the Lawrences', as if living up to the house itself, which was not only one of the most imposing of the homes of that rich little middle-western city, but had an atmosphere which other houses, outwardly equally attractive, lacked. Mrs. Lawrence had taste and hospitality; the two qualities breathed through her house. She and Edith were Freeport's most successful hostesses. The society of that town was like the particular thing known as society in other towns; not distinguished by any unique thing so much as by its likeness to the thing in general. Amy, knowing society in other places, in a larger place, was a little surprised and much pleased at what she recognized.

And she felt that people were liking her, admiring her, and that always put her at her best. Sometimes Amy's poise, rare in one so young, made her seem aloof, not cordial, and she had not been one to make friends quickly. Edith's friendliness had broken through that; she talked more than was usual with her—was gayer, more friendly. "You're making a great hit, my dear," Edith whispered to her gayly, and Amy flushed with pleasure. People about the room were talking of how charming she was; of there being something unusual in that combination of girlishness and—they called it distinction; had Amy been in different mood they might have spoken of it less sympathetically as an apparent feeling of superiority. But she felt that she was with what she called her own sort, and she was warmed in gratification by the place given herself.

She was gayly telling a little group of an amusing thing that had happened at her wedding when she overheard someone saying to Edith, by whom she was standing: "Yes, on the two o'clock train. I was down to see Helen off, and saw her myself—walking away with Ted."

Amy noticed that the other women, who also had overheard, were only politely appearing to be listening to her now, and were really discreetly trying to hear what these two were saying. She brought her story to a close.

"You mean Ruth Holland?" one of the women asked, and the two groups became one.

Amy drew herself up; her head went a little higher, her lips tightened; then, conscious of that, she relaxed and stood a little apart, seeming only to be courteously listening to a thing in which she had no part. They talked in lowered tones of how strange it seemed to feel Ruth was back in that town. They had a different manner now—a sort of carefully restrained avidity. "How does she look?" one of the women asked in that lowered tone.

"Well," said the woman who had been at the train, "she hasn't kept herself *up*. Really, I was surprised. You'd think a woman in her position would make a particular effort to—to make the most of herself, now, wouldn't you? What else has she to go on? But really, she wasn't at all good style, and sort of—oh, as if she had let herself *go*, I thought. Though,"—she turned to Edith in saying this—"there's that same old thing about her; I saw her smile up at Ted as they walked away—and she seemed all different then. You know how it always used to be with Ruth—so different from one minute to another."

Edith turned away, rather abruptly, and joined another group. Amy could not make out her look; it seemed—why it seemed pain; as if it hurt her to hear what they were saying. Could it be that she still *cared?*—after the way she had been treated? That seemed impossible, even in one who had the sweet nature Mrs. Blair certainly had.

While the women about her were still talking of Ruth Holland, Amy saw Stuart Williams' wife come out of the dining room and stand there alone for a minute looking about the room. It gave her a shock. The whole thing seemed so terrible, so fascinatingly terrible. And it seemed unreal; as a thing one might read or hear about, but not the sort of thing one's own life would come anywhere near. Mrs. Williams' eyes rested on their little group and Amy had a feeling that somehow she knew what they were talking about. As her eyes followed the other woman's about the room she saw that there were several groups in which people were drawn a little closer together and appeared to be speaking a little more intimately than was usual upon such an occasion. She felt that Mrs. Williams' face became more impassive. A moment later she had come over to Amy and was holding out her hand. There seemed to Amy something very brave about her, dignified, fine, in the way she went right on, bearing it, holding her own place, keeping silence. She watched her leave the room with a new sense of outrage against that terrible woman—that woman Deane stood up for! The resentment which in the past week she had been trying to put down leaped to new life.

The women around her resumed their talk: of Mrs. Williams, the Holland family, of the night of Edith's wedding when—in that very house—Ruth Holland had been there up to the very last minute, taking her place with the rest of them. They spoke of her betrayal of Edith, her deception of all her friends, of how she was the very last girl in the world they would have believed it of.

A little later, when she and Edith were talking with some other guests, Ruth Holland was mentioned again. "I don't want to talk of Ruth," Edith said that time; "I'd rather not." There was a catch in her voice and one of the women impulsively touched her arm. "It was so terrible for you, dear Edith," she murmured.

"Sometimes," said Edith, "it comes home to me that it was pretty terrible for Ruth." Again she turned away, leaving an instant's pause behind her. Then one of the women said, "I think it's simply wonderful that Edith can have anything but bitterness in her heart for Ruth Holland! Why there's not another person in town—oh, except Deane Franklin, of course—"

She caught herself, reddened, then turned to Amy with a quick smile. "And it's just his sympathetic nature, isn't it? That's exactly Deane—taking the part of one who's down."

"And then, too, men feel differently about those things," murmured another one of the young matrons of Deane's crowd.

Their manner of seeming anxious to smooth something over, to get out of a difficult situation, enraged Amy, not so much against them as because of there being something that needed smoothing over, because Deane had put himself and her in a situation that was difficult. How did it look?—what must people think?—his standing up for a woman the whole town had turned against! But she was saying with what seemed a sweet gravity, "I'm sure Deane would be sorry for any woman who had been so—unfortunate. And she," she added bravely, "was a dear old friend, was she not?"

The woman who had commiserated with Edith now nodded approval at Amy. "You're sweet, my dear," she said, and the benign looks of them all made her feel there was something for her to be magnanimous about, something queer. Her resentment intensified because of having to give that impression of a sweet spirit. And so people talked about Deane's standing up for this Ruth Holland! *Why* did they talk?—just what did they say? "There's more to it than I know," suspicion whispered. In that last half hour it was hard to appear gracious and interested; she saw a number of those little groups in which voices were low and faces were trying not to appear eager.

She wished she knew what they were saying; she had an intense desire to hear more about this thing which she so resented, which was so roiling to her. It fascinated as well as galled her; she wanted to know just how this Ruth Holland looked, how she had looked that night of the wedding, what she had said and done. The fact of being in the very house where Ruth Holland had been that last night she was with her friends seemed to bring close something mysterious, terrible, stirring imagination and curiosity. Had she been with Deane that night? Had he taken her to the wedding?—taken her home? She hardened to him in the thought of there being this thing she did not know about. It began to seem he had done her a great wrong in not preparing her for a thing that could bring her embarrassment. Everyone else knew about it! Coming there a bride, and the very first thing encountering something awkward! She persuaded herself that her pleasure in this party, in this opening up of her life there, was spoiled, that Deane had spoiled it. And she tormented herself with a hundred little wonderings.

She and Cora Albright went home together in Edith's brougham. Cora was full of talk of Ruth Holland, this new development, Ruth's return, stirring it all up again for her. Amy's few discreet questions brought forth a great deal that she wanted to know. Cora had a worldly manner, and that vague sympathy with evil that poetizes one's self without doing anything so definite as condoning, or helping, the sinner.

"I do think," she said, with a little shrug, "that the town has been pretty hard about it. But then you know what these middle-western towns are." Amy, at this appeal to her sophistication, gravely nodded. "I do feel sorry for Ruth," Cora added in a more personal tone.

"Will you go to see her?" Amy asked, rather pointedly.

"Oh, I couldn't do that," replied Cora. "My family—you know,—or perhaps you don't know. I'm related to Mrs. Williams," she laughed.

"Oh!" Amy ejaculated, aghast, and newly fascinated by the horror, what somehow seemed the impossibleness of the whole thing—that she should be talking of Ruth Holland to a woman related to Mrs. Williams!

"I suppose *she* felt terribly," Amy murmured.

Cora laughed a little. "Oh, I don't know. It never seemed to me that Marion would do much feeling. Feeling is so—ruffling."

"She looks," said Amy, a little aggressively, "as though she might not show all she feels."

"Oh, I suppose not," Cora agreed pleasantly. "Perhaps I do Marion an injustice. She may have suffered in silence. Certainly she's kept silence. Truth is, I never liked her so very well. I like Ruth much the better of the two. I like warmth—feeling."

She was leaning forward and looking from the window. "That's the Hollands'," she said. And under her breath, compassionately, she murmured, "Poor Ruth!"

"I should think you *would* go and see her," said Amy, curiously resentful of this feeling.

With a little sigh Cora leaned back in the luxurious corner. "We're not free to do what we might like to do in this life," she said, looking gravely at Amy and speaking as one actuated by something larger than personal feeling. "Too many people are associated with me for me to go and see Ruth—as, for my own part, I'd gladly do.

You see it's even closer than being related to Marion. Cyrus Holland,—Ruth's brother—married into my family too. Funny, isn't it?" she laughed at Amy's stare. "Yes, Cyrus Holland married a second cousin of Stuart Williams' wife."

"Why—" gasped Amy, "it's positively weird, isn't it?"

"Things are pretty much mixed up in this world," Cora went on, speaking with that good-natured sophistication which appealed to Amy as worldly. "I think one reason Cy was so bitter against Ruth, and kept the whole family so, was the way it broke into his own plans. He was in love with Louise at the time Ruth left; of course all her kith and kin—being also Marion's—were determined she should not marry a Holland. Cy thought he had lost her, but after a time, as long as no one was quite so bitter against Ruth as he, the opposition broke down a little—enough for Louise to ride over it. Oh, yes, in these small towns everybody's somehow mixed up with everyone else," she laughed. "And of course," she went on more gravely, "that is where it is hard to answer the people who seem so hard about Ruth. It isn't just one's self, or even just one's family —though it broke them pretty completely, you know; but a thing like that reaches out into so many places—hurts so many lives."

"Yes," said Amy, "it does." She was thinking of her own life, of how it was clouding her happiness.

"One has to admit," said Cora, in the tone of summing it all up, "that just taking one's own happiness is thorough selfishness. Society as a whole is greater than the individual, isn't it?"

That seemed to Amy the heart of it. She felt herself as one within society, herself faithful to it and guarding it against all who would do it harm; hard to the traitor, not because of any personal feeling—she wished to make that clear to herself—but because society as a whole demanded that hardness. After she had bade Cora good-by and as she was about to open the door of the house Deane had prepared for her, she told herself that it was a matter of taking the larger view. She was pleased with the phrase; it seemed to clear her own feeling of any possible charge of smallness.

CHAPTER FOURTEEN

Despite the fact that he knew he was going to be late getting home for dinner, Dr. Franklin was sending his car very slowly along the twelve-mile stretch of road that lay between him and home. This was not so much because it was beautiful country through which he went, and the spring freshness in the softness of late afternoon was grateful to him, nor because too tired for any kind of hurrying, as it was that he did not want to cover those twelve miles before he had thought out what he was going to say to Amy.

He had seen Ruth that afternoon. He went, as usual, to see her father, and as he entered the room Ruth was sitting beside the bed. She sat with her back to him and did not seem to know at once that he was there. She was bending forward, elbow on her knee, hand to her face, looking at her father who was asleep, or, rather, in that stupor with which death reaches out into life, through which the living are drawn to the dead. She was sitting very still, intent, as she watched the man whom life was letting go.

He had not seen Ruth since that night, eleven years before, when she clung to him as she saw the headlight of her train, then turned from him to the car that was to carry her away from the whole world she knew. It had seemed that the best of life was pulling away from him as he heard her train pull out. He fairly ran away from the sound of it; not alone because it was taking Ruth out of his own life, but because it was bearing her to a country where the way would be too hard.

He knew that that way had been hard, that the years had not spared her; and yet there had been a little shock when he saw Ruth that afternoon; he knew now that his fears for her had rather given themselves a color of romance. She looked worn, as if she had worked, and, just at first, before she saw him, she looked older than it would seem that number of years should make her.

But when she heard him and turned, coming to him with outstretched hand, it was as it used to be—feeling illumining, transforming her. She was the old flaming Ruth then, the years that lined her defied. Her eyes—it was like a steady light shining through trembling waters. No one else ever gave him that impression Ruth did of a certain deep steadiness through changing feeling. He had thought he remembered just how wonderful Ruth's eyes were—how feeling flamed in them and that steady understanding looked through from her to him—that bridge between separateness. But they were newly wonderful to him,— so live, so tender, so potent.

She had been very quiet; thinking back to it, he

pondered that. It seemed not alone the quiet that comes with the acceptance of death, the quiet that is the subduing effect of strange or moving circumstances, but an inner quiet, a quiet of power. The years had taken something from Ruth, but Ruth had won much from them. She was worn, a little dimmed, but deepened. A tragedy queen she was not; he had a little smile for himself for that subconscious romantic expectation that gave him, just at the first, a little shock of disappointment when he saw Ruth. A tragedy queen would hold herself more imposingly—and would have taken better care of her hands. But that moment of a lighted way between Ruth and him could let him afford to smile at disappointed romantic expectation.

He had been there for only a few minutes, having the long trip out in the country to make. Ruth and Ted seemed to be alone in the house. He asked her if she had seen Harriett, and she answered, simply, "Not yet."

She had said, "You're married, Deane—and happy. I'm so glad." That, too, she had said very simply; it was real; direct. As he thought of it now it was as if life had simplified her; she had let slip from her, like useless garments, all those blurring artificialities that keep people apart.

As usual he would go over again that evening to see his patient; and then he would remain for a visit with Ruth. And he wanted to take Amy with him. He would not let himself realize just how much he wanted to do that, how much he would hate not doing it. He was thinking it out, trying to arrive at the best way of putting it to Amy. If only he could make it seem to her the simple thing it was to him!

He would be so happy to do this for Ruth, but it was more than that; it was that he wanted to bring Amy within—within that feeling of his about Ruth. He wanted her to share in that. He could not bear to leave it a thing from which she was apart, to which she was hostile. He could not have said just why he felt it so important Amy become a part of what he felt about Ruth.

When at last they were together over their unusually late dinner the thing he wanted to say seemed to grow more difficult because Amy was so much dressed up. In her gown of that afternoon she looked so much the society person that what he had in mind somehow grew less simple. And there was that in her manner too—like her clothes it seemed a society manner—to make it less easy to attempt to take her into things outside the conventional round of life. He felt a little helpless before this self-contained, lovely young person. She did not seem easy to get at. Somehow she seemed to be apart from him. There was a real wistfulness in his desire to take her into what to him were things real and important. It seemed if he could not do that now that Amy would always be a little apart from him.

Her talk was of the tea that afternoon: who was there, what they wore, what they had said to her, how the house looked; how lovely Mrs. Lawrence and Edith were.

What he was thinking was that it was Ruth's old crowd had assembled there—at Edith's house —to be gracious to Amy that afternoon. She mentioned this name and that—girls Ruth had grown up with, girls who had known her so well, and cared for her. And Ruth? Had they spoken of her? Did they know she was home? If they did, did it leave them all unmoved? He thought of the easy, pleasant way life had gone with most of those old friends of Ruth's. Had they neither the imagination nor the heart to go out in the thought of the different thing it had been to her?

He supposed not; certainly they had given no evidence of any such disposition. It hardened him against them. He hated the thought of the gay tea given for Amy that afternoon when Ruth, just back after all those years away, was home alone with her father, who was dying. Amy they were taking in so graciously—because things had gone right with her; Ruth, whom they knew, who had been one of them, they left completely out. There flamed up a desire to take Amy with him, as against them, to show them that she was sweeter and larger than they, that she understood and put no false value on a cordiality that left the heart hard.

But Amy looked so much one of them, seemed so much one with them in her talk about them, that he put off what he wanted to say, listening to her. And yet, he assured himself, that was not the whole of Amy; he softened and took heart in the thought of her tenderness in moments of love, her sweetness when the world fell away and they were man and woman to each other. Those real things were stronger in her than this crust of worldliness. He would reach through that to the life that glowed behind it. If he only had the skill, the understanding, to reach through that crust to the life within, to that which was real, she would understand that the very thing bringing them their happiness was the thing which in Ruth put her apart from her friends; she would be larger, more tender, than those others. He wanted that triumph for her over them. He would glory in it so! There would be such pride in showing Amy to Ruth as a woman who was real. And most of all, because it was a thing so deep in his own life, he wanted Amy to come within, to know from within, his feeling about Ruth.

"You know, dear, that was Ruth's old crowd you were meeting this afternoon," he finally said.

He saw her instantly stiffen. Her mouth looked actually hard. That, he quickly told himself, was what those people had done to her.

"And that house," he went on, his voice remaining quiet, "was like another home to Ruth."

Amy cleared her throat. "She didn't make a very good return for the hospitality, do you think?" she asked sharply.

Flushing, he started to reply to that, but instead asked abruptly, "Does Edith know that Ruth is home?"

"Yes," Amy replied coldly, "they were speaking of her."

"*Speaking* of her!" he scoffed.

"I suppose *you* would think," she flamed, "that they ought to have met her at the train!"

"The idea doesn't seem to me preposterous," he answered.

Feeling the coldness in his own voice he realized how he was at the very start getting away from the thing he wanted to do, was estranging Amy by his resentment of her feeling about a thing she did not understand. After all—as before, he quickly made this excuse for her—what more natural than that she should take on the feeling of these people she was thrown with, particularly when they were so very kindly in their reception of her?

"Dear," he began again, "I saw Ruth this afternoon. She seems so alone there. She's gone through such—such hard things. It's a pretty sad home-coming for her. I'm going over there

again this evening, and, Amy dear, I do so want
you to go with me.''

Amy did not reply. He had not looked at her
after he began speaking—not wanting to lose
either his courage or his temper in seeing that
stiffening in her. He did not look at her now,
even though she did not speak.

''I want you to go, Amy. I ask you to. I want
it—you don't know how much. I'm terribly sorry
for Ruth. I knew her very well, we were very
close friends. Now that she is here, and in
trouble—and so lonely—I want to take my wife to
see her.''

As even then she remained silent, he turned to
her. She sat very straight; red spots burned in
her cheeks and there was a light in her eyes he
had never seen there before. She pushed back
her chair excitedly. ''And may I ask,''—her
voice was high, tight,—''if you see nothing insulting to your wife in this—proposal?''

For an instant he just stared at her. ''Insulting?'' he faltered. ''I—I—'' He stopped, helpless, and helplessly sat looking at her, sitting
erect, breathing fast, face and eyes aflame with
anger. And in that moment something in his
heart fell back; a desire that had been dear to him,
a thing that had seemed so beautiful and so necessary, somehow just crept back where it could not
be so much hurt. At the sight of her, hard, scorn-

ful, so sure in her hardness, that high desire of his love that she share his feeling fell back. And then to his disappointment was added anger for Ruth; through the years anger against so many people had leaped up in him because of their hardness to Ruth, that, as if of itself, it leaped up against Amy now.

"No," he said, his voice hard now too, "I must say I see nothing insulting in asking you to go with me to see Ruth Holland!"

"Oh, you don't!" she cried. "A woman living with another woman's husband! Why, this very afternoon I was with the wife of the man that woman is living with!—*she* is the woman I would meet! And you can ask me—your wife—to go and see a woman who turned her back on society—on decency—a woman her own family cast out, and all decent people turn away from." She paused, struggling, unable to keep her dignity and yet say the things rushing up to be said.

He had grown red, as he always did when people talked that way about Ruth. "Of course," —he made himself say it quietly—"she isn't those things to me, you know. She's—quite other things to me."

"I'd like to know what she *is* to you!" Amy cried. "It's very strange—your standing up for her against the whole town!"

He did not reply; it was impossible to tell Amy,

when she was like this, what Ruth had been—was —to him.

She looked at him as he sat there silent. And this was the man she had married!—a man who could treat her like this, asking her to go and see a woman who wasn't respectable—why, who was as far from respectable as a woman could be! This was the man for whom she had left her mother and father—and a home better than this home certainly,—yes, and that other man who had wanted her and who had so much more to offer! *He* respected her. He would never ask her to go and see a woman who wasn't decent! But she had married for love; had given up all those other things that she might have love. And now. . . . Her throat tightened and it was hard to hold back tears. And then suddenly she wanted to go over to Deane, slip down beside him, put her arms around him, tell him that she loved him and ask him to please tell her that he loved her. But there was so strange an expression on his face; it checked that warm, loving impulse, holding her where she was, hard. What was he thinking about—*that woman?* He had so strange a look. She did not believe it had anything to do with her. No, he had forgotten her. It was this other woman. Why, he was in love with her—of course! He had always been in love with her.

Because it seemed the idea would break her

heart, because she could not bear it, it was scoffingly that she threw out: "You were in love with her, I suppose? You've always been in love with her, haven't you?"

"Yes, Amy," he answered, "I was in love with Ruth. I loved her—at any rate, I sorrowed for her—until the day I met you."

His voice was slow and sad; the whole sadness of it all, all the sadness of a world in which men and women loved and hurt each other seemed closing in around him. He did not seem able to rise out of it, to go out to her; it was as if his new disappointment brought back all the hurt of old ones.

Young, all inexperienced in the ways of adjusting love to life, of saving it for life, the love in her tried to shoot through the self-love that closed her in, holding her tight. She wanted to follow that impulse, go over and put her arms around her husband, let her kisses drive away that look of sadness. She knew that she could do it, that she ought to do it, that she would be sorry for not having done it, but—she couldn't. Love did not know how to fight its way through pride.

He had risen. "I must go. I have a number of calls to make. I—I'm sorry you feel as you do, Amy."

He was not going to explain! He was just leaving her outside it all! He didn't care for her, really, at all—just took her because he couldn't get that other woman! Took *her*—Amy Forrester

—because he couldn't get the woman he wanted! Great bands of incensed pride bound her heart now, closing in the love that had fluttered there. Her face, twisted with varying emotions, was fairly ugly as she cried: "Well, I must say, I wish you had told me this before we were married!"

He looked at her in surprise. Then, surprised anew, looked quickly away. Feeling that he had failed, he tried to put it aside lightly. "Oh, come now, Amy, you didn't think, did you, that you could marry a man of thirty-four who had never loved any woman?"

"I should like to think he had loved a respectable woman!" she cried, wounded anew by this lightness, unable to hold back things she miserably knew she would be sorry she had not held back. "And if he had loved that kind of a woman—*did* love her—I should like to think he had too much respect for his wife to ask her to meet such a person!"

"Ruth Holland is not a woman to speak like that about, Amy," he said with unconcealed anger.

"She's not a decent woman! She's not a respectable woman! She's a bad woman! She's a low woman!"

She could not hold it back. She knew she looked unlovely, knew she was saying things that would not make her loved. She could not help it. Deane turned away from her. After a minute he got a little control of himself and instead of the hot things that had flashed up, said coldly: "I don't think you know what you're talking about."

"Of course I couldn't hope to know as much as *she* does," she jeered. "However," she went on, with more of a semblance of dignity, "I do know a few things. I know that society cannot countenance a woman who did what that woman did. I know that if a woman is going to selfishly take her own happiness with no thought of others she must expect to find herself outside the lives of decent people. Society must protect itself against such persons as she. I know that much—fortunately."

Her words fortified her. She, certainly, was in the right. She felt that she had behind her all those women of that afternoon. Did any of them receive Ruth Holland? Did they not all see that society must close in against the individual who defied it? She felt supported.

For the minute he stood there looking at her— so absolutely unyielding, so satisfied in her conclusions,—those same things about society and the individual that he had heard from the rest of them; like the rest of them so satisfied with the law she had laid down—law justifying hardness of heart and closing in against the sorrow of a particular human life; from Amy now that same look, those same words. For a little time he did not speak. "I'm awfully sorry, Amy," was all he said then.

He stood there in miserable embarrassment. He always kissed her good-by.

She saw his hesitancy and turned to the other room. "Hadn't you better hurry?" she laughed. "You have so many calls to make—and some of them so important!"

CHAPTER FIFTEEN

It was quiet that evening in the house of Cyrus Holland; the noises that living makes were muffled by life's awe of death, even sounds that could not disturb the dying guarded against by the sense of decorum of those living on. Downstairs were people who had come to inquire for the man they knew would not be one of them again. For forty years Cyrus Holland had been a factor in the affairs of the town. He was Freeport's senior banker, the old-fashioned kind of banker, with neither the imagination nor the daring to make of himself a rich man, or of his bank an institution using all the possibilities of its territory. In venturing days he remained cautious. His friends said that he was sane—responsible; men of a newer day put it that he was limited, lacking in that boldness which makes the modern man of affairs. He had advised many men and always on the side of safety. No one had grown rich through his suggestions, but more than one had been saved by his counsels. With the expansion of the business of the town newer banks had gone ahead of his, and when they said he was one of the good substantial men of the community they were indicating his limitations with his virtues. Such a man, not a brilliant figure through his lifetime, would be lamented in his passing. They had often said that he failed in using his opportunities; what they said now was that he had never abused them—death, as usual, inducing the living to turn the kindly side to the truth about the dying.

Ruth did not go downstairs to see the people who were coming in. Ted was down there, and Flora Copeland, a spinster cousin of the Hollands, who for several years had lived in the house. Once, in passing through the hall, she heard voices which she recognized. She stood there listening to them. It was so strange to hear them; and so good. She was hungry for voices she knew—old voices. Once there was a pause and her heart beat fast for she got a feeling that maybe they were going to ask for her. But they broke that pause to say goodnight. She had received no message about anyone asking for her.

But even though she was not seeing the people who came she felt the added strangeness her presence made in that house which had suspended the usual affairs of living in waiting for death. The nurse was one of the girls of the town, of a family Ruth knew. She had been only a little girl at the time Ruth went away. She was conscious, in the young woman's scrupulously professional manner toward herself, of a covert interest, as in something mysterious, forbidden. She could see that to this decorous young person she was a woman out of another world. It hurt her, and it made her a little angry. She wished that this professional, proper young woman, stealing glances as at a forbidden thing, could know the world in which she actually lived.

And yet it occurred to her that the strain was less great than it would have been at any other time—something about a room of death making the living a little less prone to divide themselves into good and bad, approved and condemned. With the approach of death there are likely to be only two classes—the living and the dead. After the first few hours, despite the estranging circumstances, there did seem to be some sort of a bond between her and this girl who attended her father.

Ruth and Ted and Flora Copeland had had dinner together. Her Cousin Flora had evidently pondered the difficult question of a manner with Ruth and was pursuing it scrupulously. Her plan was clearly indicated in her manner. She would seem to be acting as if nothing had happened and yet at the same time made it plain that she in no sense countenanced the person to whom she was being kind. Her manner was that most dismal of all things—a punctilious kindliness.

This same Cousin Flora, now an anæmic woman of forty-five, had not always been exclusively concerned with propriety. Ruth could remember Cousin Flora's love affair, which had so greatly disturbed the members of the family, and which, to save their own pride, they had thwarted. Cousin Flora had had the misfortune to fall in love with a man quite outside the social sphere of the Copelands and the Hollands. He was a young laboring man whom she knew through the social affairs of the church. He had the presumption to fall in love with her. She had not had love before, being less generously endowed in other respects than with social position in Freeport. There had been a brief, mad time when Cousin Flora had seemed to find love greater than exclusiveness. But the undesirable affair was frustrated by a family whose democracy did not extend beyond a working together for the good of the Lord, and Cousin Flora was, as Ruth remembered their saying with satisfaction, saved. Looking at her now Ruth wondered if there ever came times when she regretted having been saved.

She tried to make the most of all those little things that came into her mind just because this homecoming was so desolate a thing to be left alone with. She had many times lived through a homecoming. And when she had thought of coming home she had always, in spite of it all, thought of things as much the same. And now even she and Ted were strange with each other; it was Ted the little boy she knew; it was hard all at once to bridge years in which they had not shared experiences.

It was the house itself seemed really to take her in. When she got her first sight of it all the things in between just rolled away. She was back. What moved her first was not that things had changed but that they were so much the same— the gate, the walk up to the house, the big tree, the steps of the porch; as she went up the walk there was the real feeling of coming home.

Then they stepped up on the porch—and her mother was not there to open the door for her; she knew then with a poignancy even those first days had not carried that she would never see her mother again, knew as she stepped into the house that her mother was gone. And yet it would keep seeming her mother must be somewhere in that house, that in a little while she would come in the room and tell something about where she had been. And she would find herself listening for her grandfather's slow, uncertain step; and for Terror's bark—one of his wild, glad rushes into the room. Ted said that Terror had been run over by an automobile a number of years before.

Nor was it only those whom death kept away who were not there. Her sister Harriett had not been there to welcome her; now it was evening and she had not yet seen her. Ted had merely said that he guessed Harriett was tired out. He seemed embarrassed about it and had hastily be-

gun to talk of something else. And none of the
old girls had come in to see her. The fact that she
had not expected them to come somehow did not
much relieve the hurt of their not coming. When
a door opened she would find herself listening for
Edith's voice; there was no putting down the feeling that surely Edith would be running in soon.

Most of the time she sat by her father's bed;
though she was watching him dying, to sit there
by him was the closest to comfort she could come.
And as she watched the face which already had the
look of death there would come pictures of her
father at various times through the years. There
was that day when she was a tiny girl and he came
home bringing her a puppy; she could see his
laughing face as he held the soft, wriggling, fuzzy
little ball of life up to her, see him standing there
enjoying her delight. She saw him as he was one
day when she said she was not going to Sunday-
school, that she was tired of Sunday-school and
was not going any more. She could hear him saying, "Ruth, go upstairs and put on your clothes
for Sunday-school!"—see him as plainly as
though it had just happened standing there point-
ing a stern finger toward the stairs, not moving
until she had started to obey him. And once when
she and Edith and some other girls were making
a great noise on the porch he had stepped out from
the living-room, where he and some men were sitting about the table, looking over something, and

said, mildly, affectionately, "My dears, what would you think of making a little less noise?" Queer things to be remembering, but she saw just how he looked, holding the screen door open as he said it.

And as she sat there thinking of how she would never hear his voice again, he reached out his hand as if groping for something he wanted; and when with a little sob she quickly took it he clasped her hand, putting into it a strength that astonished her. He turned toward her after that and the nature of his sleep changed a little; it seemed more natural, as if there were something of peace in it. It was as if he had turned to her, reached out his hand for her, knowing she was there and wanting her. He was too far from life for more, but he had done what he could. Her longing gave the little movement big meaning. Sitting there holding the hand of her father who would never talk to her nor listen to her again, she wanted as she had never wanted before to tell her story. She had been a long time away; she had had a hard time. She wanted to tell him about it, wanted to try and make him understand how it had all happened. She wanted to tell him how homesick she had been and how she had always loved them all. It seemed if she could just make him know what it was she had felt, and what she had gone through, he would be sorry for her and love her as he used to.

Someone had come into the room; she did not turn at once, trying to make her blurred eyes clear. When she looked around she saw her sister Harriett. Her father had relaxed his hold on her hand and so she rose and turned to her sister.

"Well, Ruth," said Harriett, in an uncertain tone. Then she kissed her. The kiss, too, was uncertain, as if she had not known what to do about it, but had decided in its favor. But she *had* kissed her. Again that hunger to be taken in made much of little. She stood there struggling to hold back the sobs. If only Harriett would put her arms around her and really kiss her!

But Harriett continued to stand there uncertainly. Then she moved, as if embarrassed. And then she spoke. "Did you have a—comfortable trip?" she asked.

The struggle with sobs was over. Ruth took a step back from her sister. It was a perfectly controlled voice which answered: "Yes, Harriett, my trip was comfortable—thank you."

Harriett flushed and still stood there uncertainly. Then, "Did the town look natural?" she asked, diffidently this time.

But Ruth did not say whether the town had looked natural or not. She had noticed something. In a little while Harriett would have another baby. And she had not known about it! Harriett, to be sure, had had other babies and she had not known about it, but somehow to see Harriett, not having known it, brought it home hard that she was not one of them any more; she did not know when children were to be born; she did not know what troubled or what pleased them; did not know how they managed the affairs of living—who their neighbors were—their friends. She had not known about Harriett; Harriett did not know about her—her longing for a baby, longing which circumstances made her sternly deny herself. Unmindful of the hurt of a moment before she now wanted to pour all that out to Harriett, wanted to talk with her of those deep, common things.

The nurse had come in the room and was beginning some preparations for the night. Harriett was moving toward the door. "Harriett," Ruth began timidly, "won't you come in my room a little while and—talk?"

Harriett hesitated. They were near the top of the stairs and voices could be heard below. "I guess not," she said nervously. "Not to-night," she added hurriedly; "that's Edgar down there. He's waiting for me."

"Then goodnight," said Ruth very quietly, and turned to her room.

All day long she had been trying to keep away from her room. "Thought probably you'd like to have your old room, Ruth," Ted had said in taking her to it. He had added, a little hurriedly, "Guess no one's had it since you left."

It looked as if it was true enough no one had used it since she went out of it that night eleven years before. The same things were there; the bed was in the same position; so was her dressing table, and over by the big window that opened to her side porch was the same little low chair she always sat in to put on her shoes and stockings. It took her a long way back; it made old things very strangely real. She sat down in her little chair now and looked over at a picture of the Madonna Edith had once given her on her birthday. She could hear people moving about downstairs, hear voices. She had never in her whole life felt as alone.

And then she grew angry. Harriett had no right to treat her like that! She had worked; she had suffered; she had done her best in meeting the hard things of living. She had gone the way of women, met the things women meet. Why, she had done her own washing! Harriett had no right to treat her as if she were clear outside the common things of life.

She rose and went to the window and lowering it leaned out. She had grown used to turning from hard things within to the night. There in the South-west, where they slept out of doors, she had come to know the night. Ever since that it had seemed to have something for her, something from which she could draw. And after they had gone through those first years and the fight was not for keeping life but for making a place for it in the world, she had many times stepped from a cramping little house full of petty questions she did not know how to deal with, from a hard little routine that threatened their love out to the vast, still night of that Colorado valley and always something had risen in herself which gave her power. So many times that had happened that instinctively she turned to the outside now, leaning her head against the lowered casing. The oak tree was gently tapping against the house—that same old sound that had gone all through her girlhood; the familiar fragrance of a flowering vine on the porch below; the thrill of the toads off there in the little ravine, a dog's frolicsome barking; the laughter of some boys and girls who were going by—old things those, sweeping her back to old things. Down in the next block some boys were singing that old serenading song, "Good-night, Ladies." Long ago boys had sung it to her. She stood there listening to it, tears running down her face.

She was startled by a tap at the door; dashing her hands across her face she eagerly called, "Come in."

"Deane's here, Ruth," said Ted. "Wants to see you. Shall I tell him to come in here?"

She nodded, but for an instant Ted stood there looking at her. She was so strange. She had been crying, and yet she seemed so glad, so excited about something.

"Oh, Deane," she cried, holding out her two hands to him, laughter and sobs crowding out together, "*talk* to me! How's your mother? How's your Aunt Margaret's rheumatism? What kind of an automobile have you? What about your practice? What about your dog? Why, Deane," she rushed on, "I'm just starving for things like that! You know I'm just Ruth, don't you, Deane?" She laughed a little wildly. "And I've come home. And I want to know about things. Why I could listen for hours about what streets are being paved—and who supports old Mrs. Lynch! Don't you see, Deane?" she laughed through tears. "But first tell me about Edith! How does she look? How many children has she? Who are her friends? And oh, Deane —tell me,—does she *ever* say anything about me?"

They talked for more than two hours. She kept pouring out questions at him every time he would stop for breath. She fairly palpitated with that desire to hear little things—what Bob Horton did for a living, whether Helen Matthews still gave music lessons. She hung tremulous upon his words, laughing and often half crying as he told little stories about quarrels and jokes—about churches and cooks. In his profession he had many times seen a system craving a particular thing, but it seemed to him he had never seen any need more pitifully great than this of hers for laughing over the little drolleries of life. And then they sank into deeper channels—he found himself telling her things he had not told anyone: about his practice, about the men he was associated with, things he had come to think.

And she talked to him of Stuart's health, of their efforts at making a living—what she thought of dry farming, of heaters for apple orchards; the cattle business, the character of Western people. She told him of the mountains in winter—snow down to their feet; of Colorado air on a winter's morning. And then of more personal, intimate things—how lonely they had been, how much of a struggle they had found it. She talked of the disadvantage Stuart was at because of his position, how he had grown sensitive because of suspicion, because there were people who kept away from him; how she herself had not made friends, afraid to because several times after she had come to know the people around her they had "heard," and drawn away. She told it all quite simply, just that she wanted to let him know about their lives. He could see what it was meaning to her to talk, that she had been too tight within and was finding relief. "I try not to talk much to Stuart about things that would make him feel bad," she said. "He gets despondent. It's been very hard for

Stuart, Deane. He misses his place among men.''

She fell silent there, brooding over that—a touch of that tender, passionate brooding he knew of old. And as he watched her he himself was thinking, not of how hard it had been for Stuart, but of what it must have been to Ruth. That hunger of hers for companionship told him more than words could possibly have done of what her need had been. He studied her as she sat there silent. She was the same old Ruth, but a deepened Ruth; there was the same old sweetness, but new power. He had a feeling that there was nothing in the world Ruth would not understand; that bars to her spirit were down, that she would go out in tenderness to anything that was of life—to sorrow, to joy, with the insight to understand and the warmth to care. He looked at her: worn down by living, yet glorified by it; hurt, yet valiant. The life in her had gone through so much and circumstances had not been able to beat it down. And this was the woman Amy said it was insulting of him to ask her to meet!

She looked up at him with her bright, warm smile. ''Oh, Deane, it's been so good! You don't know how you've helped me. Why you wouldn't believe,'' she laughed, ''how much better I feel.''

They had risen and he had taken her hand for goodnight. ''You always helped me, Deane,'' she said in her simple way. ''You never failed me. You don't know''—this with one of those flashes of feeling that lighted Ruth and made her wonderful—"how many times, when things were going badly, I've thought of you—and wanted to see you."

They stood there a moment silent; the things they had lived through together, in which they had shared understanding, making a spiritual current between them. She broke from it with a light, fond: "Dear Deane, I'm so glad you're happy. I want you to be happy always."

CHAPTER SIXTEEN

Those words kept coming back to him after he had gone to bed: ''I'm so glad you're happy—I want you to be happy always.'' Amy was asleep when he came home, or he took it for granted that she was asleep and was careful not to disturb her, for it was past midnight. He wished she would turn to him with a sleepy little smile. He wanted to be made to feel that it was true he was happy, that he was going to be happy always. That night was not filled with the sweetness of love's faith in permanence. He tried to put away the thought of how Amy had looked as she said those things about Ruth. Knowing the real Ruth, his feeling about her freshened, deepened, he could not bear to think of Amy as having said those things. He held it off in telling himself again that that was what the people of the town had done, that he himself had not managed well. He would try again—a little differently. Amy was really so sweet, so loving, he told himself, that she would come to be different about this. Though he did not dwell on that, either—upon her coming to be different; her face in saying those things was a little too hard to forget. He kept up a pretence with himself on the surface, but down in his heart he asked less now;

he was not asking of love that complete sharing, that deep understanding which had been his dream before he talked to Amy. He supposed things would go on about the same—just that that one thing wouldn't be, was the thought with which he went to sleep, making his first compromise with his ideal for their love. Just as he was falling asleep there came before him, half of dreams, Ruth's face as it had been when she seemed to be brooding over the things life brought one. It was as if pain had endowed her with understanding. Did it take pain to do it?

He had an early morning call to make and left home without really talking to Amy. When he woke in the morning, yearning to be back in the new joy of her love, he was going to tell her that he was sorry he had hurt her, sorry there was this thing they looked at differently, but that he loved her with his whole heart and that they were going to be happy just the same, and then maybe some time they'd "get together" on this. It was a thing he would not have said he would do, but there are many things one will do to get from the shadow back into that necessary sunlight of love.

However, there was not opportunity then for doing it; he had to hurry to the hospital and Amy gave him no chance for such a moment with her. She had the manner of keeping up an appearance of going on as if nothing had happened; as if that thing were left behind—frosted over. She kissed him good-by, but even in that there seemed an immense reservation.   It made him unhappy, worried him.   He told himself that he would have to talk to Amy, that it wouldn't do to leave the thing that way.

It had been so easy to talk to Ruth; it seemed that one could talk to her about anything, that there was no danger of saying a thing and having it bound back from a wall of opinions and prejudices that kept him from her.   There was something resting, relaxing, in the way one could be one's self with Ruth, the way she seemed to like one for just what one was.   He had always felt more at ease with her than with anyone else, but now he more than ever had the feeling that her mind was loosened from the things that held the minds of most of the women he knew.   It was a great thing not to have those holdbacks in talking with a friend, to be freed of that fear of blundering into a thing that would be misunderstood.   He did not face the fact that that was just the way it was with Amy, that there was constantly the fear of saying something that would better have been left unsaid.   But he was thinking that being free to say what one was feeling was like drawing a long breath.

And in thinking of it as he went about his calls that morning, in various homes, talking with a number of people, it occurred to him that many of those things he had come to think, things of which he did not often try to talk to others, he had arrived at because of Ruth. It was amazing how his feeling about her, thoughts through her, had run into all his thinking. It even occurred to him that if it had not been for her he might have fallen into accepting many things more or less as the rest of the town did. It seemed now that as well as having caused him much pain she had brought rich gain; for those questionings of life, that refusal placidly to accept, had certainly brought keener satisfactions than he could have had through a closer companionship with facile acceptors. Ruth had been a big thing in his life, not only in his heart, but to his mind.

He had come out of the house of one of his patients and was standing on the steps talking with the woman who had anxiously followed him to the door. The house was directly across the street from the Lawrences'. Edith was sitting out on the porch; her little girl of eight and the boy, who was younger, were with her. They made an attractive picture.

He continued his reassuring talk to the woman whose husband was ill, but he was at the same time thinking of Ruth's eager questionings about Edith, about Edith's children, her hunger for every smallest thing he could tell her. When he went down to his car Edith, looking up and seeing him, gayly waved her hand. He returned the salute and stood there as if doing something to the car. Sit-

ting there in the morning sunshine with her two
children Edith looked the very picture of the
woman for whom things had gone happily. Life
had opened its pleasantest ways to Edith. He
could not bring himself to get in his car and start
away; he could not get rid of the thought of what
it would mean to Ruth if Edith would go to see
her, could not banish the picture of Ruth's face if
Edith were to walk into the room. And because
he could not banish it he suddenly turned abruptly
from his car and started across the street and up
the steps to the porch.

She smiled brightly up at him, holding out her
hand. "Coming up to talk to me? How nice!"

He pulled up a chair, bantering with the children.

"I know what you've come for," Edith laughed
gayly. "You've come to hear about how lovely
Amy was at the tea yesterday. You want to know
all the nice things people are saying about
her."

His face puckered as it did when he was perplexed or annoyed. He laughed with a little constraint as he said: "That would be pleasant
hearing, I admit. But it was something else I
wanted to talk to you about just now, Edith."

She raised her brows a little in inquiry, bending
forward slightly, waiting, her eyes touched with
the anticipation of something serious. He felt
sure his tone had suggested Ruth to her; that in-

dicated to him that Ruth had been much in her mind.

"I had a long visit with Ruth last night," he began quietly.

She did not speak, bending forward a little more, her eyes upon him intently, anxiously.

"Edith?"

"Yes, Deane?"

He paused, then asked simply: · "Edith, Ruth is very lonely. Won't you go to see her?"

She raised her chin in quick, startled way, some emotion, he did not know just what, breaking over her face.

"I thought I'd come and tell you, Edith, how lonely—how utterly lonely—Ruth is, because I felt if you understood you would want to go and see her."

Still Edith did not speak. She looked as though she were going to cry.

"Ruth's had a hard time, Edith. It's been no light life for her—you don't have to do more than look in her eyes to know that. I wish you could have heard the way she asked about you—poured out questions about you. She loves you just as she always did, Edith. She's sorrowed for you all through these years."

A tear brimmed over from Edith's blue eyes and rolled slowly—unheeded—down her cheek. His heart warmed to her and he took hope as he watched that tear.

"She was crazy to know about your children. That's been a grief to her, Edith. Ruth should be a mother—you know that. You must know what a mother she would have made. If you were to take your youngsters to see her—" He broke off with a laugh, as if there was no way of expressing it.

Edith looked away from him, seemed to be staring straight into a rose bush at the side of the porch.

"Couldn't you?" he gently pressed.

She turned to him. "I'd like to, Deane," she said simply, "but,"—her dimmed eyes were troubled—"I don't see how I could."

"Why not?" he pursued. "It's simple enough —just go and see her. We might go together, if that would seem easier."

She was pulling at a bit of sewing in her lap. "But, Deane, it *isn't* simple," she began hesitatingly. "It isn't just one's self. There's society—the whole big terrible question. If it were just a simple, individual matter,—why, the truth is I'd love to go and see Ruth. If it were just a personal thing—why don't you know that I'd forget everything—except that she's Ruth?" Her voice choked and she did not go on, but was fumbling with the sewing in her lap.

He hitched his chair forward anxiously, concentrated on his great desire to say it right, to win Edith for Ruth. Edith was a simple sort of being—really, a loving being; if she could only detach herself from what she pathetically called the whole terrible question—if he could just make her see that the thing she wanted to do was the thing to do. She looked up at him out of big grieving eyes, as if wanting to be convinced, wanting the way opened for the loving thing she would like to do.

"But, Edith," he began, as composedly and gently as he could, for she was so much a child in her mentality it seemed she must be dealt with gently and simply, "*is* it so involved, after all? Isn't it, more than anything else, just that simple, personal matter? Why not forget everything but the personal part of it? Ruth is back—lonely—in trouble. Things came between you and Ruth, but that was a long time ago and since that she's met hard things. You're not a vindictive person; you're a loving person. Then for heaven's sake why *wouldn't* you go and see her?"—it was impossible to keep the impatience out of that last.

"I know," she faltered, "but—society—"

"Society!" he jeered. "*Forget* society, Edith, and be just a human being! If *you* can forget—forgive—what seemed to you the wrong Ruth did *you*—if *your* heart goes out to her—then what else is there to it?" he demanded impatiently.

"But you see,"—he could feel her reaching out, as if thinking she must, to the things that had been said to her, was conscious of her mother's thinking pushing on hers as she fumbled, "but one *isn't* free, Deane. Society *has* to protect itself. What might not happen—if it didn't?"

He tried to restrain what he wanted to say to that—keep cool, wise, and say the things that would get Edith. He was sure that Edith wanted to be had; her eyes asked him to overthrow those things that had been fastened on her, to free her so that the simple, human approach was the only one there was to it, justify her in believing one dared be as kind, as natural and simple and real as one wanted to be. He was sure that in Edith's heart love for her friend was more real than any sense of duty to society.

"But after all what is society, Edith?" he began quietly. "Just a collection of individuals, isn't it? Why must it be so much harder than the individuals comprising it? If it is that—then there's something wrong with it, wouldn't you think?"

He looked around at the sound of a screen door closing. Edith's mother had stepped out on the porch. He knew by her startled look, her quick, keen glance at him, that she had heard his last words. She stepped forward holding up her hands in mock dismay, with a laughing: "What a large, solemn issue for an early morning conversation!"

Deane tried to laugh but he was not good at dissembling and he was finding it hard to conceal his annoyance at the interruption. Talking to Mrs.

Lawrence was very different from talking to Edith. Edith, against her own loving impulses, tried to think what she thought she ought to think; Mrs. Lawrence had hardened into the things she thought should be thought, and at once less loving and more intelligent than Edith, she was fixed where her daughter was uncertain, complacent where Edith was troubled. She was one of those women who, very kind to people they accept, have no tendrils of kindness running out to those whom they do not approve. Her qualities of heart did not act outside the circle of her endorsement. With the exception of Ruth's brother Cyrus, no one in the town had been harder about her than Edith's mother. He had all the time felt that, let alone, Edith would have gone back to Ruth.

He had risen and pulled up a chair for Mrs. Lawrence and now stood there fumbling with his hat, as if about to leave. It seemed to him he might as well.

"Why, my dears!" exclaimed the older woman with a sort of light dryness, "pray don't let me feel I have broken up a philosophic discussion."

"Deane was asking me to go and see Ruth, mother," said Edith, simply and not without dignity.

He saw her flush, her quick look up at him, and then the slight tightening of her lips.

"And doesn't it occur to Deane," she asked

pleasantly, "that that is rather a strange thing to ask of you?"

"She is very lonely, Deane says," said Edith tremulously.

Mrs. Lawrence was threading a needle. "I presume so," she answered quietly.

Deane felt the blood rising in him. Somehow that quiet reply angered him as no sharp retort could have done. He turned to Edith, rather pointedly leaving her mother out. "Well," he asked bluntly, "will you go?"

Edith's eyes widened. She looked frightened. She stole a look at her mother, who had serenely begun upon her embroidery.

"Why, Deane!" laughed the mother, as if tolerantly waving aside a preposterous proposal, "how absurd! Of course Edith won't go! How could she? Why should she?"

He made no reply, fearing to let himself express the things which—disappointed—he was feeling.

Mrs. Lawrence looked up. "If you will just cast your mind back," she said, her voice remaining pleasant though there was a sting in it now, "to the way Ruth treated Edith, I think it will come home to you, Deane, that you are asking a rather absurd thing."

"But Edith says,"—he made a big effort to speak as quietly as she did—"that that personal part of it is all right with her. She says that she would really like to go and see Ruth, but doesn't think she can—on account of society.''

Mrs. Lawrence flushed a little at his tone on that last, but she seemed quite unruffled as she asked: ''And you see no point in that?''

He had sat down on the railing of the porch. He leaned back against a pillar, turning a little away from them as he said with a laugh not free of bitterness: ''I don't believe I quite get this idea about society.'' Abruptly he turned back to Mrs. Lawrence. ''What is it? A collection of individuals for mutual benefit and self-protection, I gather. Protection against what? Their own warmest selves? The most real things in them?''

Mrs. Lawrence colored, though she was smiling composedly enough. Edith was not smiling. He saw her anxious look over at her mother, as if expecting her to answer that, and yet—this was what her eyes made him think—secretly hoping she couldn't.

But Mrs. Lawrence maintained her manner of gracious, rather amused tolerance with an absurd hot-headedness, perversity, on his part. ''Oh, come now, Deane,'' she laughed, ''we're not going to get into an absurd discussion, are we?''

''I beg your pardon, Mrs. Lawrence,'' he retorted sharply, ''but I don't think it an absurd discussion. I don't consider a thing that involves the happiness of as fine a human being as Ruth Holland an absurd thing to discuss!''

She laid down her work. "Ruth Holland," she began very quietly, "is a human being who selfishly—basely—took her own happiness, leaving misery for others. She outraged society as completely as a woman could outrage it. She was a thief, really,—stealing from the thing that was protecting her, taking all the privileges of a thing she was a traitor to. She was not only what we call a bad woman, she was a hypocrite. More than that, she was outrageously unfaithful to her dearest friend—to Edith here who loved and trusted her. Having no respect for marriage herself, she actually had the effrontery—to say nothing of the lack of fine feeling—to go to the altar with Edith the very night that she herself outraged marriage. I don't know, Deane, how a woman could do a worse thing than that. The most pernicious kind of woman is not the one who bears the marks of the bad woman upon her. It's the woman like Ruth Holland, who appears to be what she is not, who deceives, plays a false part. If you can't see that society must close in against a woman like that then all I can say, my dear Deane, is that you don't see very straight. You jeer about society, but society is nothing more than life as we have arranged it. It is an institution. One living within it must keep the rules of that institution. One who defies it—deceives it—must be shut out from it. So much we are forced to do in self-defence. We *owe* that to the people who are trying to live decently, to be faithful. Life, as we have arranged it, must be based on confidence. We have to keep that confidence. We have to punish a violation of it.'' She took up her sewing again. ''Your way of looking at it is not a very large way, Deane,'' she concluded pleasantly.

Edith had settled back in her chair—accepting, though her eyes were grieving. It was that combination which, perhaps even more than the words of her mother, made it impossible for him to hold back.

''Perhaps not,'' he said; ''not what you would call a large way of looking at it. But do you know, Mrs. Lawrence, I'm not sure that I care for that large way of looking at it. I'm not sure that I care a great deal about an institution that smothers the kindly things in people—as you are making this do in Edith. It sometimes occurs to me that life as we have arranged it is a rather unsatisfactory arrangement. I'm not sure that an arrangement of life which doesn't leave place for the most real things in life is going to continue forever. Ruth was driven into a corner and forced to do things she herself hated and suffered for—it was this same arrangement of life forced that on her, you know. You talk of marriage. But you must know there was no real marriage between Marion Averley and Stuart Williams. And I don't believe you can deny that there is a real

marriage between him and Ruth Holland.'' He
had risen and now moved a little toward the steps.
''So you see I don't believe I care much for your
'society,' Mrs. Lawrence,'' he laughed shortly.
''This looks to me like a pretty clear case of life
against society—and I see things just straight
enough that life itself strikes me as rather more
important than your precious 'arrangement' of
it!''

That did not bring the color to Mrs. Lawrence's
face; there seemed no color at all there when
Deane finished speaking. She sat erect, her hands
folded on her sewing, looking at him with
strangely bright eyes. When she spoke it was
with a certain metallic pleasantness. ''Why, very
well, Deane,'' she said; ''one is at perfect liberty
to choose, isn't one? And I think it quite right
to declare one's self, as you have just done, that
we may know who is of us and who is not.'' She
smiled—a smile that seemed definitely to shut him
out.

He looked at Edith; her eyes were down; he
could see that her lips trembled. ''Good-by,'' he
said.

Mrs. Lawrence bowed slightly and took up her
sewing.

''Good-by, Edith,'' he added gently.

She looked up at him and he saw then why she
she had been looking down. ''Good-by, Deane,''

she said a little huskily, her eyes all clouded with tears. "Though how absurd!" she quickly added with a rather tremulous laugh. "We shall be seeing you as usual, of course." But it was more appeal than declaration.

CHAPTER SEVENTEEN

Ruth was different after her talk with Deane that night. Ted felt the change in her when he went up to say goodnight. The constraint between them seemed somehow to have fallen away. Ruth was natural now—just Ruth, he told himself, and felt that talking to Deane had done her good. He lingered to chat with her awhile—of the arrangements for the night, various little things about the house, just the things they naturally would talk of; his feeling of embarrassment, diffidence, melted quite away before her quiet simplicity, her warm naturalness. She had seemed timid all day—holding back. Now she seemed just quietly to take her place. He had been afraid of doing or saying something that would hurt her, that had kept him from being natural, he knew. But now he forgot about that. And when Ruth put her hands up on his shoulders and lifted her face to kiss him goodnight he suddenly knew how many lonely nights there had been. "I'm so glad I've got you back, Ted," she said; "I want to talk to you about heaps of things."

And Ted, as he went to bed, was thinking that there were heaps of things he wanted to talk to Ruth about. He hadn't had much of anybody to talk to about the things one does talk to one's own folks about. His father had been silent and queer the last couple of years, and somehow one wouldn't think of "talking" to Harriett. He and Ruth had always hit it off, he told himself. He was glad she had found her feet, as he thought of it; evidently talking with Deane had made her feel more at home. Deane was a bully sort! After he had fallen into a light sleep he awakened and there came all freshly the consciousness that Ruth was back, asleep in her old room. It made him feel so good; he stretched out and settled for sleep with satisfaction, drowsily thinking that there *were* heaps of things he wanted to talk to Ruth about.

Ruth, too, was settling to sleep with more calm, something nearer peace than it had seemed just a little while before she was going to find in her father's house. Talking with Deane took her in to something from which she had long felt shut out. It was like coming on a camp fire after being overawed by too long a time in the forest— warmth and light and cheerful crackling after loneliness in austere places. Dear Deane! he was always so good to her; he always helped. It was curious about Deane—about Deane and her. There seemed a strange openness—she could not think of it any other way—between them. Things she lived through, in which he had no part, drew her to him, swung her back to him. There was something between his spirit and hers that seemed to make him part even of experiences she had had with another man, as if things of the emotions, even though not shared, drew them together through the spirit. Very deeply she hoped that Deane would be happy. She wished she might meet his wife, but probably she wouldn't. She quickly turned from that thought, wanting to stay by the camp fire. Anyway, Deane was her friend. She rested in that thought of having a friend—someone to talk to about things small and droll, about things large and mysterious. Thoughts needed to be spoken. It opened something in one to speak them. With Stuart she had been careful not to talk of certain things, fearing to see him sink into that absorption, gloom, she had come to dread.

She cried a little after she had crept into her bed—her own old bed; but they were just tears of feeling, not of desolation. The oak tree was tapping against the house, the breeze, carrying familiar scents, blew through the room. She was back home. All the sadness surrounding her homecoming could not keep out the sweet feeling of being back that stole through her senses.

Next morning she went about the house with new poise; she was quiet, but it was of a different quality from the quiet of the day before. Flora Copeland found herself thinking less about maintaining her carefully thought out manner toward

Ruth. She told herself that Ruth did not seem like "that kind of a woman." She would forget the "difficult situation" and find herself just talking with Ruth—about the death of her sister Mary's little girl, of her niece who was about to be married. There was something about Ruth that made one slip into talking to her about things one was feeling; and something in the quiet light of her tired sweet eyes made one forget about not being more than courteous. Even Laura Abbott, the nurse, found herself talking naturally to this Ruth Holland, this woman who lived with another woman's husband, who was more "talked about" than any woman in the town had ever been. But somehow a person just forgot what she really was, she told a friend; she wasn't at all like you'd expect that kind of a person to be. Though of course there were terribly embarrassing things— like not knowing what to call her.

Between Ruth and Harriett things went much better than they had the day before. Ruth seemed so much herself when they met that afternoon that unconsciously Harriett emerged from her uncertainty, from that fumbling manner of the day before. The things holding them apart somehow fell back before the things drawing them together. They were two sisters and their father was dying. The doctor had just been there and said he did not believe Mr. Holland could live another day. They were together when he told them that; for the moment, at least, it melted other things away.

They stood at the head of the stairs talking of things of common concern—the efficiency of the nurse, of Ted, who had been with his father more than any of the rest of them, for whom they feared it would be very hard when the moment came. Then, after a little pause made intimate by feeling shared, Harriett told when she would be back, adding, ''But you'll see to it that I'm telephoned at once if—if I should be wanted, won't you, Ruth?''—as one depending on this other more than on anyone else. Ruth only answered gently, ''Yes, Harriett,'' but she felt warmed in her heart. She had been given something to do. She was depended on. She was not left out.

She sat beside her father during the hour that the nurse had to be relieved. Very strongly, wonderfully, she had a feeling that her father knew she was there, that he wanted her there. In the strange quiet of that hour she seemed to come close to him, as if things holding them apart while he was of life had fallen away now that he no longer was life-bound. It was very real to her. It was communion. Things she could not have expressed seemed to be flowing out to him, and things he could not have understood seemed reaching him now. It was as if she was going with him right up to the border—a long way past the things of life that drove them apart. The nurse, coming back to resume duty, was arrested, moved, by

Ruth's face. She spoke gently in thanking her, her own face softened. Flora Copeland, meeting Ruth in the hall, paused, somehow held, and then, quite forgetful of the manner she was going to maintain toward Ruth, impulsively called after her: "Are you perfectly comfortable in your room, Ruth? Don't you—shan't I bring in one of the big easy chairs?"

Ruth said no, she liked her own little chair, but she said it very gently, understanding; she had again that feeling of being taken in, the feeling that warmed her heart.

She went in her room and sat quietly in her little chair; and what had been a pent up agony in her heart flowed out in open sorrowing: for her mother, who was not there to sit in her room with her; for her father, who was dying. But it was releasing sorrowing, the sorrowing that makes one one with the world, drawing one into the whole life of human feeling, the opened heart that brings one closer to all opened hearts. It was the sadness that softens; such sadness as finds its own healing in enriched feeling. It made her feel very near her father and mother; she loved them; she felt that they loved her. She had hurt them—terribly hurt them; but it all seemed beyond that now; they understood; and she was Ruth and they loved her. It was as if the way had been cleared between her and them. She did not feel shut in alone.

Ted hesitated when he came to her door a little later, drew back before the tender light of her illumined face. It did not seem a time to break in on her. But she held out her hand with a little welcoming gesture and, though strangely subdued, smiled lovingly at him as she said, "Come on in, Ted."

Something that the boy felt in her mood made him scowl anew at the thing he had to tell her. He went over to the window, his back to her, and was snapping his finger against the pane. "Well," he said at last, gruffly, "Cy gets in to-day. Just had a wire."

Ruth drew back, as one who has left exposed a place that can be hurt draws back when hurt threatens. Ted felt it—that retreating within herself, and said roughly: "Much anybody cares! Between you and me, I don't think father would care so very much, either."

"Ted!" she remonstrated in elder sister fashion.

"Cy's got a hard heart, Ruth," he said with a sudden gravity that came strangely through his youthfulness.

Ruth did not reply; she did not want to say what she felt about Cy's heart. But after a moment the domestic side of it turned itself to her. "Will Louise come with him, Ted?"

"No," he answered shortly.

His tone made her look at him in inquiry, but he

had turned his back to her again. "I was just wondering about getting their room ready," she said.

For a moment Ted did not speak, did not turn toward her. Then, "We don't have to bother getting any room ready for Cy," he said, with a scoffing little laugh.

Ruth's hand went up to her throat—a curious movement, as if in defense. "What do you mean, Ted?" she asked in low quick voice.

Ted's finger was again snapping the window pane. Once more he laughed disdainfully. "Our esteemed brother is going to the hotel," he jeered.

As Ruth did not speak he looked around. He could not bear her face. "Don't you care, Ruth," he burst out. "Why, what's the difference?" he went on scoffingly. "The hotel's a good place. He'll get along all right down there—and it makes it just so much the better for us."

But even then Ruth could not speak; it had come in too tender a moment, had found her too exposed; she could only cower back. Then pride broke through. "Cyrus needn't go to the hotel, Ted. If he can't stay in the same house with me —even when father is dying—then I'll go somewhere else."

"You'll not!" he blazed, with a savagery that at once startled and wonderfully comforted her. "If Cy wants to be a fool, let him be a fool! If he

can't act decent—then let him do what he pleases
—or go to the devil!''

She murmured something in remonstrance, but
flooded with gratefulness for the very thing she
tried to protest against. And then even that was
struck out. She had brought about this quarrel,
this feeling, between the two brothers. Ted's an-
tagonism against Cyrus, comforting to her, might
work harm to Ted. Those were the things she
did. That was what came through her.

The comfort, communion, peace of a few minutes before seemed a mockery. Out of her great
longing she had deluded herself. Now she was
cast back; now she knew. It was as if she had
only been called out in order to be struck back.
And it seemed that Ted, whom she had just found
again, she must either lose or harm. And the
shame of it!—children not coming together under
their father's roof when he was dying! Even
death could not break the bitterness down. It
made her know just how it was—just where she
stood. And she thought of the town's new talk
because of this.

''It's pretty bad, isn't it, Ted?'' she said finally,
looking up to him with heavy eyes.

Ted flushed. ''Cy makes it worse than it need
be,'' he muttered.

''But it is pretty bad, isn't it?'' she repeated in
a voice there was little life in. ''It was about as
bad as it could be for you all, wasn't it?''

"Well, Ruth," he began diffidently, "of course —of course this house hasn't been a very cheerful place since you went away."

"No," she murmured, "of course not." She sat there dwelling upon that, forming a new picture of just what it had been. "It really made a big difference, did it, Ted?—even for you?" She asked it very simply, as one asking a thing in order to know the truth.

Ted sat down on the bed. He was shuffling his feet a little, embarrassed, but his face was finely serious, as if this were a grave thing of which it was right they talk.

"Of course I was a good deal of a kid, Ruth," he began. "And yet—" He halted, held by kindness.

"Yes?" she pressed, as if wanting to get him past kindness.

"Well, yes, Ruth, it was—rather bad. I minded on account of the fellows, you see. I knew they were talking and—" Again he stopped; his face had reddened. Her face too colored up at that.

"And then of course home—you know it had always been so jolly here at home—was a pretty different place, Ruth," he took it up gently. "With Cy charging around, and mother and father so— different."

"And they were different, were they, Ted?" she asked quietly.

He looked at her in surprise. "Why, yes, Ruth, they certainly were—different."

Silence fell between them, separately dwelling upon that.

"Just how—different?" Ruth asked, for it seemed he was not going on.

"Why—mother stopped going out, and of course that made her all different. You know what a lot those parties and doings meant to mother."

She did not at once speak, her face working. Then: "I'm sorry," she choked. "Need she have done that, Ted?" she added wistfully after a moment.

He looked at her with that fine seriousness that made him seem older than he was—and finer than she had known. "Well, I don't know, Ruth; you know you don't feel very comfortable if you think people are—talking. It makes you feel sort of—out of it; as if there was something different about you."

"And father?" she urged, her voice quiet, strangely quiet. She was sitting very still, looking intently at Ted.

"Well, father rather dropped out of it, too," he went on, his voice gentle as if it would make less hard what it was saying. "He and mother just seemed to want to draw back into their shells. I think—" He stopped, then said: "I guess you really want to know, Ruth; it—it did make a big difference in father. I think it went deeper than you may have known—and maybe it's only fair to him you should know. It did make a difference; I think it made a difference even in business. Maybe that seems queer, but don't you know when a person doesn't feel right about things he doesn't get on very well with people? Father got that way. He didn't seem to want to be with people."

She did not raise her eyes at that. "Business hasn't gone very well, has it, Ted?" she asked after a moment of silence, still not looking up.

"Pretty bad. And of course *that* gets Cy," he added.

She nodded. "I guess there's a good deal to be said on Cy's side," she murmured after a little, her hands working and her voice not steady.

Ted grunted something disdainful, then muttered: "He played things up for all they were worth. Don't you think he ever missed anything!"

"Was that why Cy left town, Ted?" Ruth asked, speaking all the while in that low, strange voice.

"Oh, he claims so," scoffed Ted. "But he can't make me believe any family humiliation would have made him leave town if he hadn't had a better thing somewhere else. But of course he *says* that. That it was too hard for him and Louise! Too bad about that little doll-face, isn't it?"

Ruth made a gesture of remonstrance, but the boyish partisanship brought the tears she had until then been able to hold back.

Ted rose. And then he hesitated, as if not wanting to leave it like this. "Well, Ruth, I can tell you one thing," he said gently, a little bashfully; "with all Cy's grand talk about the wrong done mother and father, neither of them ever loved him the way they loved you."

"Oh, *did* they, Ted?" she cried, and all the held back feeling broke through, suffusing her. "They *did?*—in spite of everything? Tell me about that, Ted! Tell me about it!"

"Mother used to talk a lot to me," he said. "She was always coming into my room and talking to me about you."

"Oh, *was* she, Ted?" she cried again, feeling breaking over her face in waves. "She *did* talk about me? What did she say? Tell me!"

"Just little things, mostly. Telling about things you had said and done when you were a kid; remembering what you'd worn here and there —who you'd gone with. Oh,—you know; just little things.

"Of course," he went on, Ruth leaning forward, hanging on his words, "I was a good deal of a kid then; she didn't talk to me much about the—serious part of it. Maybe that was the reason she liked to talk to me—because she could just talk about the little things—old things. Though once or twice—"

"Yes, Ted?" she breathed, as he paused there.

"Well, she did say things to me, too. I remember once she said, 'It wasn't like Ruth. Something terrible happened. She didn't know what she was doing.'"

Ruth's hands were pressed tight together; unheeded tears were falling on them.

"And she used to worry about you, Ruth. When it was cold and she'd come into my room with an extra cover she'd say—'I wish I knew that my girl was warm enough tonight.'"

At that Ruth's face went down in her hands and she was sobbing.

"I don't know what I'm talking like this for!" muttered the boy angrily. "Making you feel so bad!"

She shook her head, but for a little could not look up. Then she choked: "No, I want to know. Never mind how it hurts, I want to know." And then, when she had controlled herself a little more she said, simply: "I didn't know it was like that. I didn't know mother felt—like that."

"She'd start to write to you, and then lots of times she wouldn't seem to know how. She wanted to write to you lots more than she did. But I don't know, Ruth, mother was queer. She seemed sort of bewildered. She—wasn't herself. She was just kind of powerless to do anything about things. She'd come in this room a lot. Sit in here by herself. One of the last days mother was around she called me in here and she had that dress you wore to Edith Lawrence's wedding spread out on the bed and was—oh, just kind of fussing with it. And the reason she called me in was that she wanted to know if I remembered how pretty you looked in it that night.''

But Ruth had thrown out a hand for him to stop, had covered her face as if shutting something out. ''Oh, I'm sorry, Ruth!'' murmured Ted. ''I'm a fool!'' he cried angrily. But after a minute he added haltingly, ''And yet—you did want to know, and—maybe it's fairer to mother, Ruth. Maybe —'' but he could not go on and went over and stood by the window, not wanting to leave her like that, not knowing what to do.

''Well, one thing I want you to know, Ruth,'' he said, as he did finally turn to the door. ''I've been talking along about how hard it was for the rest of us, but don't for a minute think I don't see how terrible it was for *you*. I get that, all right.''

She looked up at him, wanting to speak, but dumb; dumb in this new realization of how terrible it had been for them all.

CHAPTER EIGHTEEN

An hour later she had to get away from that room. She did not know where she was going, but she had to have some escape. Just the physical act of getting away was something.

Ted and Harriett were talking in the lower hall. They looked in inquiry at the hat she held and her face made Ted lay a hand on her arm. She told them she had to have exercise—air—and was going out for a little walk. She thought Harriett looked aghast—doubtless preferring Ruth be seen as little as possible. But she could not help that; she had to get away—away from that room, that house, away from those old things now newly charged. Something left with them shut down around her as a fog in which she could not breathe. Ted asked if he should go with her, but she shook her head and started for the side door, fearing he might insist. He called after her that Harriett was going to have Cyrus stay at her house, that she could make room for him. He said it with a relief which told how he had really hated having his brother go to the hotel. As she turned with something about that being better, she noticed how worn and worried Harriett looked, and then hurried on, wanting to get away, to escape for a little while from that crushing realization of how hard she made things for them all. But she could not shut out the thought of the empty rooms upstairs at their house—Cyrus's old home—and the crowded quarters at Harriett's. Yet of course this would be better than the hotel; she was glad Harriett and Ted had been able to arrange it; she hoped, for their sakes, that Cyrus would not, to emphasize his feeling, insist upon staying downtown.

She walked several blocks without giving any thought to where she was going. She was not thinking then of those familiar streets, of the times she had walked them. She was getting away, trying, for a little while, to escape from things she had no more power to bear. She could not have stayed another minute in her old room.

A little ahead of her she saw a woman sitting in a market wagon, holding the horse. She got the impression that the woman was selling vegetables. She tried to notice, to be interested. She could see, as she came along toward the wagon, that the vegetables looked nice and fresh. She and Stuart had raised vegetables once; they had done various things after what money they had was exhausted and, handicapped both by his lack of ruggedness and by the shrinking from people which their position bred in them, they had to do the best they could at making a living. And so she noticed these vegetables, but it was not until she was close to her that she saw the woman had relaxed her hold on the lines and was leaning forward, peering at her. And when she came a little nearer this woman—a thin, wiry little person whose features were sharp, leaned still further forward and cried: "Why, how do you do? How d'do, Ruth!"

For a moment Ruth was too startled to make any reply. Then she only stammered, "Why, how do you do?"

But the woman leaned over the side of the wagon. Ruth was trying her best to think who she was; she knew that she had known her somewhere, in some way, but that thin, eager little face was way back in the past, and that she should be spoken to in this way—warm, natural—was itself too astonishing, moving, to leave her clear-headed for casting back.

And then, just as she seemed about to say something, her face changed a little. Ruth heard a gate click behind her and then a man, a stolid farmer, he appeared, came up to the wagon. The woman kept nodding her head, as if in continued greeting, but she had leaned back, as though she had decided against what she had been about to say. Ruth, starting on, still bewildered, stirred, nodded and smiled too; and then, when the man had jumped in the wagon and just as the horse was starting, the woman called: "It seems awful good to have you back on these streets, Ruth!"

Ruth could only nod in reply and hurried on; her heart beat fast; her eyes were blurring. "It seems awful good to have you back on these streets, Ruth!'' Was *that* what she had said? She turned around, wanting to run after that wagon, not wanting to lose that pinched, shabby, eager little woman who was glad to have her back on those streets. But the wagon had turned a corner and was out of sight. Back on those streets! It opened her to the fact that she was back on them. She walked more slowly, thinking about that. And she could walk more slowly; she was less driven.

After a block of perplexed thinking she knew who that woman was; it flashed from her memory where she had known that intent look, that wistful intentness lighting a thin little face. It was Annie Morris, a girl in her class at the high-school, a plain, quiet girl—poor she believed she was, not in Ruth's crowd. Now that she searched back for what she remembered about it she believed that this Annie Morris had always liked her; and perhaps she had taken more notice of her than Edith and the other girls had. She could see her now getting out of the shabby buggy in which she drove in to school—she lived somewhere out in the country. She remembered talking to her sometimes at recess—partly because she seemed a good deal alone and partly because she liked to talk to her. She remembered that she was what they called awfully bright in her classes.

That this girl, whom she had forgotten, should welcome her so warmly stirred an old wondering: a wondering if somewhere in the world there were not people who would be her friends. That wondering, longing, had run through many lonely days. The people she had known would no longer be her friends. But were there not other people? She knew so little about the world outside her own life; her own life had seemed to shut down around her. But she had a feeling that surely somewhere—somewhere outside the things she had known—were people among whom she could find friends. So far she had not found them. At the first, seeing how hard it would be, how bad for them both, to have only each other, she had tried to go out to people just as if there were nothing in her life to keep her back from them. And then they would "hear"; that hearing would come in the most unforeseen little ways, at the most unexpected times; usually through those coincidences of somebody's knowing somebody else, perhaps meeting someone from a former place where they had already "heard"; it was as if the haphazardness of life, those little accidents of meetings that were without design, equipped the world with a powerful service for "hearing," which after a time made it impossible for people to feel that what was known in one place would not come to be known in another. After she had several times been hurt by the drawing away of people whom she had grown to like, she herself drew back where she could not be so easily hurt. And so it came about that her personality changed in that; from an outgoing nature she came to be one who held back, shut herself in. Even people who had never "heard" had the feeling she did not care to know them, that she wanted to be let alone. It crippled her power for friendship; it hurt her spirit. And it left her very much alone. In that loneliness she wondered if there were not those other people— people who could "hear" and not draw away. She had not found them; perhaps she had at times been near them and in her holding back—not knowing, afraid—had let them go by. Of that, too, she had wondered; there had been many lonely wonderings.

She came now to a corner where she stopped. She stood looking down that cross street which was shaded by elm trees. That was the corner where she had always turned for Edith's. Yes, that was the way she used to go. She stood looking down the old way. She wanted to go that way now!

She went so far as to cross the street, and on that far corner again stood still, hesitating, wanting to go that old way. It came to her that if this other girl—Annie Morris—a girl she could barely remember, was glad to see her back, then surely Edith—*Edith*—would be glad to see her. But after a moment she went slowly on—the other way. She remembered; remembered the one letter she had had from Edith—that letter of a few lines sent in reply to her two letters written from Arizona, trying to make Edith understand.

"Ruth"—Edith had written—she knew the few words by heart; "Yes, I received your first letter. I did not reply to it because it did not seem to me there was anything for me to say. And it does not seem to me now that there is anything for me to say." It was signed, "Edith Lawrence Blair." The full signature had seemed even more formal than the cold words. It had hurt more; it seemed actually to be putting in force the decree that everything between her and Edith was at an end. It was never to be Ruth and Edith again.

As she walked slowly on now, away from Edith's, she remembered the day she walked across that Arizona plain, looking at Edith's letter a hundred times in the two miles between the little town and their cabin. She had gone into town that day to see the doctor. Stuart had seemed weaker and she was terribly frightened. The doctor did not bring her much comfort; he said she would have to be patient, and hope—probably it would all come right. She felt very desolate that day in the far-away, forlorn little town. When she got Edith's letter she did not dare to open it until she got out from the town.

And then she found those few formal, final words
—written, it was evident, to keep her from writing any more. The only human thing about it
was a little blot under the signature. It was the
only thing a bit like Edith; she could see her making it and frowning over it. And she wondered
—she had always wondered—if that little blot
came there because Edith was not as controlled,
as without all feeling, as everything else about her
letter would indicate. As she looked back to it
now it seemed that that day of getting Edith's
letter was the worst day of all the hard years.
She had been so lonely—so frightened; when she
saw Edith's handwriting it was hard not to burst
into tears right there at the little window in the
queer general store where they gave out letters as
well as everything else. But after she had read
the letter there were no tears; there was no feeling of tears. She walked along through that flat,
almost unpeopled, half desert country and it
seemed that the whole world had shrivelled up.
Everything had dried, just as the bushes along
the road were alive and yet dried up. She knew
then that it was certain there was no reach
back into the old things. And that night, after
they had gone to bed out of doors and Stuart had
fallen asleep, she lay there in the stillness of that
vast Arizona night and she came to seem in
another world. For hours she lay there looking
up at the stars, thinking, fearing. She reached

over and very gently, meaning not to wake him, put her hand in the hand of the man asleep beside her, the man who was all she had in the world, whom she loved with a passion that made the possibility of losing him a thing that came in the night to terrorize her. He had awakened and understood, and had comforted her with his love, lavishing upon her tender, passionate assurance of how he was going to get strong and make it all come right for them both. There was something terrible in that passion for one another that came out of the consciousness of all else lost. They had each other—there were moments when that burned with a terrible flame through the feeling that they had nothing else. That night they went to sleep in a wonderful consciousness of being alone together in the world. Time after time that swept them together with an intensity of which finally they came to be afraid. They stopped speaking of it; it came to seem a thing not to dwell upon.

The thought of Edith's letter had brought some of that back now. She turned from it to the things she was passing, houses she recognized, new houses. Walking on past them she thought of how those homes joined. With most of them there were no fences between—one yard merging into another. Children were running from yard to yard; here a woman was standing in her own yard calling to a woman in the house adjoining.

She passed a porch where four women were sitting sewing; another where two women were playing with a baby. There were so many meeting places for their lives; they were not shut in with their own feeling. That feeling which they as individuals knew reached out into common experiences, into a life in common growing out of individual things. Passing these houses, she wanted to share in that life in common. She had been too long by herself. She needed to be one with others. Life, for a time, had a certain terrible beauty that burned in that sense of isolation. But it was not the way. One needed to be one with others.

She thought of how it was love, more than any other thing, that gave these people that common life. Love was the fabric of it. Love made new combinations of people—homes, children. The very thing in her that had shut her out was the thing drawing them into that oneness, that many in one. Homes were closed to her because of that very impulse out of which homes were built.

She had, without any plan for doing so, turned down the little street where she used to go to meet Stuart. And when she realized where she was going thoughts of other things fell away; the feeling of those first days was strangely revivified, as if going that old way made her for the moment the girl who had gone that way. Again love was not a thing of right or wrong, it was the thing

that had to have its way—life's great imperative.
Going down that old street made the glow of those
days—the excitement—come to life and quicken
her again. It was so real that it was as if she
were living it again—a girl palpitating with love
going to meet her lover, all else left behind, only
love now! For the moment those old surround-
ings made the old days a living thing to her. The
world was just one palpitating beauty; the earth
she walked was vibrant; the sweetness of life
breathed from the air she breathed. She was
charged with the joy of it, bathed in the wonder.
Love had touched her and taken her, and she was
different and everything was different. Her
body was one consciousness of love; it lifted her
up; it melted her to tenderness. It made life
joyous and noble. She lived; she loved!

Standing on the spot where they had many
times stood in moments of meeting a very real
tenderness for that girl was in the heart of this
woman who had paid so terribly for the girl's
love. It brought a feeling that she had not paid
too much, that no paying was ever too much for
love. Love made life; and in turn love was what
life was for. To live without it would be going
through life without having been touched alive.
In that moment it seemed no wrong love could
bring about would be as deep as the wrong of
denying love. There was again that old feeling
of rising to something higher in her than she had

known was there, that feeling of contact with all the beauty of the world, of being admitted to the inner sweetness and wonder of life. She had a new understanding of what she had felt; that was the thing added; that was the gift of the hard years.

And of a sudden she wanted terribly to see her mother. It seemed if she could see her mother now that she could make her understand. She saw it more simply than she had seen it before. She wanted to tell her mother that she loved because she could not help loving. She wanted to tell her that after all those years of paying for it she saw that love as the thing illumining her life; that if there was anything worthy in her, anything to love, it was in just this—that she had fought for love, that she would fight for it again. She wanted to see her mother! She believed she could help the hurt she had dealt.

She had walked slowly on, climbing a little hill. From there she looked back at the town. With fresh pain there came the consciousness that her mother was not there, that she could not tell her, that she had gone—gone without understanding, gone bewildered, broken. Her eyes dimmed until the town was a blur. She wanted to see her mother!

She was about to start back, but turned for a moment's look the other way, across that lovely country of little hills and valleys—brooks, and cattle in the brooks, and fields of many shades of green.

And then her eye fixed upon one thing and after that saw no other thing. Behind her was the place where the living were gathered together; but over there, right over there on the next hill, were the dead. She stood very still, looking over there passionately through dimmed eyes. And then swiftly, sobbing a little under her breath, she started that way. She wanted to see her mother!

And when she came within those gates she grew strangely quiet. Back there in the dwelling place of the living she had felt shut out. But she did not feel shut out here. As slowly she wound her way to the hillside where she knew she would find her mother's grave, a strange peace touched her. It was as if she had come within death's tolerance; she seemed somehow to be taken into death's wonderful, all-inclusive love for life. There seemed only one distinction: they were dead and she still lived; she had a sense of being loved because she still lived.

Slowly, strangely comforted, strangely taken in, she passed the graves of many who, when she left, had been back there in the place of the living. The change from dwelling place to dwelling place had been made in the years she was away. It came with a shock to find some of those tombstones; she found many she had thought of as back there, a few hills away, where men still lived. She would pause and think of them, of the strangeness of finding them here when she had known them there—of life's onward movement, of death's inevitability. There were stones marking the burial places of friends of her grandfather—old people who used to come to the house when she was a little girl; she thought with a tender pleasure of little services she had done them; she had no feeling at all that they would not want her to be there. Friends of her father and mother too were there; yes, and some of her own friends—boys and girls with whom she had shared youth.

She sat a long time on the hillside where her mother had been put away. At first she cried, but they were not bitter tears. And after that she did not feel that, even if she could have talked to her mother, it would be important to say the things she had thought she wanted to say. Here, in this place of the dead, those things seemed understood. Vindication was not necessary. Was not life life, and should not one live before death came? She saw the monuments marking the graves of the Lawrences, the Blairs, the Williams', the Franklins,—her mother's and her father's people. They seemed so strangely one: people who had lived. She looked across the hills to the town which these people had built. Right beside her was her grandfather's grave; she thought of his stories of how, when a little boy, he came with his people to that place not then a town; his stories of the beginnings of it, of the struggles and conflicts that had made it what it was. She thought of their efforts, their disappointments, their hopes, their loves. Their loves. . . . She felt very close to them in that. And as she thought of it there rose a strange feeling, a feeling that came strangely strong and sure: If these people who had passed from living were given an after moment of consciousness, a moment when they could look back on life and speak to it, she felt that their voices, with all the force they could gather, would be raised for more living. Why did we not live more abundantly? Why did we not hold life more precious? Were they given power to say just one word, would they not, seeing life from death, cry—Live!

Twilight came; the world had the sweetness of that hour just before night. A breeze stirred softly; birds called lovingly—loving life. The whole fragrance of the world was breathed into one word. It was as if life had caught the passionate feeling of death; it was as if that after consciousness of those who had left life, and so knew its preciousness, broke through into things still articulate. The earth breathed—Live!

CHAPTER NINETEEN

Cyrus Holland died just before daybreak next morning. It seemed to Deane Franklin that he had only just fallen asleep when the telephone beside him was ringing. When tired out he slept through other noises, but that one always instantly reached—a call to him that got through sleep. He wakened just enough to reach out for the 'phone and his "Hello!" was cross. Was there never a time when one could be let alone? But the voice that came to him banished both sleep and irritation. It was Ruth's voice, saying quietly, tensely: "Deane? I'm sorry—but we want you. There's a change. I'm sure father's going."

He was dressing almost the instant he hung up the receiver. To Amy, who had roused, he said: "It's Ruth. Her father's going. I can't do a thing—but they want me there."

At first Amy made no reply. He thought nothing about that, engrossed in getting dressed as quickly as possible. When she burst out, "So of course you're going!" he was dumbfounded at the passionateness of her voice. He looked at her in astonishment; then, for the first time the other side of it, as related to their quarrel about Ruth,

213

turned itself to him. "Why, of course I'm going, Amy," he said quietly.

"It makes a difference who it is, doesn't it?" she cried, stormily. "The other night when somebody called you and there wasn't a thing you could do, you *said* so! You *told* them they mustn't ask you! But *this* is different, isn't it?"

The words had piled up tumultuously; she seemed right on the verge of angry, tumultuous tears. He paused in what he was doing. "Why, Amy," he murmured in real astonishment. And then helplessly repeated in tender reproach, "Why, Amy!"

But she laughed, it seemed sneeringly. He colored, quickly finished dressing and left the room without saying anything more.

When she heard the front door close, heard Deane running down the steps, she sat up in bed and burst into tears of rage. Always that woman! Running away to her in the middle of the night! He didn't *have* to go! There was nothing for him to do as a doctor—he could do nothing for a man who had been dying for a couple of days. He *said* that—just a couple of nights before when someone wanted him to come. But this was Ruth Holland! She had only to telephone. Of course he'd go anywhere—any time—for her! Her sobs grew more and more passionate. Her head down on her knees she rocked back and forth in that miserable fury only jealousy and wounded pride can create.

This gathered together, brought to a head, the resentment accumulating through a number of incidents. That afternoon she had gone over to the Lawrences' to thank Edith and her mother for the flowers from the tea which they had sent her that morning. They had urged her to run in often, to be friendly. Her unhappiness about her talk with Deane the night before, when he had actually proposed that she go to see this Ruth Holland, made her want to be with friends; she wanted to see people who felt as she did that— though it did not so present itself to her—she might fortify herself in the conviction that Deane was preposterously wrong, and she taking the only course a good woman could take in relation to a bad one. She was prepared to feel that men did not see those things as clearly as women did, that it was woman who was the guardian of society, and that she must bear with man in his failure to see some things right. She had been eager to strengthen herself in that feeling, not alone because it would, in her own mind, get her out of reach of any possible charge of hardness or narrowness, but because it would let her break through her feeling against Deane; she wanted to get back to the days of his complete adoration of her, back where his passion for her would sweep all else out of their world. She knew well enough that Deane loved her, but there was a tightened up place around her knowing that. It made her miserable. Things would not be right until she found a way through that tightened up place—a way that would make her right and Deane wrong, but would let her forgive, largely and gently understanding. Such, not thought out, were the things that took her to the Lawrences' that afternoon.

It was apparent that Edith had been crying. She and her mother were gracious to Amy, but there was a new constraint. She felt uncomfortable. When they were alone Edith broke out and told her how she was just sick at heart about Ruth. Deane had been there that morning urging her to go and see Ruth—instantly there was all anew that tightening up that held her from Deane, that feeling against him and against this Ruth Holland that was as if something virulent had been poured into her blood, changing her whole system. Edith cried as she told how Deane and her mother had quarreled because he felt so strongly on the subject, and didn't seem able to understand her mother's standpoint. Then, she too wanting to set herself right with herself, she went over the whole story—the shock to her, how it had hurt her ideal of friendship, had even seemed to take something from the sanctity of her own marriage. She silenced something within herself in recounting the wrong done her, fortified herself in repeating the things she had from her mother about one's not being free, about what the individual owed to society.

Amy went home in a turmoil of resentment against her husband. It was hard to hold back the angry tears. A nice position he was putting himself in—going about the town pleading for this woman whom nobody would take in!—estranging his friends—yes, probably hurting his practice. And *why?* *Why* was he so wrought up about it? Why was he making a regular business of going about fighting her battles? Well, *one* thing it showed! It showed how much consideration he had for his own wife. When she came in sight of their house it was harder than ever to hold back the tears of mortification, of hot resentment. She had been so sure she was going to be perfectly happy in that house! Now already her husband was turning away from her—humiliating her—showing how much he thought of another woman, and *such* a woman! She did not know what to do with the way she felt, did not know how to hold from the surface the ugly things that surged through her, possessed her. Until now she had had nothing but adulation from love. A pretty, petted girl she had formed that idea of pretty women in youth that it was for men to give love and women graciously to accept it. For her vanity to be hurt by a man who had roused her passion turned that passion to fury against him and made it seem that a great wrong had been done her.

As she approached she saw that Deane was standing before the house talking to a woman in a vegetable wagon. He had one foot up on the spoke of the wheel and was talking more earnestly than it seemed one would be talking to a vegetable woman. Doubtless she was one of his patients. As she came up he said: "Oh, Amy, I want you to know Mrs. Herman."

She stiffened; his tone in introducing her to a woman of what she thought of as the lower classes seeming just a new evidence of his inadequate valuation of her.

"Your husband and I went to school together," said Mrs. Herman, pleasantly, but as if explaining.

"Oh?" murmured Amy.

Deane abruptly moved back from the wagon. "Well, you do that, Annie. Ruth would love to see you, I know."

So *that* was it! She turned away with a stiff little nod to the woman in the wagon. Always the same thing!—urging Tom, Dick and Harry to go and see that woman!—taking up with a person like this, introducing his wife in that intimate way to a woman who peddled vegetables just because she was willing to go and see Ruth Holland! She didn't know that she had to stand such things! —she didn't know that she *would*. She guessed she could show him that she wasn't going to play second fiddle to that Ruth Holland!

Deane came to the door of the room where she was taking off her hat. Her fingers were trembling so that she could scarcely get the pins. "That little woman you were so chilly to is a pretty fine sort, Amy," he said incisively.

"Because she is going to see Ruth Holland?" she retorted with an excited laugh.

"Oh, you were pretty stand-offish before you knew that," he answered coolly.

Vanity smarting from deeper hurts made her answer, haughtily: "I'm rather inexperienced, you know, in meeting people of that class."

In his heart too there were deeper disappointments than this touched. "Well, I must say—" he began hotly, "I think if I felt as snobbish as that I'd try pretty hard to conceal it!"

Amy was carefully putting away her hat; she had an appearance of cold composure, of a sense of superiority. It was because she wanted to keep that that she did not speak. The things within would so completely have destroyed it.

"I guess you don't understand, Amy," said Deane, quieted by her silence; "if you knew all about Annie Morris I think you'd see she is a woman worth meeting." Thinking of his talk with Edith and her mother that morning, he added, a good deal of feeling breaking into his voice:

"A good sight more so than some of the people you are meeting!"

"And of course," she could not hold back, "they —those inferior people—won't go to see Ruth Holland, and this wonderful woman will! That's the secret of it, isn't it?"

"It's one thing that shows her superiority," he replied coolly. "Another thing is her pluck— grit. Her husband is a dolt, and she's determined her three children shall have some sort of a show in life, so she's driven ahead—worked from daylight till dark many a time—to make decent things possible for them."

"Well, that's very commendable, I'm sure," replied Amy mildly, appearing to be chiefly concerned with a loose button on the wrap she had just taken off.

"And with all that she's kept her own spirit alive; she's not going to let life get clear ahead of *her*, either. She's pretty valiant, I think." He was thinking again of Edith and her mother as he added contentiously, "I don't know any woman in this town I'd rather talk to!"

Amy, appearing quite outside the things that were disturbing him, only smiled politely and threaded a needle for sewing on the button. He stood there in the doorway, fidgeting, his face red. She seemed so uncaring; she seemed so far away. "Oh, Amy!" he cried, miserably, appealingly.

Quickly she looked up; her mouth, which had

been so complacent, twitched. He started toward her, but just then the doorbell rang. "I presume that's your mother," she said, in matter of fact tone.

Mrs. Franklin was with them for dinner that night. Amy's social training made it appear as if nothing were disturbing her. She appeared wholly composed, serene; it was Deane who seemed ill at ease, out of sorts.

After dinner he had to go to the hospital and when she was alone with his mother Amy was not able to keep away from the subject of Ruth Holland. For one thing, she wanted to hear about her, she was avid for detail as to how she looked, things she had done and said—that curious human desire to press on a place that hurts. And there was too the impulse for further self-exoneration, to be assured that she was right, to feel that she was injured.

All of those things it was easy to get from Mrs. Franklin. Amy, not willing to reveal what there had been between her and Deane, and having that instinct for drawing sympathy to herself by seeming self-depreciation, spoke gently of how she feared she did not altogether understand about Deane's friend Ruth Holland. Was she wrong in not going with Deane to see her?

Mrs. Franklin's explosion of indignation at the idea, and the feeling with which, during the hour that followed, she expressed herself about Deane's friend Ruth Holland, acted in a double fashion as both fortification and new hurt. Mrs. Franklin, leader in church and philanthropic affairs, had absolutely no understanding of things which went outside the domain of what things should be. The poor and the wicked did terrible things that society must do something about. There was no excuse whatever for people who ought to know better. That people should be dominated by things they ought not to feel was perversity on their part and the most wilful kind of wickedness. She had Mrs. Lawrence's point of view, but from a more provincial angle. Deane did not get his questioning spirit, what she called his stubbornness, from his mother.

Added to what she as a church woman and worker for social betterment felt about the affair was the resentment of the mother at her son's having been, as she put it, dragged into the outrage. She grew so inflamed in talking of how this woman had used Deane that she did not take thought of how she was giving more of an impression of her power over him than might be pleasant hearing for Deane's young wife. The indignation of the whole Franklin family at what they called the way Deane had been made a cat's paw was fanned to full flame in this preposterous suggestion that Amy should go to see Ruth Holland. In her indignation at the idea she gave a new sense of what the town felt about Ruth, and she was more vehement than tactful in her expressions against Deane for holding out that way against the whole town. "It just shows, my dear," she said, "what a woman of no principle can do with a man!"

Amy, hurt to the quick in this thought of the mysterious lure of a woman of no principle, remarked casually, "She's wonderfully attractive, I presume."

Mrs. Franklin was not too blunted by indignation to miss the pain that was evident in the indifferently asked question. Hastily—more hastily than subtly, she proceeded to depreciate the attractions of Ruth Holland, but in the depreciation left an impression of some quality—elusive, potent—which more than beauty or definite charm gave her power. Edith too had spoken of that "something" about Ruth; a something one never forgot; a something, she said, that no one else had.

And now, awakened by Deane's having been called by this woman in the night, herself alone there and he hurrying to Ruth Holland, the barriers of pride broke down and she cried because she was sorry for herself, because she was hurt and outraged that she should be hurt, because for the first time in her whole life she was thwarted— not having her way, set aside. She completely lost her hold on herself, got up and stormed about the room. When she looked at her face in the mirror she saw that it was hideous. She couldn't help it!—she didn't care! The resentment, rage, in her heart was like a poison that went all through her. She was something that didn't seem herself. She thought horrible things and ground her teeth and clenched her hands and let her face look as ugly as it could. She hated this woman! She wished some horrible thing would happen to her! She hated Deane Franklin! The passion he had roused in her all turned into this feeling against him. She wouldn't stand it! She wouldn't stay there and play second fiddle to another woman—she, a bride! Fresh tears came with that last. Her mother and father would never have treated her that way. They didn't think Deane Franklin good enough for her, anyway! She would go back home! *That* would make things pretty hard for him! That would show what this woman had done! And he'd be sorry then—would want her back—and she wouldn't come. She finally found control in that thought of her power over him used to make him suffer.

Deane, meanwhile, was hurrying through the streets that had the unrealness of that hour just before morning. That aspect of things was with him associated with death; almost always when he had been on the streets at that hour it was because someone was fighting death. It was so still —as if things were awed. And a light that seemed apart from natural things was formed by the way the street lights grew pale in the faint light of coming day. Everyone was sleeping—all save those in a house half a dozen blocks away, the house where they were waiting for death.

He was on foot, having left his car down at the garage for some repairs after taking his mother home. As he slowed for a moment from a walk that was half run he thought of how useless his hurrying was. What in the world could he do when he got there? Nothing save assure them he could do nothing. Poor Ruth!—it seemed she had so much, so many hard things. This was a time when one needed one's friends, but of course they couldn't come near her—on account of society. Though—his face softened with the thought— Annie Morris would come, she not being oppressed by this duty to society. He thought of the earnestness of her thin face as she talked of Ruth. That let in the picture of Amy's face as he introduced them. He tried not to keep seeing it. He did think, however, that it was pretty unnecessary of Amy to have talked to his mother about Ruth. All that was unyielding in him had been summoned by the way his mother talked to him going home—"going for him" like that because he had wanted Amy to go and see Ruth. That, it seemed to him, was something between him and Amy. He would not have supposed she would be so ready to talk with some one else about a thing that was just between themselves. There had been that same old hardening against his mother when she began talking of Ruth, and that feeling that shut her out excluded Amy with her. And he had wanted Amy with him.

Hurrying on, he tried not to think of it. He didn't know why Amy had talked to his mother about it—perhaps it just happened so, perhaps his mother began it. He seized upon that. And Amy didn't understand; she was young—her life had never touched anything like this. He was going to talk to her—really talk to her, not fly off the handle at the first thing she would say. He told himself that he had been stupid, hard—a bungler. It made him feel better to tell himself that. Yes, he certainly had been unsympathetic, and it was a shame that anything had come to make Amy unhappy—and right there at first, too! Why, it was actually making her sick! When he went back after taking his mother home Amy said she had a bad headache and didn't want to talk. She was so queer that he had taken her at her word and had not tried to talk to her—be nice to her. It seemed now that he hadn't been kind; it helped him to feel that he hadn't been kind. And it was the headache, being roused in the night when she was not well that had made her so—well, so wrought up about his answering to the call of the Hollands—old patients, old friends. He was going to be different; he was going to be more tender with Amy—that would be the way to make her understand. Such were the things his troubled mind and hurt heart tried to be persuaded of as, thinking at the same time of other things—the death to which he was hurrying, how hard it would be for Ruth if Cyrus didn't speak to her—he passed swiftly by the last houses where people slept and turned from a world tinged with the strangeness of an hour so little known to men's consciousness, softly opened the door and stepped into the house where death was touching life with that same unreality with which, without, day touched night.

Miss Copeland, wrapped in a bathrobe, sat in the upstairs hall. "He's still breathing," she whispered in that voice which is for death alone. In the room Ruth and Ted stood close together, the nurse on the other side of the bed. Ruth's hair was braided down her back; he remembered when she used to wear it that way, he had one of those sudden pictures of her—on her way to school, skipping along with Edith Lawrence. She turned, hearing him, and there was that rush of feeling to her eyes that always claimed him for Ruth, that quick, silent assumption of his understanding that always let down bars between them. But Ruth kept close to Ted, as if she would shield him; the boy looked as Deane had seen novices look in the operating room.

There was nothing for him to do beyond look at his patient and nod to the nurse in confirmation that it would be any minute now. He walked around to Ted and Ruth, taking an arm of each of them and walking with them to the far side of the room.

"There's nothing to do but wait," he said.

"I wish Harriett and Cyrus would get here," whispered Ruth.

"You telephoned?"

"Before I did you—but of course it's a little farther."

They stood there together in that strange silence, hearing only the unlifelike breathing of the man passing from life. Listening to it, Ruth's hand on Deane's arm tightened. Soothingly he patted her hand.

Then, at a movement from the nurse, he stepped quickly to the bed. Ruth and Ted, close together, first followed, then held back. A minute later he turned to them. "It's over," he said, in the simple way final things are said.

There was a choking little cry from Ted. Ruth murmured something, her face all compassion for him. But after a moment she left her brother and stood alone beside her father. In that moment of seeing her face, before turning away because it seemed he should turn away, Deane got one of the strangest impressions of his life. It was as if she was following her father—reaching him; as if there was a fullness of feeling, a rising passionate intensity that could fairly overflow from life. Then she turned back to Ted.

Cyrus and Harriett had entered. There was a moment when the four children were there together. Cyrus did not come up to the bed until Ruth had left. Deane watched his face as—perfunctorily subdued, decorous, he stood where Ruth had stood a moment before. Then Cyrus turned to him and together they walked from the room, Cyrus asking why they had not been telephoned in time.

Deane lingered for a little while, hating to go without again seeing Ruth and Ted. He tapped at Ruth's door; he was not answered, but the unlatched door had swung a little open at his touch. He saw that the brother and sister were out on the little porch opening off Ruth's room. He went out and stood beside them, knowing that he would be wanted. The sun was just rising, touching the dew on the grass. The birds were singing for joy in another day. The three who had just seen death stood there together in silence.

CHAPTER TWENTY

The two days when the natural course of life was arrested by death had passed. Their father had been buried that afternoon, and in the early evening Ted and Ruth were sitting on the little upper porch, very quiet in the new poignant emptiness of the house. Many people had been coming and going in those last few days; now that was over and there was a pause before the routine of life was to be resumed. The fact that the nurse had gone seemed to turn the page.

Ruth had just asked how long Cyrus was going to stay and Ted replied that he wanted to stay on a week or perhaps more, attending to some business. She knew how crowded it must be for them at Harriett's, knew that if she went away Cyrus would come home. There seemed nothing more to keep her; she would like to be with Ted awhile, but it seemed she could not do that without continuing a hard condition for them all. They could settle into a more natural order of things with her not there. It was time for her to go.

It was hard to have to think that. She would love to have stayed a little while. She had been away so long—wanting home for so long. She knew now, facing the going away, how much she

had secretly hoped might result from this trip
back home.

She had seen a number of people in the past
few days—relatives, old friends of the family,
friends of Ted. She had done better in meeting
them than, just a little while before, she would
have thought possible. Something remained with
her from that hour at her mother's grave, that
strange hour when she had seemed to see life from
outside, beyond it. That had summoned something within herself that no personal hurt could
scatter, as if taking her in to something from
which no circumstance could drive her out. She
had felt an inner quiet, a steadiness within; there
was power in it, and consolation. It took her out
of that feeling of having no place—no right to a
place, the feeling that had made her wretched and
powerless. She was of life; her sure inner sense
of the reality and beauty of that seemed a thing
not to be broken down from without. It was hers,
her own. It sustained her; it gave her poise.
The embarrassment of other people gave way before her simple steadiness. She had had but the
one point of contact with them—that of her
father's death; it made her want more, made going away hard. It was hard to leave all the old
things after even this slight touch with them
again.

And that new quiet, that new force within was
beginning to make for new thinking. She had

thought much about what she had lived through—she could not help doing that, but she was thinking now with new questionings. She had not questioned much; she had accepted. What was gathering within her now was a feeling that a thing so real, so of life as her love had been should not be a thing to set her apart, should not be a thing to blight the lives that touched hers. This was not something called up in vindication, a mere escape from hard thinking, her own way out from things she could not bear; it was deeper than that, far less facile. It came from that inner quiet—from that strange new assurance—this feeling that her love should not have devastated, that it was too purely of life for that; that it was a thing to build up life, to give to it; this wondering, at once timid and bold, if there was not something wrong with an order that could give it no place, that made it life's enemy.

She had been afraid of rebellious thinking, of questionings. There had been so much to fight, so much to make her afraid. At first all the strength of her feeling had gone into the fight for Stuart's health; she was afraid of things that made her rebellious—needing all of herself, not daring to break through. The circumstances had seemed to make her own life just shut down around her; and even after those first years, living itself was so hard, there were so many worries and disappointments—her feeling about it was so tense, life so stern—that her thoughts did not shoot a long way out into questionings. She had done a thing that cut her off from her family; she had hurt other people and because of that she herself must suffer. Life could not be for her what it was for others. She accepted much that she did not try to understand. For one thing, she had had no one to talk to about those things. Seeing how Stuart's resentment against the state of things weakened him, keeping him from his full powers to meet those hard conditions, she did not encourage their talking of it and had tried to keep herself from the thinking that with him went into brooding and was weakening. She had to do the best she could about things; she could not spend herself in rebellion against what she had to meet. Like a man who finds himself on a dizzy ledge she grew fearful of much looking around.

But now, in these last few days, swept back into the wreckage she had left, something fluttered to life and beat hard within her spirit, breaking its way through the fearfulness that shut her in and sending itself out in new bolder flights. Not that those outgoings took her away from the place she had devastated; it was out of the poignancy of her feeling about the harm she had done, out of her new grief in it that these new questionings were born. The very fact that she did see so well, and so sorrowingly, what she had done, brought this new feeling that it should not have been that way, that what she had felt, and her fidelity to that feeling—ruthless fidelity though it was—should not have blighted like this. There was something that seemed at the heart of it all in that feeling of not being ashamed in the presence of death—she who had not denied life.

Silence had fallen between her and Ted, she saddened in the thought of going away and open to the puzzling things that touched her life at every point; looking at Ted—proud of him—hating to leave him now just when she had found him again, thinking with loving gratefulness and pride of how generous and how understanding he had been with her, how he was at once so boyish and so much more than his years. The fine seriousness of his face tonight made him very dear and very comforting to her. She wanted to keep close to him; she could not bear the thought of again losing him. If her hard visit back home yielded just that she would have had rich gain from it. She began talking with him about what he would do. He talked freely of his work, as if glad to talk of it; he was not satisfied with it, did not think there was much "chance" there for him. Ted had thought he wanted to study law, but his father, in one of his periods of depression, had said he could not finish sending him through college and Ted had gone into one of the big manufactories there. He was in the sales department, and he talked to Ruth of the work. He told her of his friends, of what they were doing; they talked of many things, speaking of the future with that gentle intimacy there can be between those sorrowing together for things past. Their sensitive consciousness of the emptiness of the house—the old place, their home,—brought them together through a deep undercurrent of feeling. Their voices were low as they spoke of more intimate things than it is usual to speak of without constraint, something lowered between them as only a grief shared can lower bars to the spirit, their thinking set in that poignant sense of life which death alone seems able to create.

Ted broke a pause to say that he supposed it was getting late and he must be starting for Harriett's. Cyrus had asked him to come over awhile that evening. Mr. McFarland, their family lawyer, was going out of town for a few days, leaving the next morning. He was coming in that evening, more as the old friend than formally, to speak to them about some business matters, Cyrus's time being limited and there being a number of things to arrange.

"I hate leaving you alone, Ruth," said Ted, lingering.

She looked over to him with quick affectionate smile. "I don't mind, Ted. Somehow I don't mind being alone tonight."

That was true. Being alone would not be loneliness that evening. Things were somehow opened;

all things had so strangely opened. She had been looking down the deep-shadowed street, that old street down which she used to go. The girl who used to go down that street was singularly real to her just then; she had about her the fresh feeling, the vivid sense, of a thing near in time. Old things were so strangely opened, old feeling was alive again: the wild joy in the girl's heart, the delirious expectancy—and the fear. It was strange how completely one could get back across the years, how things gone could become living things again. That was why she was not going to mind being alone just then; she had a sense of the whole flow of her life—living, moving. It did not seem a thing to turn away from; it was not often that things were all open like that.

"I shouldn't wonder if Deane would drop in," said Ted, as if trying to help himself through leaving her there alone.

"He may," Ruth answered. She did not say it with enthusiasm, much as she would like to talk with Deane. Deane was just the one it would be good to talk with that night. But Deane never mentioned his wife to her. At first, in her preoccupation, and her pleasure in seeing him, she had not thought much about that. Then it had come to her that doubtless Deane's wife would not share his feeling about her, that she would share the feeling of all the other people; that brought the fear that she might, again, be making things hard for Deane. She had done enough of that; much as his loyalty, the rare quality of his affectionate friendship meant to her, she would rather he did not come than let the slightest new shadow fall upon his life because of her. And yet it seemed all wrong, preposterous, to think anyone who was close to Deane, anyone whom he loved, should not understand this friendship between them. She thought of how, meeting after all those years, they were not strange with each other. That seemed rare—to be cherished.

"What's Deane's wife like, Ted?" she asked.

"I haven't met her," he replied, "but I've seen her. She's awfully good-looking; lots of style, and carries herself as if—oh, as if she knew she was somebody," he laughed. "And I guess Deane thinks she *is*," he added with another laugh. "Guess he decided that first time he met her. You know he stopped in Indianapolis to see a classmate who was practising there—met her at a party, I believe, and—good-by Deane! But somehow she isn't what you'd expect Deane's wife to be," he went on more seriously. "Doesn't look that way, anyhow. Looks pretty frigid, I thought, and, oh—fixed up. As if she wasn't just real."

Ruth's brows puckered. If there was one thing it seemed the wife of Deane Franklin should be, it was real. But doubtless Ted was wrong—not knowing her. It did not seem that Deane would be drawn to anyone who was not real.

She lingered in the thought of him. Real was just what Deane was. He had been wonderfully real with her in those days—days that had made the pattern of her life. Reality had swept away all other things between them. That carried her back to the new thinking, the questions. It seemed it was the things not real that were holding people apart. It was the artificialities people had let living build up around them made those people hard. People would be simpler—kinder—could those unreal things be swept away. She dwelt on the thought of a world like that—a world of people simple and real as Deane Franklin was simple and real.

She was called from that by a movement and exclamation from Ted, who had leaned over the railing. "There goes Mildred Woodbury," he said,—"and alone."

His tone made her look at him in inquiry and then down the street at the slight figure of a girl whose light dress stood out clearly between the shadows. Mildred was the daughter of a family who lived in the next block. The Woodburys and the Hollands had been neighbors and friends as far back as Ruth could remember. Mildred was only a little girl when Ruth went away—such a pretty little girl, her fair hair always gayly tied with ribbons. She had been there with her mother the night before and Ruth had been startled by her coming into the room where she was and saying impulsively: "You don't remember me, do you? I'm Mildred—Mildred Woodbury."

"And you used to call me Wuth!" Ruth had eagerly replied.

It had touched her, surrounded as she was by perfunctoriness and embarrassment that this young girl should seek her out in that warm way. And something in the girl's eyes had puzzled her. She had returned to thought of it more than once and that made her peculiarly interested in Ted's queer allusion to Mildred now.

"Well?" she inquired.

"Mildred's getting in rather bad," he said shortly.

"Getting—what do you mean, Ted?" she asked, looking at him in a startled way.

"People are talking about her," he said.

"People are—?" she began, but stopped, looking at him all the while in that startled way.

"Talking about her," he repeated. "I guess it's been going on for some time—though I didn't hear about it until a little while ago."

"About what, Ted?" Her voice faltered and it seemed to make him suddenly conscious of what he was saying, to whom he spoke.

"Why,"—he faltered now too, "Mildred's acting sort of silly—that's all. I don't know—a flirtation, or something, with Billy Archer. You don't know him; he came here a few years ago on some construction work. He's an engineer. He is a fascinating fellow, all right," he added.

Ruth pushed back her chair into deeper shadow. "And—?" she suggested faintly.

"He's married," briefly replied Ted.

She did not speak for what seemed a long time. Ted was beginning to fidget. Then, "How old is Mildred, Ted?" Ruth asked in a very quiet voice.

"About twenty, I guess; she's a couple of years younger than I am."

"And this man?—how old is he?" That she asked a little sharply.

"Oh, I don't know; he's in the older crowd; somewhere in the thirties, I should say."

"Well—" But she abruptly checked what she had sharply begun to say, and pushed her chair still further back into shadow. When Ted stole a timid glance at her a minute later he saw that she seemed to be holding her hands tight together.

"And doesn't Mildred's mother—?" It seemed impossible for her to finish anything, to say it out.

He shook his head. "Guess not. It's funny— but you know a person's folks—"

There was another silence; then Ted began to whistle softly and was looking over the railing as if interested in something down on the lawn.

"And you say people are really—talking about Mildred, Ted?" Ruth finally asked, speaking with apparent effort.

He nodded. "Some people are snubbing her.

You know this town is long on that," he threw in with a short laugh. "I saw Mrs. Brewer—remember her?—she used to be Dorothy Hanlay—out and out snub Mildred at a party the other night. She came up to her after she'd been dancing with Billy—Lord knows how many times she'd danced with him that night—and Mrs. Brewer simply cut her. I saw it myself. Mildred got white for a moment, then smiled in a funny little way and turned away. Tough on her, wasn't it?—for really, she's a good deal of a kid, you know. And say, Ruth, there's something mighty decent about Edith—about Mrs. Blair. She saw it and right afterwards she went up to Mildred, seemed particularly interested in her, and drew her into her crowd. Pretty white, don't you think? That old hen—Mrs. Brewer—got red, let me tell you, for Edith can put it all over her, you know, on being somebody, and that *got* her—good and plenty!"

There was a queer little sound from Ruth, a sound like a not quite suppressed sob; Ted rose, as if for leaving, and stood there awkwardly, his back to her. He felt that Ruth was crying, or at least trying not to cry. Why had he talked of a thing like that? Why did he have to bring in Edith Lawrence?

It seemed better to go on talking about it now, as naturally as he could. "I never thought there was much to Mildred," he resumed, not turning round. "She always seemed sort of stuck up with the fellows of our crowd. But I guess you never can tell. I saw her look at Billy Archer the other night." He paused with a little laugh. "There wasn't anything very stuck up about that look."

As still Ruth did not speak he began to talk about the property across the street being for sale. When he turned around for taking leave—it being past the time for going to Harriett's—it made him furious at himself to see how strained and miserable Ruth's face was. She scarcely said good-by to him; she was staring down the street where Mildred had disappeared a few moments before. All the way over to Harriett's he wondered just what Ruth was thinking. He was curious as well as self-reproachful.

CHAPTER TWENTY-ONE

When Ted entered the living-room at his sister Harriett's he felt as if something damp and heavy had been thrown around him. He got the feeling of being expected to contribute to the oppressiveness of the occasion. The way no one was sitting in a comfortable position seemed to suggest that constraint was deemed fitting. Cyrus was talking to Mr. McFarland with a certain self-conscious decorousness. Harriett's husband, the Rev. Edgar Tyler, sat before the library table in more of his pulpit manner than was usual with him in his household, as if—so it seemed to Ted—the relation of death to the matter in hand brought it particularly within his province. Ted had never liked him; especially he had hated his attitude about Ruth—his avowed sorrowfulness with which the heart had nothing to do. He resented the way his brother-in-law had made Harriett feel that she owed it to the community, to the church, not to countenance her sister. Harriett had grown into that manner of striving to do the right thing. She had it now—sitting a little apart from the others, as if not to intrude herself. Sitting there with those others his heart went out to Ruth; he was *for* her, he told himself warmly, and he'd take nothing off of Cy about her, either! He watched Cyrus and thought of how strange it was that a brother and sister should be as different as he and Ruth were. They had always been different; as far back as he could remember they were different about everything. Ruth was always keyed up about something—delighted, and Cy was always "putting a crimp" in things. As a little boy, when he told Ruth things he was pleased about they always grew more delightful for telling her; and somehow when you told Cyrus about a jolly thing it always flattened out a little in the telling.

A shrinking from the appearance of too great haste gave a personal color to the conversation. It was as old friend quite as much as family solicitor that the lawyer talked to them, although the occasion for getting together that night was that Cyrus might learn of an investment of his father's which demanded immediate attention.

Mr. McFarland spoke of that, and then of how little else remained. He hesitated, then ventured: "You know, I presume, that your father has not left you now what he would have had ten years ago?"

Ted saw Cyrus's lips tighten, his eyes lower. He glanced at Harriett, who looked resigned; though he was not thinking much of them, but of his father, who had met difficulties, borne disappointments. He was thinking of nights when his father came home tired; mornings when he went away in that hurried, harassed way. He could see him sitting in his chair brooding. The picture of him now made him appear more lonely than he had thought of him while living. And now his father was dead and they were sitting there talking over his affairs, looking into things that their father had borne alone, things he had done the best he could about. He wished he had tried harder to be company for him. In too many of those pictures which came now his father was alone.

He heard Cyrus speaking. "Yes," he was saying, "father was broken by our personal troubles." There was a pause. Ted did not raise his eyes to his brother. He did not want to look at him, not liking his voice as he said that. "It is just another way," Cyrus went on, "in which we all have to suffer for our family disgrace."

Ted felt himself flushing. Why need Cy have said that? Mr. McFarland had turned slightly away, as if not caring to hear it.

And then Cyrus asked about their father's will.

The attorney's reply was quiet. "He leaves no will."

Ted looked at him in surprise. Then he looked at Cyrus and saw his startled, keen, queer look at the attorney. It was after seeing his brother's face that he realized what this meant—that if his father left no will Ruth shared with the rest of them. Suddenly his heart was beating fast.

"How's that?" Cyrus asked sharply.

"There was a will, but he destroyed it about two month's ago."

"He—? Why?" Cyrus pressed in that sharp voice.

Ted felt certain that the lawyer liked saying what he had to say then. He said it quietly, but looking right at Cyrus. "He destroyed his will because it cut off his daughter Ruth."

Ted got up and walked to the window, stood there staring out at the street lights. Bless dad! He wished he could see him; he would give almost anything to see him for just a minute. He wished he had known; he would love to have told his father just how corking he thought that was. He stood there a minute not wanting to show the others how much he was feeling—this new, warm rush of love for his father, and his deep gladness for Ruth. He thought of what it would mean to her, what it would mean to know her father had felt like that. He had had to leave her there at home alone; now he could go home and tell her this news that would mean so much.

When he turned back to the group it was to see that he was not alone in being moved by what they had heard. Harriett too had turned a little away from the others and was looking down. He saw a tear on her face—and liked her better than he ever had before. Then he looked at her husband and in spite of all he was feeling it was hard not to smile; his brother-in-law's face looked so comical to him, trying to twist itself into the fitting emotions. Ted watched him unsparingly for a minute, maliciously saying to himself: "Keep on, old boy, you'll make it after a little!"

Then he looked at his brother and his face hardened, seeing too well what new feeling this roused in Cyrus against Ruth, reading the resentment toward their father for this final weakening in his stand against her.

"Well—" Cyrus began but did not go on, his lips tightening.

"Your father said," the lawyer added, "that if there was one of his children—more than the others—needed what he could do for her, it was his daughter Ruth."

He was looking at Ted, and Ted nodded eagerly, thinking now of what, in the practical sense, this would mean to Ruth. Mr. McFarland turned back to Cyrus as he remarked: "He spoke of Ruth with much feeling."

Cyrus flushed. "I guess father was pretty much broken—in mind as well as body—at that time," he said unpleasantly.

"His mind was all right," answered the lawyer curtly.

He left a few minutes later; Harriett, who went with him to the door, did not return to the room.

The two men and Ted sat for a moment in silence. Then Cyrus turned upon him as if angered by what he divined him to be feeling. "Well," he said roughly, "I suppose you're pleased?"

"I'm pleased, all right," replied Ted with satisfaction. He looked at the minister. "Good thing, for I guess I'm the only fellow here who is."

Harriett's husband colored slightly. "I am neither pleased nor displeased," was his grave reply. "Surely it was for your father to do as he wished. For a father to forgive a child is—moving. I only hope," he added, "that it will not seem in the community to mean the countenancing—" He paused, looking to Cyrus for approval.

Then Ten blazed out. "Well, if you want to know what I think, I don't think a little 'countenancing' of Ruth is going to do this community— or anybody else—any harm!"

' Cyrus looked at him with that slightly sneering smile that always enraged Ted. "You're proud of your sister, I suppose?" he inquired politely.

Ted reddened. Then he grew strangely quiet. "Yes," he said, "I believe I am. I've come pretty close to Ruth these last few days, and I think that's just what I am—proud of her. I can't say I'm proud of what Ruth did; I'd have to think more about that. But I'm proud of what she *is*. And I don't know—I don't know but what it's what a person *is* that counts." He fell silent, thinking of what he meant by that, of the things he felt in Ruth.

Cyrus laughed mockingly. "Rather a curious thing to be proud of, I should say. What she 'is' is—"

Ted jumped up. "Don't say it, Cy! Whatever it is you're going to say—just don't say it!"

Cyrus had risen and was putting in his pocket a paper Mr. McFarland had given him. "No?" he said smoothly, as if quite unperturbed. "And why not?"

At that uncaring manner something seemed to break inside Ted's head, as if all the things Cyrus had said about Ruth had suddenly gathered there and pressed too hard. His arm shot out at his brother.

"That's why not!" he cried.

He had knocked Cyrus back against the wall and stood there threatening him. To the minister, who had stepped up, protesting, he snapped: "None of *your* put-in! And after this, just be a little more careful in *your* talk—see?"

He stepped back from Cyrus but stood there glaring, breathing hard with anger. Cyrus, whose face had gone white, but who was calm, went back to the table and resumed what he had been doing there.

"A creditable performance, I must say, for the

day of your father's funeral," he remarked after a moment.

"That's all right!" retorted Ted. "Don't think I'm sorry! I don't know any better way to start out new—start out alone—than to tell you what I think of you!—let you know that I'll not take a thing off of you about Ruth. You've done enough, Cy. Now you quit. You kept mother and father away when they didn't want to be kept away—and I want to tell you that I'm *on* to you, anyway. Don't think for a minute that I believe it's your great virtue that's hurting you. You can't put that over on me. It's pride and stubbornness and just plain meanness makes you the way you are! Yes, I'm glad to have a chance to tell you what I think of you—and then I'm through with you, Cy. I think you're a pin-head! Why, you haven't got the heart of a flea! I don't know how anybody as fine as Ruth ever came to have a brother like you!"

His feeling had grown as he spoke, and he stopped now because he was too close to losing control; he reddened as his brother—calm, apparently unmoved—surveyed him as if mildly amused. That way Cyrus looked at him when they were quarrelling always enraged him. If he would only *say* something—not stand there as if he were too superior to bother himself with such a thing! He knew Cyrus knew it maddened him—that that was why he did it, and so it was quietly that he resumed: "No, Cy, I'm not with you, and you might as well know it. I'm for Ruth. You've got the world on your side—and I know the arguments you can put up, and all that, but Ruth's got a—" he fumbled a minute for the words—"Ruth's got a power and an understanding about her that you'll never have. She's got a heart. More than that, she's got—character."

He paused, thinking, and Cyrus did speak then. "Oh, I don't think I'd use that word," he said suavely.

"No, you wouldn't; you wouldn't see it, but that's just what I mean." He turned to the minister. "Character, I say, is what my sister Ruth has got. Character is something more than putting up a slick front. It's something more than doing what's expected of you. It's a kind of—a kind of being faithful to yourself. *Being* yourself. Oh, I know—" at a sound from his brother—"just how you can laugh at it, but there's something to it just the same. Why, Ruth's got more real stuff in her than you two put together! After being with her these days you, Cy, strike a fellow as pretty shallow."

That brought the color to his brother's face. Stung to a real retort, he broke out with considerable heat: "If to have a respect for decency is 'shallow'—!" He quickly checked himself as the door opened and Harriett's maid entered.

She paused, feeling the tension, startled by their

faces. "Excuse me, sir," she said to the minister, "but Mrs. Tyler said I was to tell you she had gone out for a few minutes. She said to tell you she had gone to see her sister."

She looked startled at Ted's laugh. After she had gone he laughed again. "Hard luck!" he said to his brother-in-law, and walked from the room.

He did not go directly home. He was too upset to face Ruth just then; he did not want her to know, it would trouble her. And he wanted to walk—walk as fast as he could, walk off steam, he called it. His heart was pounding and there seemed too much blood in his head. But he wasn't sorry, he told himself. Cy would have it in for him now, but what did he care for that? He could get along without him. But his lips trembled as he thought that. He had had to get along without his mother; from now on he would have to get along without his father. He had a moment of feeling very much alone. And then he thought of Ruth. Yes,—there was Ruth! He wheeled toward home. He wanted to tell her. He hoped Harriett hadn't got it told; he wanted to tell her himself. Bless dad! He loved him for doing that. If only he'd known it in time to let him know what he thought of him for doing it!

CHAPTER TWENTY-TWO

Harriett had been with Ruth for half an hour and still she had not told her what she had come to tell her. She was meaning to tell it before she left, to begin it any minute now, but, much as she wanted to tell it, she shrank from doing so. It seemed that telling that would open everything up—and they had opened nothing up. Harriett had grown into a way of shrinking back from the things she really wanted to do, was unpracticed in doing what she felt like doing.

Acting upon an impulse, she had started for Ruth. There had been a moment of real defiance when she told Mamie to tell Mr. Tyler that she had gone to see her sister. She had a right to go and see her sister! No one should keep her from it. Her heart was stirred by what her father had done about Ruth. It made her know that she too felt more than she had shown. His having done that made her want to do something. It moved her to have this manifestation of a softening she had not suspected. It reached something in her, something that made her feel a little more free, more bold, more loving. His defiance, for she felt that in it too, struck a spark in her. She even had a secret satisfaction in the discomfiture she knew this revelation of her father's—what they would call weakening—caused her husband and her brother. Unacknowledged dissatisfactions of her own sharpened her feeling about it. She had not looked at either her husband or Cyrus when the announcement was made, but beneath her own emotion was a secret, unacknowledged gloating at what she knew was their displeasure, at their helplessness to resent. Ted was a dear boy! Ted's shining eyes somehow made her know just how glad she herself was.

So she had hurried along, stirred, eager to tell Ruth. But once with her she held back from telling her, grew absurdly timid about it. It seemed so much else might come when that came—things long held back, things hard to let one's self talk about.

And then Ruth was so strange tonight. After that first day it had been easy to talk with Ruth; that first embarrassment over, she had seemed simple and natural and Harriett could talk with her about the little things that came up and at times just forget the big thing that held them apart. After that first meeting she had felt much more comfortable with Ruth than she would have supposed the terrible circumstances would let her feel. But tonight Ruth was different, constrained, timid; she seemed holding herself back, as if afraid of something. It made Harriett conscious of what there was holding them apart. She did not know how to begin what she had been so eager to tell.

And so they talked of surface things—current things: the service that afternoon; some of the relatives who had been there; of old friends of their father's. They kept away from the things their hearts were full of.

Ruth had been glad to see Harriett; it touched her that Harriett should come. But she was nervous with her; it was true that she was holding back. That new assurance which had helped her through the last few days had deserted her. Since Ted told her of Mildred that inner quiet from which assurance drew was dispelled. She seemed struck back—bewildered, baffled. Was it always to be that way? Every time she gained new ground for her feet was she simply to be struck back to new dismays, new incertitudes, new pain? Had she only deluded herself in that feeling which had created the strengthening calm of the last few days?

After Ted left her she had continued to sit looking down the street where Mildred had gone; just a little while before she had been looking down that street as the way she herself had gone— the young girl giving herself to love, facing all perils, daring all things for the love in her heart. But now she was not thinking of the love in Mildred's heart; she was thinking of the perils around her—the pity of it—the waiting disaster.

A little while before it had seemed there should
always be a place in the world for love, that
things shutting love out were things unreal. And
now she longed to be one with Edith in getting
Mildred back to those very things—those unreal
things that would safeguard. The mockery of it
beat her back, robbing her of the assurance that
had been her new strength. That was why Harriett found her strange, hard to talk to. She
wanted to cower back. She tried not to think of
Mildred—to get back to herself. But that she
could not do; Mildred was there in between—
confusing, a mockery.

Harriett spoke of the house, how she supposed
the best thing to do would be to offer it for sale.
Ruth looked startled and pained. "It's in bad re-
pair," Harriett said; "it's all run down. And
then—there's really no reason for keeping it."

And then they fell silent, thinking of years
gone—years when the house had not been all run
down, when there was good reason for keeping it.
To let the house go to strangers seemed the final
acknowledgment that all those old things had
passed away. It was a more intimate, a sympathetic silence into which that feeling flowed—each
thinking of old days in that house, each knowing
that the other was thinking of those days. Harriett could see Ruth as a little girl running
through those rooms. She remembered a certain
little blue gingham dress—and Ruth's hair braided

down her back; pictures of Ruth with their grandfather, their mother, their father—all those three gone now. ˉShe started to tell Ruth what she had come to tell her, then changed it to something else, still holding back, afraid of emotion, of breaking through, seeming powerless and hating herself for being powerless. She would tell that a little later—before she left. She would wait until Ted came in. She seized upon that, it let her out—let her out from the thing she had been all warm eagerness to do. To bridge that time she asked a few diffident questions about the West; she really wanted very much to know how Ruth lived, how she "managed." But she put the questions carefully, it would seem reluctantly, just because almost everything seemed to lead to that one thing,—the big thing that lay there between her and Ruth. It was hard to ask questions about the house Ruth lived in and not let her mind get swamped by that one terrible fact that she lived there with Stuart Williams—another woman's husband.

Harriett's manner made Ruth bitter. It seemed Harriett was afraid to talk to her, evidently afraid that at any moment she would come upon something she did not want to come near. Harriett needn't be so afraid!—she wasn't going to contaminate her.

And so the talk became a pretty miserable affair. It was a relief when Flora Copeland came in the room. "There's someone here to see you, Ruth," she said.

"Deane?" inquired Ruth.

"No, a woman."

"A woman?"—and then, at the note of astonishment in her own voice she laughed in an embarrassed little way.

"Yes, a Mrs. Herman. She says you may remember her as Annie Morris. She says she went to school with you."

"Yes," said Ruth, "I know." She was looking down, pulling at her handkerchief. After an instant she looked up and said quietly: "Won't you ask her to come in here?"

The woman who stood in the doorway a moment later gave the impression of life, work, having squeezed her too hard. She had quick movements, as if she were used to doing things in a hurry. She had on a cheap, plain suit, evidently bought several years before. She was very thin, her face almost pinched, but two very live eyes looked out from it. She appeared embarrassed, but somehow the embarrassment seemed only a surface thing. She held out a red, rough hand to Ruth and smiled in quick, bright way as she said: "I don't know that you remember me, Ruth."

"Oh, yes I do, Annie," Ruth replied, and held on to the red, rough hand.

"I didn't know; I'm sure," she laughed, "that

you've always meant more to me than I could to you."

After Ruth had introduced Harriett the stranger explained that with: "I thought a great deal of Ruth when we were in school together. She never knew it—she had so many friends." A little pause followed that.

"So I couldn't bear to go away," Annie went on in her rather sharp, bright way, "without seeing you, Ruth. I hope I'm not intruding, coming so —soon."

"You are not intruding, Annie," said Ruth; her voice shook just a little.

Ted had come home, and came in the room then and was introduced to Annie, with whom, though frankly surprised at seeing her, he shook hands warmly. "But we do know each other," he said.

"Oh, yes," she laughed, "I've brought you many a cauliflower."

"And oh, those eggs!" he laughed back.

Again there was a slight pause, and then Annie turned to Ruth with the manner of being bound to get right into the thing she had come to say. "I didn't wait longer, Ruth, because I was afraid you might get away and I wondered,"—this she said diffidently, as one perhaps expecting too much— "if there was any chance of your coming out to make me a little visit before you go back.

"You know,"—she turned hastily to Ted, turning away from the things gathering in Ruth's eyes, "the country is so lovely now. I thought it might do Ruth good. She must be tired, after the long journey—and all. I thought a good rest—" She turned back to Ruth. "Don't you think, Ruth," she coaxed, "that you'd like to come out and play with my baby?"

And then no one knew what to do for suddenly Ruth was shaken with sobs. Ted was soothing her, telling Annie that naturally she was nervous that night. "Ted," she choked, in a queer, wild way, laughing through the sobs, "did you *hear?* She wants me to come out and play with her *baby!*"

Harriett got up and walked to the other side of the room. Ruth—laughing, crying—was repeating: "She wants me to play with her *baby!*" Harriett thought of her own children at home, whom Ruth had not seen. She listened to the plans Annie and Ted and Ruth were making and wretchedly wished she had done differently years before.

CHAPTER TWENTY-THREE

Ruth had been with Annie for five days now; the original three days for which she had said she could come had been lengthened to a week, and she knew that she would not want to go even then. For here was rest. Here she could forget about herself as set apart from others. Here she did not seem apart. After the stress of those days at home it was good to rest in this simple feeling of being just one with others. It was good to lie on the grass under the trees, troubled thoughts in abeyance, and feel spring in the earth, take it in by smell and sound. It was wonderfully good to play with the children, to lie on the grass and let the little two year old girl—Annie's baby—pull at her hair, toddling around her, cooing and crowing. There was healing in that. It was good to be some place where she did not seem to cause embarrassment, to be where she was wanted. After the strain of recent events the simple things of these days were very sweet to her. It had become monstrous always to have to feel that something about her made her different from other people. There was something terrible in it—something not good for one. Here was release from that.

And it was good to be with Annie; they had not

talked much yet—not seriously talked. Annie seemed to know that it was rest in little things Ruth needed now, not talk of big ones. They talked about the chickens and the cows, the flowers and the cauliflowers, about the children's pranks. It was restoring to talk thus of inconsequential things; Ruth was beginning to feel more herself than she had felt in years. On that fifth day her step was lighter than when she came; it was easier to laugh. Hers had once been so sunny a nature; it was amazingly easy to break out of the moroseness with which circumstances had clouded her into that native sunniness. That afternoon she sat on the knoll above the house, leaning back against a tree and smiling lazily at the gamboling of the new little pigs.

Annie was directing the boy who had been helping her cut asparagus to carry the baskets up where Ruth was sitting. "I'm going to talk to you while I make this into bunches, Ruth," she called.

"I'll help," Ruth called back with zest.

They talked at first of the idiosyncrasies of asparagus beds, of the marketing of it; then something Annie said set Ruth thinking of something that had happened when they were in high school. "Oh, do you remember, Annie—" she laughingly began. There was that sort of talk for awhile— "Do you remember . . . ?" and "Oh, whatever became of . . . ?"

As they worked on Ruth thought of the strangeness of her being there with this girl who, when they were in school together, had meant so little to her. Her own work lagged, watching Annie as with quick, sure motions she made the asparagus into bunches for market. She did things deftly and somehow gave the feeling of subordinating them to something else, of not letting them take all of her. Ruth watched her with affectionate interest; she wore an all-over gingham apron, her big sun hat pushed back from her browned, thin face; she was not at all attractive unless one saw the eager, living eyes—keenly intelligent eyes. Ruth thought of her other friends—the girls who had been her friends when she was in school and whom she had not seen now; she wondered why it was Annie had none of the feeling that kept those other girls away.

Annie's husband was a slow, stolid man; Ruth supposed that in his youth, when Annie married him, he had perhaps been attractive in his stalwartness. He was sluggish now; good humored enough, but apparently as heavy in spirit as in body. Things outside the material round of life —working, eating, sleeping—simply did not seem to exist for him. At first she wondered how Annie could be content with life with him, Annie, who herself was so keenly alive. Thinking of it now it seemed Annie had the same adjustment to him that she had to the asparagus,—something subordinated, not taking up very much of herself. She had about Annie, and she did not know just why she had it, the feeling that here was a person who could not be very greatly harmed, could not be completely absorbed by routine, could not, for some reason she could not have given, be utterly vanquished by any circumstance. She went about her work as if that were one thing—and then there were other things; as if she were in no danger of being swallowed up in her manner of living. There was something apart that was dauntless. Ruth wondered about her, she wanted to find out about her. She wanted for herself that valiant spirit, a certain unconquerableness she felt in Annie.

Annie broke a pause to say: "You can't know, Ruth, how much it means to have you here."

Ruth's face lighted and she smiled; she started to speak, but instead only smiled again. She wanted to tell what it meant to her to be there, but that seemed a thing not easily told.

"I wish you could stay longer," Annie went on, all the while working. "So—" she paused, and continued a little diffidently—"so we could really get acquainted; really talk. I hardly ever have anyone to talk to," she said wistfully. "One gets pretty lonely sometimes. It would be good to have someone to talk to about the things one thinks."

"What are the things you think, Annie?" Ruth asked impulsively.

"Oh, no mighty thoughts," laughed Annie; "but of course I'm always thinking about things. We keep alive by thinking, don't we?"

Ruth gave her a startled look.

"Perhaps it's because I haven't had from life itself much of what I'd like to have," Annie was going on, "that I've made a world within. Can't let life cheat us, Ruth," she said brightly. "If we can't have things in one way—have to get them in another."

Again Ruth looked at her in that startled way. Annie did not see it, reaching over for more asparagus; she was all the time working along in that quick, sure way—doing what she was doing cleverly and as if it weren't very important. "Perhaps, Ruth," she said after a minute, "that that's why my school-girl fancy for you persisted—deepened—the way it has." She hesitated, then said simply: "I liked you for not letting life cheat you."

She looked up with a quick little nod as she said that but found Ruth's face very serious, troubled. "But I don't think I've done what you mean, Annie," she began uncertainly. "I did what I did —because I had to. And I'm afraid I haven't— gone on. It begins to seem to me now that I've stayed in a pretty small place. I've been afraid!" she concluded with sudden scorn.

"That isn't much wonder," Annie murmured gently.

"But with me," she took it up after a little, "I've had to go on." Her voice went hard in saying it. "Things would have just shut right down on me if I would have let them," she finished grimly.

"I married for passion," she began quietly after a minute. "Most people do, I presume. At least most people who marry young."

Ruth colored. She was not used to saying things right out like that.

"Romantic love is a wonderful thing," Annie pursued; "I suppose it's the most beautiful thing in the world—while it lasts." She laughed in a queer, grim little way and gave a sharp twist to the knot she was tying. "Sometimes it opens up to another sort of love—love of another quality—and to companionship. It must be a beautiful thing—when it does that." She hesitated a moment before she finished with a dryness that had that grim quality: "With me—it didn't.

"So there came a time," she went on, and seemed newly to have gained serenity, "when I saw that I had to give up—go under—or get through myself what I wasn't going to get through anyone else. Oh, it's not the beautiful way—not the complete way. But it's one way!" she flashed in fighting voice. "I fought for something, Ruth. I held it. I don't know that I've a name for it—but it's the most precious thing in life. My life itself is pretty limited; aside from the children"

—she softened in speaking of them—"my life is—pretty barren. And as for the children"—that fighting spirit broke sharply through, "they're all the more reason for not sinking into things—not sinking into *them,*" she laughed.

As she stopped there Ruth asked eagerly, eyes intently upon her: "But just what is it you mean, Annie? Just what is it you fought for—kept?"

"To be my *own!*" Annie flashed back at her, like steel.

Then she changed; for the first time her work fell unheeded in her lap; the eyes which a minute before had flashed fight looked far off and were dreamy; her face, over which the skin seemed to have become stretched, burned by years of sun and wind, quivered a little. When she spoke again it was firmly but with sadness. "It's what we think that counts, Ruth. It's what we feel. It's what we *are.* Oh, I'd like richer living—more beauty —more joy. Well, I haven't those things. For various reasons, I won't have them. That makes it the more important to have all I can take!"—it leaped out from the gentler thinking like a sent arrow. "Nobody holds my thoughts. They travel as far as they themselves have power to travel. They bring me whatever they can bring me—and I shut nothing out. I'm not afraid!"

Ruth was looking at her with passionate earnestness.

"Over there in that town,"—Annie made a little

gesture toward it, "are hundreds of women who would say they have a great deal more than I have. And it's true enough," she laughed, "that they have some things I'd like to have. But do you think I'd trade with them?. Oh, no! Not much! The free don't trade with the bond, Ruth."

And still Ruth did not speak, but listened with that passionate intentness.

"There in that town," Annie went on, "are people—most a whole townful of them—who are going through life without being really awake to life at all. They move around in a closed place, doing the same silly little things—copy-cats—repeaters. They're not their *own*—they're not awake. They're like things run by machinery. Like things going in their sleep. Take those girls we used to go to school with. Why, take Edith Lawrence. I see her sometimes. She always speaks sweetly to me; she means to be nice. But she moves round and round in her little place and she doesn't even *know* of the wonderful things going on in the world today! Do you think I'd trade with *her?*—social leader and all the rest of it!" She was gathering together the bundles of asparagus. She had finished her work. "Very sweet—very charming," she disposed of Edith, "but she simply doesn't count. The world's moving away from her, and she,"—Annie laughed with a mild scorn—"doesn't even know that!"

CHAPTER TWENTY-FOUR

It was late when Ruth went to sleep that night; she and Annie talked through the evening—of books Annie was reading, of the things which were interesting her. She was rich in interests; ideas were as personal things to her; she found personal satisfactions in them. She was following things which Ruth knew little about; she had been long away from the centers of books, and out of touch with awakened people. A whole new world seemed to open from these things that were vital to Annie; there was promise in them—a quiet road out from the hard things of self. There were new poets in the world; there were bold new thinkers; there was an amazing new art; science was reinterpreting the world and workers and women were setting themselves free. Everywhere the old pattern was being shot through with new ideas. Everywhere were new attempts at a better way of doing things. She had been away from all that; what she knew of the world's new achievement had seemed unreal, or at least detached, not having any touch with her own life. But as disclosed by Annie those things became realities—things to enrich one's own life. It kindled old fires of her girlhood, fanned the old desire to know. Personal things had seemed to quell that; the storm in her own life had shut down around her. Now she saw that she, like those others whom Annie scorned, had not kept that openness to life, had let her own life shut her in. She had all along been eager for books, but had not been fortunate in the things she had come upon. She had not had access to large libraries—many times not even to small ones; she had had little money for buying books and was so out of touch with the world that she had not had much initiative in trying to get hold of things. She felt now that she had failed miserably in that, but there were years when she was like a hurt thing that keeps in hiding, most of all wanting to escape more hurt. It had been a weakness—she clearly saw that now, and it had been weakening to her powers. Most of the books she had come upon were of that shut-in life Annie scorned, written from within that static living, and for it. People in them had the feeling it was right people should have, unless there were bad people in the book, and then they were very definitely bad. Many of those books had been not only unsatisfying, but saddening to her, causing her to feel newly apart from the experiences of people of her kind.

But now Annie's books let her glimpse a new world—a world which questioned, a world of protest, of experiment, a world in which people unafraid were trying to find the truth, trying to build freshly, to supplant things outworn with the vital forms of a new reality. It was quickening. It made her eager. She was going to take some of those books home, she would send for others, would learn how to keep in touch with this new world which was emerging from the old. It was like breaking out from a closed circle. It was adventure!

Even after she went to her room that night, late though it was, she did not go at once to bed. She sat for a time looking off at the lights of that town for which she had so long grieved, the town that had shut her out. The fact that it had shut her out had been a determining thing in her life, to her spirit. She wondered now if perhaps she had not foolishly spent herself in grieving for a thing that would have meant little could she have had it. For it seemed now that it had remained very much a fixed thing, and now she knew that, with it all, she herself had not been fixed. The things of which Annie talked, things men of this new day were expressing, roused her like this, not because they were all new, but because of her own inner gropings. Within herself she had been stumbling toward some of those things. Here was the sure expression of some halting thoughts of her own. It was exciting to find that there were people who were feeling the things that, even in that timid, uncertain way, she had come to feel by herself. She had been half afraid to formulate some of the things that had come into her mind. This gathered together the timid little shoots. She was excited about the things of which Annie talked— those new ideals of freedom—not so much because they were new and daring and illumining things, as because they did not come all alien. There was something from within to go out to them. In that —not that there were interesting things she could have from without—but that she, opened to the new stimulus, could become something from within, was the real excitation, the joy of the new promise was there. And this new stir, this promise of new satisfactions, let her feel that her life was not all mapped out, designed ahead. She went to sleep that night with a wonderful new feeling of there being as much for her in life as she herself had power to take.

And she woke with that feeling; she was eager to be up, to be out in the sunshine. Annie, she found, had gone early to town with her vegetables. Ruth helped eleven-year-old Dorothy, the eldest child, get off for school and walked with her to the schoolhouse half a mile down the road. The little girl's shyness wore away and she chatted with Ruth about school, about teachers and lessons and play. Ruth loved it; it seemed to set the seal of a human relationship upon her new feeling. What a wonderful thing for Annie to have these children! Today gladness in there being children in the world went out past sorrow in her own deprivation. The night before she had said to Annie, "You have your children. That makes life worth while to you, doesn't it?" And Annie, with that hard, swift look of being ruthless for getting at the truth— for getting her feeling straight and expressing it truly, had answered, "Not in itself. I mean, it's not all. I think much precious life has gone dead under that idea of children being enough —letting them be all. *We* count—*I* count! Just leaving life isn't all; living it while we're here— that counts, too. And keeping open to it in more than any one relationship. Suppose they, in their turn, have that idea; then life's never really lived, is it?—always just passed on, always *put off.*" They had talked of that at some length. "Certainly I want my children to have more than I have," Annie said. "I am working that they may. But in that working for them I'm not going to let go of the fact that I count too. Now's my only chance," she finished in that grim little way as one not afraid to be hard.

Thinking back to that it seemed to Ruth a bigger mother feeling than the old one. It was not the sort of maternal feeling to hem in the mother and oppress the children. It was love in freedom— love that did not hold in or try to hold in. It would develop a sense of the preciousness of life. It did not glorify self-sacrifice—that insidious foe to the fullness of living.

Thinking of that, and going out from that to

other things, she sat down on a log by the roadside, luxuriating in the opulence and freshness of the world that May morning, newly tuned to life, vibrant with that same fresh sense of it, glad gratefulness in return to it, that comes after long sickness, after imprisonment.   The world was full of singing birds that morning,—glorious to be in a world of singing birds!   The earth smelled so good!   There were plum trees in bloom behind her; every little breeze brought their fragrance. The grass under her feet was springy—the world was vibrant, beautiful, glad.   The earth seemed so strong, so full of still unused powers, so ready to give.

She sat there a long time; she had the courage this morning to face the facts of her life.   She was eager to face them, to understand them that she might go on understandingly.   She had the courage to face the facts relating to herself and Stuart.   That was a thing she had not dared do. With them, love *had* to last, for love was all they had.   They had only each other.   They did not dare let themselves think of such a thing as the love between them failing.

Well, it had not failed; but she let herself see now how greatly it had changed.   There was something strangely freeing in just letting herself see it.   Of course there had been change; things always changed.   Love changed within marriage —she did not know why she should expect it to be different with her. But in the usual way—within marriage—it would matter less for there would be more ways of adapting one's self to the changing. Then one could reach out into new places in life, gaining new channels, taking on new things as old ones slipped away, finding in common interests, common pleasures, the new adjustment for feeling. But with them life had seemed to shut right down around them. And they had never been able to relax in the reassuring sense of the lastingness of their love. She had held herself tense in the idea that there was no change, would be none. She had a feeling now of having tried too hard, of being tired through long trying. There was relief in just admitting that she was tired. And so she let herself look at it now, admitting that she had been clutching at a vanished thing.

It would have been different, she felt, had the usual channels of living been opened to them. Then together they could have reached out into new experiences. Their love had been real—great. Related to living, surely it could have remained the heart of life. Her seeing now that much of the life had gone out of it did not bear down upon her with the great sadness she would have expected. She knew now that in her heart she had known for a long time that passion had gone. Facing it was easier than refusing to see. It ceased to be a terrible thing once one looked at it. Of this she was sure: love should be able to be a part of the rest of life; the big relationship, but one among others; the most intense interest, but one with other interests. Unrooted, detached, it might for the time be the more intense, but it had less ways of saving itself. If simply, naturally, they could have grown into the common life she felt they might have gone on without too much consciousness of change, growing into new things as old ones died away, half unconsciously making adjustments, doubtless feeling something gone but in the sharing of new things not left desolate through that sense of the passing of old ones. Frightened by the thought of having nothing else, they had tried too hard. She was tired; she believed that Stuart too was tired.

There was a certain tired tenderness in her thinking of him. Dear Stuart, he loved easy pleasant living. It seemed he was not meant for the too great tests, for tragically isolated love. She knew that he had never ceased to miss the things he had let go—his place among men, the stimulus of the light, pleasant social relationships with women. He was meant for a love more flexibly related to living, a love big and real but fitted more loosely, a little more carelessly, to life. There was always so deep a contrition for his irritations with her. The whole trouble was indicated right there, that the contrition should be all out of proportion to the offence. It would have been better had he felt more free to be irritated; one should not have to feel frightened at a little bit of one's own bad temper—appalled at crossness, at hours of ennui. Driving them back together after every drifting apart all of that made for an intensity of passion—passion whipped to life by fear. But that was not the way to grow into life. Flames kindled by fear made intense moments but after a time left too many waste places between them and the lives of men.

Today her hope for the future was in the opening of new places. She was going back with new vision, new courage. They must not any longer cling together in their one little place, coming finally to actual resentment of one another for the enforced isolation. They must let themselves go out into living, dare more, trust more, lose that fear of rebuff, hope for more from life, *claim* more. As she rose and started towards home there was a new spring in her step. For her part, she was through with that shrinking back! She hoped she could bring Stuart to share her feeling, could inspire in him this new trust, new courage that had so stimulated and heartened her. Her hope for their future lay there.

Climbing a hill she came in sight of the little city which they had given up, for which they had grieved. Well, they had grieved too much, she resolutely decided now. There were wider horizons than the one that shut down upon that town.

She was not conquered! She would not be conquered. She stood on the hilltop exulting in that
sense of being free. She had been a weakling to
think her life all settled! Only cowards and the
broken in spirit surrendered the future as pay-
ment for the past. Love was the great and beautiful wonder—but surely one should not stay with it
in the place where it found one. Why, loving
should light the way! Far from engulfing all the
rest of life it seemed now that love should open
life to one. Whether one kept it or whether one
lost it, it failed if it did not send one farther along
the way. She had been afraid to think of her love
changing because that had seemed to grant that it
had failed. But now it seemed that it failed if it
did not leave her bigger than it had found her.
Her eyes filled in response to the stern beauty of
that. Not that one stay with love in the same
place, but rather the meaning of it all was in just
this: that it send one on.

Eyes still dimmed with the feeling of it, she
stood looking as if in a final letting go at that town
off there on the bend of the river. It became to
her the world of shut-in people, people not going
on, people who loved and never saw the meaning
of love, whose experiences were not as wings to
carry them, but as walls shutting them in. She
was through grieving for those people. She was
going on—past them—so far beyond them that
her need for them would fall away.

She was conscious of an approaching horse and
buggy and stepped aside; then walked on, so aglow
with her own thoughts that a passing by did not
break in upon her. She did not even know that
the girl in the run-about had stopped her horse.
At the cry: "Oh—I'm so glad!" she was as
startled as if she had thought herself entirely
alone.

It was a big effort to turn, to gather herself
together and speak. She had been so far away,
so completely possessed that it took her an instant
to realize that the girl leaning eagerly toward her
was Mildred Woodbury.

Mildred was moving over on the seat, inviting
her to get in. "I'm so glad!" she repeated. "I
went to Mrs. Herman's, and was so disappointed
to miss you. I thought maybe I'd come upon you
somewhere," she laughed gladly, though not without embarrassment.

There was a moment of wanting to run away, of
really considering it. She knew now—had remembered, realized—what it was about Mildred.

CHAPTER TWENTY-FIVE

Her instinct to protect herself from this young girl was the thing that gained composure for her. At first it was simply one of those physical instincts that draw us back from danger, from pain; and then she threw the whole force of her will to keeping that semblance of composure. Her instinct was not to let reserves break down, not to show agitation; to protect herself by never leaving commonplace ground. It was terribly hard —this driving back the flood-tide of feeling and giving no sign of the struggle, the resentment. It was as if every nerve had been charged to full life and then left there outraged.

But she could do it; she could appear pleasantly surprised at Mildred's having come to take her for a drive, could talk along about the little things that must be her shield against the big ones. Something in her had gone hard in that first moment of realizing who Mildred was. She was not going to be driven back again! And so she forced herself to talk pleasantly of the country through which they went, of Mildred's horse, of driving and riding.

But it was impossible not to grow a little interested in this young Mildred Woodbury. She sat

erect and drove in a manner that had the little
tricks of worldliness, but was somehow charming
in spite of its artificiality.   Ruth was thinking that
Mildred was a more sophisticated young person
than she herself had been at that age.   She wondered if sophistication was increasing in the world,
if there was more of it in Freeport than there used
to be.

They talked of Ruth's father, of Mildred's
people, of the neighborhood both knew so well.
From that it drifted to the social life of the town.
She was amused, rather sadly amused, at Mildred's air of superiority about it; it seemed so
youthful, so facile.   Listening to Mildred now
pictures flashed before her: she and Edith Lawrence—girls of about fifteen—going over to the
Woodburys' and eagerly asking, "Could we take
the baby out, Mrs. Woodbury?"   "Now you'll be
very, very careful, girls?" Mrs. Woodbury would
say, wrapping Mildred all up in soft pink things.
"Oh, *yes*, Mrs. Woodbury," they would reply, a
little shocked that she could entertain the thought
of their not being careful.   And then they would
start off cooing girlish things about the cunning
little darling.   This was that baby—in spite of her
determination to hold aloof from Mildred there
was no banishing it; no banishing the apprehension that grew with the girl's talk.   For Mildred
seemed so much a part of the very thing for which
she had this easy scorn.   Something in the way she

held the lines made it seem she would not belong anywhere else. She looked so carefully prepared for the very life for which she expressed disdain.

She tried to forget the things that were coming back to her—how Mildred would gleefully hold up her hands to have her mittens put on when she and Edith were about to take her out, and tried too to turn the conversation—breaking out with something about Mrs. Herman's children. But it became apparent that Mildred was not to be put off. Everything Ruth would call up to hold her off she somehow forced around to an approach for what she wanted to say.

And then it came abruptly, as if she were tired of trying to lead up to it. "I've been wanting to see you—Ruth," she hesitated over the name, but brought it out bravely, and it occurred to Ruth then that Mildred had not known how to address her. "When I heard you were here," she added, "I was determined you shouldn't get away without my seeing you."

Ruth looked at her with a little smile, moved, in spite of herself, by the impetuousness of the girl's tone, by something real that broke through the worldly little manner.

"I don't feel as the rest of them do." She flushed and said it hurriedly, a little tremulously; and yet there was something direct and honest in her eyes, as if she were going to say it whether it seemed nice taste or not. It reached Ruth, went through her self-protective determination not to be reached. Her heart went out to Mildred's youth, to this appeal from youth, moved by the freshness and realness beneath that surface artificiality, saddened by this defiance of one who, it seemed, could so little understand how big was the thing she defied, who seemed so much the product of the thing she scorned, so dependent on what she was apparently in the mood to flout. "I don't know that they are to be blamed for their feeling, Mildred," she answered quietly.

"Oh, yes, they are!" hotly contended the girl. "It's because they don't understand. It's because they *can't* understand!" The reins had fallen loose in her hand; the whip sagged; she drooped—that stiff, chic little manner gone. She turned a timid, trusting face to Ruth—a light shining through troubled eyes. "It's love that counts, isn't it,—Ruth?" she asked, half humble, half defiant.

It swept Ruth's heart of everything but sympathy. Her hand closed over Mildred's. "What is it, dear?" she asked. "Just what is it?"

Mildred's eyes filled. Ruth could understand that so well—what sympathy meant to a feeling shut in, a feeling the whole world seemed against. "It's with me—as it was with you," the girl answered very low and simply. "It's—like that."

Ruth shut her eyes for an instant; they were passing something fragrant; it came to her—an old fragrance—like something out of things past; a robin was singing; she opened her eyes and looked at Mildred, saw the sunshine finding gold in the girl's hair. The sadness of it—of youth and suffering, of pain in a world of beauty, that reach of pain into youth, into love, made it hard to speak. "I'm sorry, dear," was all she could say.

They rode a little way in silence; Ruth did not know how to speak, what to say; and then Mildred began to talk, finding relief in saying things long held in. Ruth understood that so well. Oh, she understood it all so well—the whole tumult of it, the confused thinking, the joy, the passion,—the passion that would sacrifice anything, that would let the whole world go. Here it was again. She knew just what it was.

"So you can see," Mildred was saying, "what you have meant to me."

Yes, she could see that.

They were driving along the crest of the hills back of the town. Mildred pointed to it. "That town isn't the whole of the world!" she exclaimed passionately, after speaking of the feeling that was beginning to form there against herself. "What do I care?" she demanded defiantly. "It's not the whole of the world!"

Ruth looked at it. She could see the Lawrence house—it had a high place and was visible from all around; Mildred's home was not far from there; her own old home was only a block farther on. She had another one of those flashing pictures from things far back: Mrs. Woodbury—Mildred's mother—standing at the door with a bowl of chicken broth for Mrs. Holland—Ruth's mother—who was ill. "I thought maybe this would taste good," she could hear Mrs. Woodbury saying. Strange how things one had forgotten came back. Other things came back as for a moment she continued to look at the town where both she and Mildred had been brought up, where their ties were. Then she turned back to Mildred, to this other girl who, claimed by passionate love, was in the mood to let it all go. "But that's just what it is, Mildred," she said. "The trouble is, it *is* the whole of the world."

"It's the whole of the social world," she answered the look of surprise. "It's just the same everywhere. And it's astonishing how united the world is. You give it up in one place—you've about given it up for every place."

"Then the whole social world's not worth it!" broke from Mildred. "It's not worth—enough."

Ruth found it hard to speak; she did not know what to say. She had a flashing sense of the haphazardness of life, of the power, the flame this found in Mildred that the usual experiences would never have found, of how, without it, she would doubtless have developed much like the other girls of her world—how she might develop because of it—how human beings were shaped by chance.

She looked at Mildred's face—troubled, passionate, a confused defiance, and yet something real there looking through the tumult, something flaming, something that would fight, a something, she secretly knew, more flaming, more fighting, than might ever break to life in Mildred again. And then she happened to look down at the girl's feet —the very smart low shoes of dull kid, perfectly fitted, high arched—the silk stockings, the slender ankle. They seemed so definitely feet for the places prepared, for the easier ways, not fitted for going a hard way alone. It made her feel like a mother who would want to keep a child from a way she herself knew as too hard.

"But what are you going to put in the place of that social world, Mildred?" she gently asked. "There must be something to fill its place. What is that going to be?"

"Love will fill its place!" came youth's proud, sure answer.

Ruth was looking straight ahead; the girl's tone had thrilled her—that faith in love, that courage for it. It was so youthful!—so youthfully sure, so triumphant in blindness. Youth would dare so much—youth knew so little. She did not say anything; she could not bear to.

"Love can fill its place!" Mildred said again, as if challenging that silence. And as still Ruth did not speak she demanded, sharply, "Can't it?"

Ruth turned to her a tender, compassionate

face, too full of feeling, of conflict, to speak.
Slowly, as if she could not bear to do it, she shook
her head.

Mildred looked just dazed for a moment, then so
much as if one in whom she had trusted, on whom
she had counted for a great deal had failed her
that Ruth made a little gesture as if to say it was
not that, as if to say she was sorry it seemed like
that.

Mildred did not heed it. "But it has with you,"
she insisted.

"It has *not!*" leaped out the low, savage answer that startled the woman from whom it came.
"It has not!" she repeated fiercely.

Her rage was against the feeling that seemed
to trick one like that; the way love *got* one—made
one believe that nothing else in the world mattered
but just itself. It wasn't fair! It was cruel!
That made her savage—savage for telling Mildred the other side of it, the side love blinded her
to. In that moment it seemed that love was a
trap; it took hold of one and persuaded one things
were true that weren't true! Just then it seemed
a horrible thing the way love got one through
lovely things, through beauty and tenderness,
through the sweetest things—then did as it pleased
with the life it had stolen in upon. Fiercely she
turned the other face, told Mildred what love in
loneliness meant, what it meant to be shut away
from one's own kind, what that hurting of other

lives did to one's self, what isolation made of one, what it did to love. Things leaped out that she had never faced, had never admitted for true; the girl to whom she talked was frightened and she was frightened herself—at what she told of what she herself had felt, feeling that she had never admitted she had had. She let the light in on things kept in the dark even in her own soul—a cruel light, a light that spared nothing, that seemed to find a savage delight in exposing the things deepest concealed. She would show the other side of it! There was a certain gloating in doing it—getting ahead of a thing that would trick one. And then that spent itself as passion will and she grew quieter and talked in a simple way of what loneliness meant, of what longing for home meant, of what it meant to know one had hurt those who had always been good to one, who loved and trusted. She spoke of her mother—of her father, and then she broke down and cried and Mildred listened in silence to those only half-smothered sobs.

When Ruth was able to stop she looked up, timidly, at Mildred. Something seemed to have gone out of the girl—something youthful and superior, something radiant and assured. She looked crumpled up. The utter misery in her eyes, about her mouth, made Ruth whisper: "I'm sorry, Mildred."

Mildred looked at her with a bitter little laugh and then turned quickly away.

Ruth had never felt more wretched in her life than when, without Mildred having said a word, they turned in the gate leading up to Annie's. She wanted to say something to comfort. She cast around for something. "Maybe," she began, "that it will come right—anyway."

Again Mildred only laughed in that hard little way.

When they were half way up the hill Mildred spoke, as if, in miserable uncertainty, thinking things aloud. "Mrs. Blair has asked me to go to Europe with her for the summer," she said, in a voice that seemed to have no spring left in it. "She's chaperoning a couple of girls. I could go with them."

"Oh, *do*, Mildred!" cried Ruth. "Do that!" It seemed to her wonderfully tender, wonderfully wise, of Edith. She was all eagerness to induce Mildred to go with Edith.

But there was no answering enthusiasm. Mildred drooped. She did not look at Ruth. "I could do that," she said in a lifeless way, as if it didn't matter much what she did.

When they said good-by Mildred's broken smile made Ruth turn hastily away. But she looked back after the girl had driven off, wanting to see if she was sitting up in that sophisticated little way she had. But Mildred was no longer sitting that way. She sagged, as if she did not care anything about how she sat. Ruth stood looking after her, watching as far as she could see her, longing to see her sit up, to see her hold the whip again in that stiff, chic little fashion. But she did not do it; her horse was going along as if he knew there was no interest in him. Ruth could not bear it. If only the whip would go up at just that right little angle! But it did not. She could not see the whip at all—only the girl's drooping back.

CHAPTER TWENTY-SIX

When Mildred had passed from sight Ruth slowly turned toward the house. She noticed the vegetable wagon there in front of the barn—so Annie had come home. She turned away from the kitchen door she had been about to enter; she did not want to talk to Annie just then. But when she had passed around to the other side of the house she saw, standing with their backs to her in the little flower garden, Annie and a woman she was astonished to recognize as her sister Harriett.

She made a move toward the little hill that rose behind the house. She would get away! But Mr. Herman appeared just then at the top of the hill. He saw her; he must see that she had seen the others. So she would have to stay and talk to Harriett. It seemed a thing she absolutely could not do. It had come to seem she was being made some kind of sport of, as if the game were to buffet her about between this feeling and that, let her gain a little ground, get to a clearing, then throw her back to new confusion. That day, anyway, she could bear no more of it. It was hard to reply to Mr. Herman when he called something to her. Annie heard their voices and then she had to join her and Harriett.

"Why, Ruth!" Annie cried in quick solicitude upon seeing Ruth's face, "you went too far. How hateful of you," she laughed, as if feeling there was something to laugh off, "to come looking like this just when I have been boasting to your sister about how we've set you up!"

"You do look tired, Ruth," said Harriett compassionately.

Harriett said she had come for a little visit with Ruth, and Annie proposed that they go up under the trees at the crest of the hill back of the house. It was where Ruth had sat with Annie just the day before. As she sat down there now it seemed it was ages ago since she and Annie had sat there tying the asparagus into bunches.

Annie had come up with some buttermilk for them. As she handed Ruth hers she gave her shoulder an affectionate little pat, as if, looking at her face, she wanted to tell her to take heart. Then she went back to the house, leaving the two sisters alone.

They drank their buttermilk, talking of it, of Annie's place, of her children. In a languid way Ruth was thinking that it was good of Harriett to come and see her; had she come the day before, she would have been much pleased. In that worn way, she was pleased now; doubtless it had been hard for Harriett to come—so busy, and not well. Perhaps her coming meant real defiance. Anyway, it was good of her to come. She tried to be nice to Harriett, to talk about things as if she liked having her there to talk with. But that final picture of Mildred's drooping back was right there before her all the time. As she talked with Harriett about the price of butter and eggs—the living to be had in selling them, she was all the while seeing Mildred—Mildred as she had been when Ruth got into the buggy; as she said, "Love can take its place!"—as she was when she drove away. She had a sick feeling of having failed; she had failed the very thing in Mildred to which she had elected to be faithful in herself. And *why?* What right had one to say that another was not strong enough? How did one *know?* And yet she wanted Mildred to go with Edith; she believed that she would—now. That blighting sense of failure, of having been unfaithful, could not kill a feeling of relief. Did it mean that she was, after all, just like Edith? Had her venturing, her experience, left her much as she would have been without it? Just before meeting Mildred she was strong in the feeling of having gained something from the hard way she had gone alone. She was going on! That was what it had shown her— that one was to go on. Then she had to listen to Mildred—and she was back with the very people she had felt she was going on past—one with those people she had so triumphantly decided were not worth her grieving for them.

She had been so sure—so radiantly sure, happy

in that sense of having, at last, found herself, of being rid of fears and griefs and incertitudes. Then she met Mildred. It came to her then— right while she was talking with Harriett about what Flora Copeland was going to do now that the house would be broken up—that it was just that thing which kept the world conservative. It was fear for others. It was that feeling she had when she looked down at Mildred's feet.

One did not have that feeling when one looked at one's own feet. Fear of pain for others was quite unlike fear for one's self. Courage for one's self one could gain; in the fires of the heart that courage was forged. When the heart was warm with the thing one wanted to do one said no price in pain could be too great. But courage for others had to be called from the mind. It was another thing. When it was some one else,—one younger, one who did not seem strong—then one distrusted the feeling and saw large the pain. One *knew* one could bear pain one's self. There was something not to be borne in thinking of another's pain. That was why, even among venturers, few had the courage to speak for venturing. There was something in humankind—it was strongest in womankind—made them, no matter how daring for themselves, cautious for others. And perhaps that, all crusted round with things formal and lifeless, was the living thing at the heart of the world's conservatism.

Harriett was talking of the monument Cyrus thought there should be at the cemetery; Ruth listened and replied—seemed only tired, and all the while these thoughts were shaping themselves in her inner confusion and disheartenment. She would rather have stopped thinking of it, but could not. She had been too alive when checked; there was too much emotion in that inner confusion. She wondered if she would ever become sure of anything; if she would ever have, and keep, that courage of confidence which she had thought, for just a few radiant moments, she had. She would like to talk to Annie about it, but she had a feeling that she was not fit to talk to Annie. Annie was not one of those to run back at the first thought of another's pain. That, too, Annie could face. Better let them in for pain than try to keep them from life, Annie would say. She could hear her saying it—saying that even that concern for others was not the noblest thing. Fearing would never set the world free, would be Annie's word. Not to keep people in the safe little places, but to shape a world where there need not be safe little places! While she listened to what Harriett said of how much such a monument as Cyrus wanted would cost, she could hear Annie's sharp-edged little voice making those replies to her own confusion, could hear her talking of a sterner, braver people—hardier souls—who would one day make a world where fear was not the part of kindness. Annie would say that it was not the women who would protect other women who would shape the future in which there need not be that tight little protection.

She sighed heavily and pushed back her hair with a gesture of great weariness. "Poor Ruth!" it made Harriett murmur, "you haven't really got rested at all, have you?"

She pulled herself up and smiled as best she could at her sister, who had spoken to her with real feeling. "I did," she said with a little grimace that carried Harriett back a long way, "then I got so rested I got to thinking about things—then I got tired again." She flushed after she had said it, for that was the closest they had come to the things they kept away from.

"Poor Ruth," Harriett murmured again. "And I'm afraid," she added with a little laugh, "that now I'm going to make you more tired."

"Oh, no," said Ruth, though she looked at her inquiringly.

"Because," said Harriett, "I've come to talk to you about something, Ruth."

Ruth's face made her say, "I'm sorry, Ruth, but I'm afraid it's the only chance. You see you're going away day after tomorrow."

Ruth only nodded; it seemed if she spoke she would have to cry out what she felt—that in common decency she ought to be let alone now as any worn-out thing should be let alone, that it was not fair—humane—to talk to her now. But of course she could not make that clear to Harriett, and with it all she did wonder what it was Harriett had to say. So she only looked at her sister as if waiting. Harriett looked away from her for an instant before she began to speak: Ruth's eyes were so tired, so somber; there was something very appealing about her face as she waited for the new thing that was to be said to her.

"I have felt terribly, Ruth," Harriett finally began, as if forcing herself to do so, "about the position in which we are as a family. I'll not go into what brought it about—or anything like that. I haven't come to talk about things that happened long ago, haven't come with reproaches. I've just come to see if, as a family, we can't do a little better about things as they are now."

She paused, but Ruth did not speak; she was very still now as she waited. She did not take her eyes from Harriett's face.

"Mother and father are gone, Ruth," Harriett went on in a low voice, "and only we children are left. It seems as if we ought to do the best we can for each other." Her voice quivered and Ruth's intense eyes, which did not leave her sister's face, dimmed. She continued to sit there very still, waiting.

"I had a feeling," Harriett went on, "that father's doing what he did was as a—was as a sign, Ruth, that we children should come closer together. As if father couldn't see his way to do it in his lifetime, but did this to leave word to us that we were to do something. I took it that way," she finished simply.

Ruth's eyes had brimmed over; but still she did not move, did not take her eyes from her sister's face. She was so strange—as if going out to Harriett and yet holding herself ready at any moment to crouch back.

"And so," Harriett pursued, all the while in that low voice, "that is the way I talked to Edgar and Cyrus. I didn't bring Ted into it," she said, more in her natural way, "because he's just a boy, and then—" she paused as if she had got into something that embarrassed her—"well, he and Cyrus not feeling kindly toward each other just now I thought I could do better without Ted."

Ruth flushed slightly at the mention of the feeling between her brothers; but still she did not speak, scarcely moved.

Harriett was silent a moment. "That's one of the reasons," she took it up, "why I am anxious to do something to bring us together. I don't want Ted to be feeling this way toward Cyrus. And Edgar, too, he seems to be very bitter against. It makes him defiant. It isn't good for him. I think Ted has a little disposition to be wild," she said in a confidential tone.

Ruth spoke then. "I hadn't noticed any such disposition," she said simply.

"Well, he doesn't go to church. It seems to me he doesn't—accept things as he ought to."

Ruth said nothing to that, only continued to look at her sister, waiting.

"So I talked to them," Harriett went on. "Of course, Ruth, there's no use pretending it was easy. You know how Cyrus feels; he isn't one to change much, you know." She turned away and her hand fumbled in a little patch of clover.

"But we do want to do something, Ruth," she came back to it. "We all feel it's terrible this way. So this is what Edgar proposed, and Cyrus agreed to it, and it seems to me the best thing to do." She stopped again, then said, in a blurred sort of voice, fumbling with the clover and not looking at Ruth: "If you will leave the—your— if you will leave the man you are—living with, promising never to see him again,—if you will give that up and come home we will do everything we can to stand by you, go on as best we can as if nothing had happened. We will try to—"

She looked up—and did not go on, but flushed uncomfortably at sight of Ruth's face—eyes wide with incredulity, with something like horror.

"You don't *mean* that, do you, Harriett?" Ruth asked in a queer, quiet voice.

"But we wanted to do something—" Harriett began, and then again halted, halted before the sudden blaze of anger in Ruth's eyes.

"And you thought *this*—" She broke off with

a short laugh and sat there a moment trying to gain control of herself. When she spoke her voice was controlled but full of passion. "I don't think," she said, "that I've ever known of a more monstrous—a more insulting proposal being made by one woman to another!"

"Insulting?" faltered Harriett.

Ruth did not at once reply but sat there so strangely regarding her sister. "So this is your idea of life, is it, Harriett?" she began in the manner of one making a big effort to speak quietly. "This is your idea of marriage, is it? Here is the man I have lived with for eleven years. For eleven years we've met hard things together as best we could—worked, borne things together. Let me tell you something, Harriett. If *that* doesn't marry people—tell *me* something. If that doesn't marry people—just tell me, Harriett, *what does?*"

"But you know you're not married, Ruth," Harriett replied, falteringly—for Ruth's burning eyes never left her sister's face. "You know—really—you're not married. You know he's not divorced, Ruth. He's not your husband. He's Marion Averley's."

"You think so?" Ruth flung back at her. "You really think so, do you, Harriett? After those years together—brought together by love, united by living, by effort, by patience, by courage—I

ask you again, Harriett,—if the things there have
been between Stuart Williams and me can't make
a marriage real—*what can?*"

"The law is the law," murmured Harriett.
"He is married to her. He never was married to
you."

Ruth began hotly to speak, but checked it with
a laugh and sat there regarding her sister in silence. When she spoke after that her voice was
singularly calm. "I'm glad to know this, Harriett; glad to know just what your ideas are—
yours and Edgar's and Cyrus's. You have done
something for me, after all. For I've grieved a
great deal, Harriett, for the things I lost, and you
see I won't do that any more. I see now—see
what those things are. I see that I don't want
them."

· Harriett had colored at that, and her hand was
fumbling in the little patch of clover. When she
looked up at Ruth there were tears in her eyes.
"But what could we do, Ruth?" she asked, gently,
a little reproachfully. "We wanted to do something—what else could we do?"

Her tone touched Ruth. After all, what else—
Harriett being as she was—could she do? Monstrous as the proposal seemed to her, it was Harriett's way of trying to make things better. She
had come in kindness, and she had not been kindly
received. It was in a different voice that Ruth

began: "Harriett, don't you see, when you come to look at it, that I couldn't do this? Down in your heart—way down in your heart, Harriett—don't you see that I couldn't? Don't you see that if I left Stuart now to do the best he could by himself, left him, I mean, for this reason—came creeping back myself into a little corner of respectability—the crumbs that fall from the tables of respectability—! You *know*, Harriett Holland," she flamed, "that if I did that I'd be less a woman, not a better one!"

"I—I knew it would be hard," granted Harriett, unhappily. "Of course—after such a long time together— But you're not married to him, Ruth," she said again, wretchedly. "Why"—her voice fell almost to a whisper—"you're living in —adultery."

"Well if I am," retorted Ruth—"forgive me for saying it, Harriett—that adultery has given me more decent ideas of life than marriage seems to have given you!"

Her feeling about it grew stronger as the day wore on. That evening she got the Woodburys' on the telephone and asked for Mildred. She did not know just what she would say, she had no plan, but she wanted to see Mildred again. She was told, however, that Mildred had gone to Chicago on a late afternoon train. At the last minute she had decided to go to Europe with Mrs. Blair, the servant who was speaking said, and had gone over to Chicago to see about clothes.

Ruth hung up the receiver and sat looking into the telephone. Then she laughed. So Mildred had been "saved."

CHAPTER TWENTY-SEVEN

On the afternoon of her last day in Freeport Ruth took a long tramp with Deane. She was going that night; she was all ready for leaving when Deane came out and asked if he couldn't take her for a ride in his car. She suggested a walk instead, wanting the tramp before the confinement of travelling. So they cut through the fields back of Annie's and came out on a road well known to them of old. They tramped along it a long way, Ruth speaking of things she remembered, talking of old drives along that road which had been a favorite with all of their old crowd. They said things as they felt like it, but there was no constraint in their silences. It had always been like that with her and Deane. Finally they sat down on a knoll a little back from the road, overlooking pastures and fields of blowing green.

"I love these little hills," Ruth murmured; "so many little hills," she laughed affectionately— "and so green and blowy and fruitful. With us it's a great flat valley—a plain, and most of it dry —barren. You have to do such a lot to make things grow. Here things just love to grow. And trees!" she laughed.

"But mountains there," suggested Deane.

"Yes, but a long way off from us, and sometimes they seem very stern, Deane. I've so many times had the feeling I couldn't get beyond them. Sometimes they have seemed like other things I couldn't hope to cross." After a little she said: "These little hills are so gentle; this country so open."

Deane laughed shortly. "Yes, the hills are gentle. The country is open enough!"

She laughed too. "It is beautiful country, Deane," she said, as if that were the thing mattering just then. There was an attractive bit of pasture just ahead of them: a brook ran through it—a lovely little valley between two of those gentle hills.

Deane was lying on the grass a little way from her—sprawled out in much his old awkward way, his elbow supporting his head, hat pulled down over his eyes. It was good to be with him this last afternoon. It seemed so much as it used to be; in that moment it was almost as if the time in between had not been. It was strange the way things could fall away sometimes—great stretches of time fall away and seem, for a little while, to leave things as they had been long before.

"Well, Ruth," Deane said at last, "so you're going back."

"Going back, Deane," she answered.

So much they did not say seemed to flow into that; the whole thing was right there, opened, living, between them. It had always been like that with her and Deane. It was not necessary to say things out to him, as it was with everyone else. Their thinking, feeling, seemed to come together naturally, of itself; not a matter of direction. She looked at Deane stretched out there on the grass—older, different in some ways—today he looked as if something was worrying him—yet with it all so much the Deane of old. It kept recurring as strange that, after all there had been in between, they should be together again, and that it could be as it used to be. Just as of old, a little thing said could swing them to thinking, feeling, of which perhaps they did not speak, but which they consciously shared. Many times through the years there had come times when she wanted nothing so much as to be with Deane, wanted to say things to him that, she did not know just why, there would have been no satisfaction in saying to Stuart. Even things she had experienced with Stuart she could, of the two, more easily have talked of with Deane. It was to Deane she could have talked of the things Stuart made her feel. Within a certain circle Stuart was the man to whom she came closest; somehow, with him, she did not break from that circle. She had always had that feeling of Deane's understanding what she felt, even though it was not he who inspired the feeling. That seemed a little absurd to her— to live through things with one man, and have what that living made of her seem to swing her to some one else.

Thinking of their unique companionship, which time and distance and circumstances had so little affected, she looked at Deane as he lay there near her on the grass. She was glad to have this renewal of their old friendship, which had always remained living and dear to her. And now she was going away for another long time. It was possible she would never see him again. It made her wish she could come closer to what were now the big things in his life.

"I'm so glad, Deane," she said, somewhat timidly, "about you."

He pushed back his hat and looked up in inquiry.

"So glad you got married, goose!" she laughed.

At his laugh for that she looked at him in astonishment, distinctly shocked. He was chewing a long spear of grass. For a moment he did not speak. Then, "Amy's gone home," he said shortly.

Ruth could only stare at him, bewildered.

He was running his hand over the grass near him. She noticed that it moved nervously. And she remarked the puckered brows that had all along made her think he was worried about something that day—she had thought it must be one of his cases. And there was that compression of the lips that she knew of old in Deane when he was hurt. Just then his face looked actually old, the face of a man who has taken hard things.

"Yes, Amy's gone home for a little while," he said in a more matter of fact voice, but a voice that had a hard ring. He added: "Her mother's not well," and looked up at Ruth with that characteristic little screwing up of his face, as if telling her to make what she could of it.

"Why, that's too bad," she stammered.

Again he looked up at her in that queer way of mixed feeling, his face showing the marks of pain and yet a touch of teasing there too, mocking her confusion, looking like a man who was suffering and yet a little like a teasing boy. Then he abruptly pulled his hat down over his eyes again, as if to shade them from the sun, and lay flat on his back, one heel kicking at the grass. She could not see his eyes, but she saw his mouth; that faint touch of pleasure in teasing which had perversely lurked in pain had gone now; that twist of his compressed lips was pure pain.

She was utterly bewildered, and so deeply concerned that she had to get ahead of Deane some way, not let him shut himself in with a thing that made his mouth look as if he was bearing physical pain. And then a new thought shot into her concern for him, a thought that seemed too preposterous to entertain, but that would not go away. It did not seem a thing she could speak of; but as she looked at Deane, his mouth more natural now, but the suggestion of pain left there, she had a sudden new sense of all that Deane had done for her. She couldn't leave things like this, no matter how indelicate she might seem.

"Deane," she began timidly, "I don't—in any way—for any reason—make things hard for you, do I?"

For the moment he did not speak, did not push his hat back so she could see his eyes. Then she saw that he was smiling a little; she had a feeling that he was not realizing she could see the smile; it was as if smiling to himself at something that bitterly amused him. It made her feel rather sick; it let that preposterous idea spread all through her.

Then he sat up and looked quizzically at her. "Well, Ruth, you don't expect me to deny, do you, that you did make a thing or two rather hard?" He said it with that touch of teasing. "Was I so magnanimous," he added dryly, "that I let you lose sight of the fact that I wanted you?"

Ruth colored and felt baffled; she was sure he knew well enough that was not what she referred to. He looked at her, a little mockingly, a little wistfully, as if daring her to go on.

"I wasn't talking about things long ago, Deane," she said. "I wondered—" She hesitated, looking at him in appeal, as if asking him to admit he understood what she meant without forcing her to say such a thing.

For a minute he let the pain look out of his eyes at her, looked for all the world as if he wanted her to help him. Then quickly he seemed to shut himself in. He smiled at her in a way that seemed to say, half mockingly, "I've gone!" He hurt her a little; it was hard to be with Deane and feel there was something he was not going to let her help him with. And it made her sick at heart; for surely he knew what she was driving at, driving at and edging away from, and if he could have laughed at her fears wouldn't he have done so? She thought of all Deane had done for her, borne for her. It would be bitter indeed if it were really true she was bringing him any new trouble. But how *could* it be true? It seemed too preposterous; surely she must be entirely on the wrong track, so utterly wrong that he had no idea what it was she had in mind.

As they sat there for a moment in silence she was full of that feeling of how much Deane had done for her, of a longing to do something for him. Gently she said: "I must have made things very hard for you, Deane. The town—your friends—your people, because of me you were against them all. That does make things hard—to be apart from the people you are with." She looked at him, her face softened with affectionate regret, with a newly understanding gratitude. "I've not been very good for your life, have I, Deane?'' she said, more lightly, but her voice touched with wistfulness.

He looked at her, as if willing to meet that, as if frankly considering it. ''I can't say that you've been very good for my happiness, Ruth,'' he laughed. And then he said simply, with a certain simple manliness, ''But I should say, Ruth, you have been very good for my life.'' His face contracted a little, as if with pain. That passed, and he went on in that simple way: ''You see you made me think about things. It was because of you—through you—I came to think about things. That's good for our lives, isn't it?'' That he said sternly, as if putting down something that had risen in him. ''Because of you I've questioned things, felt protest. Why, Ruth,'' he laughed, ''if it hadn't been for you I might have taken things in the slick little way *they* do,''—he waved a hand off toward the town. ''So just see what I owe you!'' he said, more lightly, as if leaving the serious things behind. Then he began to speak of other things.

It left Ruth unsatisfied, troubled. And yet it seemed surely a woman would be proud of a man who had been as fine in a thing, as big and true and understanding, as Deane had been with her. Surely a woman would be proud of a man who had so loyally, at such great cost, been a woman's friend, who, because of friendship, because of fidelity to his own feeling, would stand out that way against others. She tried to think that, for she could not go back to what Deane had left behind. And yet she could not forget that she had not met Amy.

They walked toward home talking quietly about things that happened to come up, more as if they were intimate friends who had constant meetings than as if they had been years apart and were about to part for what would probably be years more. But that consciousness was there underneath; it ruled the silences, made their voices gentler. It was very sweet to Ruth, just before again leaving all home things behind, to be walking in the spring twilight with Deane along that road they knew when they were boy and girl together.

Twilight was deepening to evening when they came to the hill from which they could see the town. They stood still looking off at it, speaking of the beauty of the river, of the bridge, of the strangeness of the town lights when there was still that faint light of day. And then they stood still and said nothing, looking off at that town where they had been brought up. It was beautiful from there, bent round a curve in the broad river, built upon hills. She was leaving it now—again leaving it. She had come home, and now she was going away again. And now she knew, in spite of her anger of the day before, in spite of all there had been to hurt her, in spite of all that had been denied her, that she was not leaving it in bitterness. In one sense she had not had much from her days back home; but in a real sense, she had had much. She looked at that town now with a feeling of new affection. She believed she would always have that feeling of affection for it. It stood to her for things gone—dear things gone; for youth's gladness, for the love of father and mother, for many happy things now left behind. But now that she had come back, had gone through those hard days, she was curiously freed from that town. She had this new affection for it in being freed of it. She would always love it because of what it had meant in the past, but love it as one does love a thing past. It seemed she had to come back to it to let it lose its hold on her. It was of the past, and she knew now that there was a future. What that future was to be she did not know, but she would turn from this place of the past with a new sense of the importance of the future. Standing there with Deane on the hilltop at evening, looking off at that town where they had both been brought up, she got a sense of the significance of the whole thing—the eleven years away, and the three years preceding those years; a sense too of the meaning of those days just past, those recent days at home when there were times of being blinded by the newly seen significance of those years of living. They had been hard days because things had been crowded so close; it had come too fast; currents had met too violently and the long way between cause and effect had been lighted by flashes too blinding. It had been like a great storm in which elements rush together. It had almost swept her down, but she had come through it and this was what she had brought out of it: a sense of life as precious, as worth anything one might have to pay for it, a stirring new sense of the future as adventure. She had been thinking of her life as defined, and now it seemed that the future was there, a beautiful untouched thing, a thing that was left, hers to do what she could with. Somehow she had broken through, broken through the things that had closed in around her. A great new thing had happened to her: she was no longer afraid to face things! In those last few days she had been tossed, now this way, now that; it seemed she had rather been made a fool of, but things had got through to her—she was awake, alive, unafraid. Something had been liberated in her. She turned to Deane, who was looking with a somber steadiness ahead at the town. She touched his arm and he looked at her, amazed at her shining eyes, shining just as they used to when as a girl she was setting out for a good time, for some mischief, excitement.

"Well, anyway, Deane," she said in a voice that seemed to brush everything else aside, "we're alive!"

CHAPTER TWENTY-EIGHT

The summer had gone by and Ted Holland, who had gone West with Ruth in May, was back in Freeport "breaking up the house." The place was offered for sale; things had to be cleared out in one way or another. What none of the children wanted was being sold to anybody who did happen to want it; what nobody wanted was to be given away to such people as had to take what they could get. And there was a great deal of it not even in the class for giving away; "just truck" Ted kept callously calling it to Harriett and their Cousin Flora. He whistled vigorously over some of the "truck,"—a worn dog's collar, an old pair of the queer kind of house shoes his mother wore, a spectacle case he had used to love to hear his father snap shut, dusty, leaky sofa-pillows that had bristled with newness in the "den" which was the delight of his sixteen-year-old heart. He kept saying to Cousin Flora that there was no end to the junk—old school readers, Ruth's party slippers. Just burn it all up, he said, in a crisp voice of efficiency; what was it good for, anyhow? Certainly it had taught him a lesson. He'd never keep anything.

They had been at it for a week—sorting, destroying, disbursing, scattering what a family's life through a generation had assembled, breaking up "the Hollands." Ted, in his own room that morning, around him the things he was going to put in his trunk for taking back West, admitted to himself that it was gruesome business.

Things were over; things at home were all over. This pulling to pieces drove that home hard. Father and mother were gone and now "their stuff" was being got out of the way. After this there would not even be a place where the things they had used were. But he would be glad when they could get through with it; he was finding that there was something wrenching about things that were left, things that had been used and that now there was no longer any use for. The sight of them stabbed as no mere thinking about things could do. It was hard work throwing away "truck" that something seemed to cling to. It was hard to really *get* it, he was thinking; a family lived in a place—seemed really a part of that place, an important part, perhaps; then things changed—people died, moved away, and that family simply *wasn't* any more—and things went on just about the same. Whistling, he put some shirts in his trunk, trying to fix his mind on how many new shirts he needed.

He was going back West—to live, to work. Not right where Ruth was, in southwestern Colorado, but in the country a little to the north. He and a fellow he had made friends with out there had bought an apple orchard—the money he was to have from his father would go into it and some of Ruth's money—she wanted him to invest some of hers with his. It was that had made it possible for him to go in with this fellow. He was glad he could do it. The West had "got" him. He believed he could make things go.

And he shouldn't have liked staying on in Freeport. Too many things were different for him to want to stay there. And too many things hurt. Ruth had come to mean too much to him to let him be happy with people who felt as the people there did about her.

He heard Harriett downstairs and went down to speak to her about the price the stove man offered for the kitchen range. He remembered his mother's delight in that range as new; somehow it made him hate selling it for this pittance.

Harriett thought, however, that they had better let it go. One couldn't expect to get much for old things, and they didn't want it on their hands.

They stayed there awhile in the dining-room, considering the problem of getting out of the way various other things there was no longer any use for. Harriett was looking at the bay window. "If the Woodburys take the house," she said, "they won't want these shades."

"Oh, no," replied Ted, "they wouldn't be good enough for Mildred."

The Woodburys had been there the night before to look at the house; they thought of buying it and Mildred, just recently home from Europe with Edith Blair—they had had a hard time getting home, because of the war—had, according to his own way of putting it, made Ted tired. She was so fretful with her father and her ideas of how the place could perhaps be made presentable by being all done over had seemed to Ted "pretty airy." He'd rather strangers had the house. He heard that Mildred was going about a lot with Bob Gearing—one of the fellows in town who had money.

Ted pulled out his watch. "I want to get down and see Deane at his noon office hours," he said.

Harriett turned from the window. "What have you got to see him about?" she asked sharply.

"Why—just see him," he answered in surprise. "Why shouldn't I want to see him? Haven't seen him since I got back. He'll want to hear about Ruth."

Harriett seemed about to speak, then looked at the door of the kitchen, where a man was packing dishes. "I don't think I'd go to him for *that*," she said in lowered voice.

Ted looked at her in bewildered inquiry.

"Mrs. Franklin has left him," she said shortly. She glanced at the kitchen door, then added in a voice that dropped still lower: "And the talk is that it's because of Ruth."

For a minute Ted just stood staring at her. Then his face was aflame with angry blood. "The *talk!*" he choked. "So that's the new 'talk'! Well—"

"S—h," warned Harriett, and stepped over and closed the kitchen door.

"I'd like to tell some of them what I think of their 'talk,'" he blazed. "Oh, I'd like to tell some of these *warts*—"

"Ted!" she admonished, nodding her head toward the closed door.

"What do I care? I'd like to have 'em hear me! I *want* them to know that I—" He broke off and stood looking at her. "It doesn't seem to worry you much!" he thrust at her.

"It did, Ted," she said patiently. "I—it did." She looked so distressed, so worn as she said it that it mollified him until she added: "And still, you mustn't be too hard on people. A woman who has put herself in that position—"

"There you go! 'Put herself' in that position! Put herself!" he jeered angrily, "in that position! As if the position was something Ruth got into on purpose! And after all these years!—still talking about her 'position.' Let me tell you something! I'll tell you the woman that's 'put herself' in the position I'd think would make her

hate herself! That's Mrs. Williams! *She's* the
one that's 'put herself'—"

"Ted," she broke in sternly, "you must *not!*"

But, "You make me *sick!*" he flung back at her
and snatched hat and coat from the hall rack
and left the house with a violent bang of the front
door.

He did not go down to Deane's office. He
stalked ahead, trying to hold down the bitter
rage that was almost choking him. At one time
when he looked up he saw that he was passing
the house Deane Franklin had built before his
marriage and noted that it was closed, all the
shades were clear down. Flower beds that had
been laid out in the spring had been let go. It
looked all wrong to see a new place so deserted,
so run down. He remembered seeing Deane
working out in that yard in the spring. He hurried on by. His heart was hot with resentment—
real hatred—of the town through which he walked.
He loathed the place! he told himself. Picking
on Ruth for *this*—ready to seize on her for anything that put her in bad! He had been with Ruth
for four months. He knew now just how things
were with her. It gave him some idea of what it
was she had gone through. It made him hate the
town that had no feeling for her.

He had walked out from town, not giving any
thought to where he was going, just walking because he had to be doing something. He was

about to cross a little bridge and stepped to the side of the road to let the vehicle right behind him get ahead. He stood glaring down at the creek and did not look up until he heard the wagon, just as it struck the bridge, stop. Then he saw that it was a woman driving the market wagon and recognized her as Mrs. Herman, who had been so good to Ruth.

He stepped up eagerly to greet her; his face quickly cleared as he held out his hand and he smiled at her with a sudden boyish warmth that made her face—it was thin, tired—also light with pleasure. He kept shaking her hand; it seemed wonderfully good of her to have come along just then—she was something friendly in a hostile world. He went out eagerly, gratefully, to the something friendly. He had had about all he could stand of the other things, other feelings. He had told Ruth that he would be sure to go and see Mrs. Herman. He got in with her now and they talked of Ruth as they jogged through the country which he now noticed was aflame with the red and gold of October.

He found himself chatting along about Ruth just as if there was not this other thing about her—the thing that made it impossible to speak of her to almost anyone else in the town. It helped a lot to talk of Ruth that way just then. He had seemed all clogged up with hatred and resentment, fury at the town made him want to do something to somebody, and pity for Ruth made him feel sick in his sense of helplessness. Now those ugly things, those choking, blinding things fell away in his talking about Ruth to this woman who wanted to hear about her because she cared for her, who wanted to hear the simple little things about her that those other people had no interest in. He found himself chatting along about Ruth and Stuart—their house, their land, the field of peas into which they turned their sheep, the potatoes grown on their place that summer. He talked of artesian wells and irrigation, of riding western horses and of camping in the mountains. Thinking of it afterwards he didn't know when he had talked so much. And of course, as everyone was doing those days, they talked about the war. She was fairly aflame with feeling about it.

He rode all the way home with Mrs. Herman, stayed for lunch and then lingered about the place for an hour or more after that. He felt more like himself than he had at any time since coming home; he could forget a little about that desolate house that was no longer to be his home, and the simple friendly interest of this woman who was Ruth's friend helped to heal a very sore place in his heart.

But afterwards, back there at home where it was as if he was stripping dead years, what came over him was the feeling that things were not as they had seemed out there with Mrs. Herman. She was like that, but in being that way she was different from the whole world, at least from practically the whole of the world that he knew. Working with old things cast him back to it all. He brooded over it there in the desolate place of things left behind; the resentful feeling toward the town, together with that miserable, helpless feeling of passionate pity for Ruth settled down upon him and he could not throw it off.

He saw Deane that night; he saw him at the Club where he went to play a game of pool, because he had to get away from the house for awhile. Deane was sitting apart from the various groups, reading a magazine. Ted stood in the door of that room looking at him a minute before Deane looked up from the page. He saw that his face was thinner; it made him look older; indeed he looked a good deal older than when, just the spring before, Ted used to see him working around that place that was all shut up now. And in that moment of scrutiny he saw something more than just looking older. If you didn't know Deane you'd think—well, you'd think you didn't want to know him. And he looked as if he didn't care about your knowing him, either; he looked as if he'd thank people to let him alone. Then he glanced up and saw Ted and it seemed there were a few people he didn't want to have let him alone.

But though he brightened on seeing him, looked like himself as he came quickly up to shake hands, he was not like himself in the talk that followed. It was as if he wanted to be, tried to be, but he was constrained in asking about the West, "the folks." He seemed to want to hear, yet he wasn't like himself, though Ted could scarcely have defined the difference. He was short in what he said, cut things off sharply, and in little pauses his face would quickly settle to that moroseness. Ted told of his own plans and Deane was enthusiastic about that. Then he fell silent a moment and after that said with intensity: "I wish *I* was going to pull out from here!"

"Well, why don't you?" laughed Ted, a little diffidently.

"Haven't got the gumption, I guess," said Deane more lightly, and as he smiled gave Ted the impression of trying to pull himself out from something.

Later in the evening a couple of men were talking of someone who was ill. "They have Franklin, don't they?" was asked, and the answer came, "Not any more. They've switched."

Walking home, he thought it had been said as if there was more to it, as if there had been previous talk about other people who had "switched." Why, surely it couldn't be that because—for some reason or other—his wife had left him people were taking it out on his practice? That seemed not only too unfair but too preposterous. Deane was the best doctor in town. What had his private affairs—no matter what the state of them—got to do with him as a physician? Surely even *that* town couldn't be as two-by-four as that!

But it troubled him so persistently that next morning, when they were alone together in the attic, he brought himself to broach it to Harriett, asking, in the manner of one interested in a thing because of its very absurdity, just what the talk was about Ruth and the Franklins.

Harriett went on to give the town's gossip of how Deane had gone to Indianapolis to see his wife, to try and make it right, but her people were strongly of the feeling that she had been badly treated and it had ended with her going away somewhere with her mother. Harriett sighed heavily as she said she feared it was one of those things that would not be made right.

"I call it the limit!" cried Ted. "The woman must be a fool!"

Harriett sadly shook her head. "You don't understand women, Ted," she said.

"And I don't want to—if *that's* what they're like!" he retorted hotly.

"I'm afraid Deane didn't—manage very well," sighed Harriett.

"Who wants to manage such a little fool!" snapped Ted.

"Now, Ted—" she began, but "You make me *tired*, Harriett!" he broke in passionately, and no more was said of it then.

They worked in silence for awhile, Ted raising a great deal of dust in the way he threw things about, Harriett looking through a box of old books and papers, sighing often. Harriett sighed a great deal, it seemed to Ted, and yet something about Harriett made him sorry for her. From across the attic he looked at her, awkwardly sitting on the floor, leaning against an old trunk. She looked tired and he thought with compassion and remorse for the rough way he had spoken to her, of how her baby was only a little more than two months old, that it must be hard for her to be doing the things she was doing that week. Harriett had grown stout; she had that settled look of many women in middle life; she looked as if she couldn't change much—in any way. Well, Ted considered, he guessed Harriett couldn't change much; she was just fixed in the way she was and that was all there was to it. But she did not look happy in those things she had settled into; she looked patient. She seemed to think things couldn't be any different.

She was turning the pages of an old album she had taken from the box of her mother's things she was sorting. "Oh!" she exclaimed in a low voice, bending over the pages. Her tone brought Ted over to her. "A picture of Ruth as a baby," she murmured.

He knelt down and looked over her shoulder into the dusty, old-fashioned album at a picture of a baby a year or so old whose face was all screwed up into a delighted laugh, tiny hands raised up and clenched in the intensity of baby excitement, baby abandonment to the joyousness of existence.

"She *was* like that," murmured Harriett, a little tremulously. "She was the *crowingest* baby!"

They bent over it in silence for a minute. "Seems pretty tickled about things, doesn't she?" said Ted with a queer little laugh. Harriett sighed heavily, but a moment later a tear had fallen down to one of the baby hands clenched in joyousness; the tear made him forgive the sigh, and when he saw her carefully take the picture from the album and put it in the pocket of her big apron, it was a lot easier, somehow, to go on working with Harriett. It was even easy, after a little, to ask her what he wanted to know about Deane's practice.

It was true, she feared, that the talk had hurt him some. Mrs. Lawrence had stopped having him. It seemed she had taken a great fancy to Amy Franklin and felt keenly for her in this. She had made other people feel that Deane had not been fair or kind and so there was some feeling against him.

"I suppose she can't claim," Ted cried hotly, "that it hurts him as a doctor?"

"No," Harriett began uncertainly, "except that a doctor—of course the personal side of things—"

"Now, there you *go*, Harriett," he interrupted furiously. "You make me *tired!* If it wasn't that you've a sneaking feeling for Ruth you'd fall for such a thing yourself!"

"There's no use trying to talk to you, Ted," said Harriett patiently.

Two days later the house was about dismantled. Ted was leaving the next day for the West. He was so sick of the whole thing that it had gone a little easier toward the last, blunted to everything but getting things done. When Harriett, her eyes reddened, came downstairs with a *doll* and wanted to know if he didn't think Ruth might like to have it, saying that it was the doll Ruth had loved all through her little girl days, and that she had just come upon it where her mother had carefully packed it away, he snatched the doll from her and crammed it into the kitchen stove and poked at it savagely to make it burn faster. Then he slammed down the lid and looked ruthlessly up at Harriett with, "We've had about enough of this sobbing around over *junk!*"

Harriett wanted him to come over to her house

that last night but he said he'd either go home
with one of the fellows or bring one of them home
with him. She did not press it, knowing how little her brother and her husband liked each other.

He went to the theatre that night with a couple
of his friends. He was glad to go, for it was as
good a way as he could think of for getting
through the evening. They were a little early and
he sat there watching the people coming in; it was
what would be called a representative audience,
the society of the town, the "best people" were
there. They were people Ted had known all his
life; people who used to come to the house, people his own family had been one with; friends of
his mother came in, associates of his father, old
friends of Ruth. That gathering of people represented the things in the town that he and his
had been allied with. He watched them, thinking
of his own going away, of how it would be an entirely new group of people he would come to
know, would become one with, thinking of the Hollands, how much they had been a part of it all
and how completely they were out of it now. As
he saw all these people, such pleasant, good-looking people, people he had known as far back as
he could remember, in whose homes he had had
good times, people his own people had been associated with always, a feeling of really hating to
leave the town, of its being hard to go away, crept
up in him. He talked along with the friend next

him and watched people taking their seats with a new feeling for them all; now that he was actually leaving them he had a feeling of affection for the people with whom he sat in the theatre that night. He had known them always; they were "mixed up" with such a lot of old things.

Some people came into one of the boxes during the first act and when the lights went up for the intermission he saw that one of the women was Stuart Williams' wife.

He turned immediately to his friends and began a lively conversation about the play, painfully wondering if the fellows he was with had seen her too, if they were wondering whether he had seen her, whether he was thinking about it. His feeling of gentle regret about leaving the town was struck away. He was glad this was his last night. Always something like this! It was forever coming up, making him feel uncomfortable, different, making him wonder whether people were thinking about "it," whether they were wondering whether he was thinking about it.

Through the years he had grown used to seeing Mrs. Williams; he had become blunted to it; sometimes he could see her without really being conscious of "it," just because he was used to seeing her. But now that he had just come home, had been with Ruth, there was an acute new shock in seeing her.

During the first intermission he never looked

back after that first glance; but when the house
was darkened again it was not at the stage he
looked most. From his place in the dress circle
across the house he could look over at her, secured by the dim light could covertly watch her.
It was hard to keep his eyes from her. She sat
well to the front of the box; he could see every
move she made, and every little thing about her
wretchedly fascinated him. She sat erect, hands
loosely clasped in her lap, seemingly absorbed in
the play. Her shoulders seemed very white above
her gauzy black dress; in that light, at least, she
was beautiful; her neck was long and slim and
her hair was coiled high on her head. He saw a
woman bend forward from the rear of the box
and speak to her; it brought her face into the
light and he saw that it was Mrs. Blair—Edith
Lawrence, Ruth's old chum. He crumpled the program in his hand until his friend looked at him in
inquiry; then he smiled a little and carefully
smoothed the program out. But when, in the
next intermission, he was asked something about
how he thought the play was going to turn out,
he was at a loss for a suggestion. He had not
known what that act was about. And he scarcely
knew what the other acts were about. It was all
newly strange to him, newly sad. He had a new
sense of it, and a new sense of the pity of it, as
he sat there that last night watching the people
who had been Ruth's and Stuart's friends; he

thought of how they had once been a part of all this; how, if things had gone differently it was the thing they would still be a part of. There was something about seeing Edith Lawrence there with Mrs. Williams made him so sorry for Ruth that it was hard to keep himself pulled together. And that house, this new sense of things, made him deeply sorry for Stuart Williams. He knew that he missed all this, terribly missed the things this represented. His constant, off-hand questionings about things—about the growth of the town, whether so and so was making good, who was running this or that, showed how he was missing the things he had turned away from, of which he had once been so promising a part. Here to-night, among the things they had left, something made him more sorry for Ruth and Stuart than he had ever been before. And he kept thinking of the strangeness of things; of how, if there had not been that one thing, so many things would have been different. For their whole family, for the Williams' family, yes, for Deane Franklin, too, it would have been all different if Ruth had just fallen in love with some one else. Somehow that seemed disloyalty to Ruth. He told himself she couldn't help it. He guessed *she* got it the worst; everything would have been different, easier, for her, certainly, if she, like the other girls of her crowd, had fallen in love with one of the fellows she could have married. Then she would be there with Edith Lawrence tonight; probably they would be in a box together.

It was hard, even when the lights were up, to keep his eyes from that box where Ruth's old friend sat with Mrs. Williams. He would seem to be looking the house over, and then for a minute his eyes would rest there and it would be an effort to let go. Once he found Mrs. Williams looking his way; he thought she saw him and was furious at himself for the quick reddening. He could not tell whether she was looking at him or not. She had that cool, composed manner she always had. Always when he met her so directly that they had to speak she would seem quite unperturbed, as if he stirred in her no more feeling than any other slight acquaintance would stir. She was perfectly poised; it would not seem that he, what he must suggest, had any power to disturb her.

Looking across at her in the house darkened for the last act, covertly watching her as she sat there in perfect command of herself, apparently quite without disturbing feeling, he had a rough desire to know what she actually *did* feel. A light from the stage surprised her face and he saw that it showed it more tired than serene. She looked bored; and she did not look content. Seeing her in that disclosing little shaft of light— she had drawn back from it—the thought broke into the boy's mind—What's *she* getting out of it?

He had never really considered it purely in the light of what it must be to her. He thought of her as a hard, revengeful woman, who, because hurt herself, was going to harm to the full measure of her power. He despised the pride, the poise, in which she cloaked what he thought of as her hard, mean spirit; he thought people a pretty poor sort for admiring that pride. But now, as he saw her face when she was not expecting it to be clearly seen, he wondered just what she was actually like, just what she really felt. It would seem that revenge must be appeased by now; or at least that that one form of taking it—not getting a divorce—must have lost its satisfaction. It would not seem a very satisfying thing to fill one's life with. And what else was there? What *was* she getting out of it? The question gave him a new interest in her.

Caught in the crowd leaving the theatre he watched her again for a moment, standing among the people who were waiting for motors and carriages. The thin black scarf around her head blew back and Edith Lawrence adjusted it for her. Her car came up and one of the men helped her into it. There was a dispute; it seemed someone was meaning to go with her and she was protesting that it was not necessary. Then they were saying goodnight to her and she was going away alone. He watched the car for a moment as it was halted by a carriage, then skirted it and sharply turned the corner.

He had intended to take one of his friends home with him, had thought it would be too dismal alone there in the bare place that last night. But now he did not want anyone with him, did not want to have to talk. Though when he let himself in the front door he wished he was not alone. It was pretty dismal to be coming into the abandoned house. He had a flashing sense of how absolutely empty the place was—empty of the people who had lived there, empty even of those people's things. There was no one to call out to him. His step made a loud noise on the bare stairs. He went back down stairs for a drink of water; he walked through the living-room, the dining-room, the kitchen. There used to be people there—things doing. Not any more. A bare house now—so empty that it was *queer*. He hurried back upstairs. At the head of the stairs he stood still and listened to the stillness from the bedrooms. Then he shook himself angrily, stamped on to his own room, loudly banged the door behind him and whistled as he hurriedly got ready for bed.

He tried to go right to sleep, but could not get sleepy. He was thinking of the house—of things that had gone on there. He thought of Ruth and Stuart—of the difference they had made in that house. And he kept thinking of Mrs. Williams, thinking in this new way of the difference it must have meant to her, must have made in *her* house. He wondered about the house she had just gone home to, wondered if she got lonely, wondered about the feeling there might be beneath that manner of not seeming to mind. He wondered just what it was made her keep from getting a divorce. And suddenly the strangest thought shot into his mind—Had anyone ever *asked* her to get a divorce?

Then he laughed; he had to make himself laugh at the preposterousness of his idea. The laugh made such a strange sound in the bare room that he lay there very still for a moment. Then loudly he cleared his throat, as if to show that he was not afraid of making another noise.

But the house was so strangely still, empty in such a queer way; it was too strange to let him go to sleep, and he lay there thinking of things in a queer way. That preposterous idea kept coming back. Maybe nobody ever *had* asked her to get the divorce; maybe it had just been taken for granted that she would be hard, would make it as hard as she could. He tried to keep away from that thought, something made him want to keep away from it, but he could not banish that notion that there were people who would be as decent as it was assumed they would be. He had noticed that with the fellows. Finally he got a little sleepy and he had a childish wish that he were not alone, that it could all be again as it had been long ago when they were all there together—before Ruth went away.

He slept heavily toward morning and was at last awakened by the persistent ringing of the door-bell. It was a special delivery letter from Ruth. She said she hoped it would catch him before he started West. She wanted him to stop in Denver and see if he could get one of those "Jap" men of all work. She said: "Maggie Gordon's mother has 'heard' and came and took her home. I turn to the Japanese—or Chinese, if it's a Chinaman you can get to come,—as perhaps having less fear of moral contamination. Do the best you can, Ted; I need someone badly."

He was to leave at five o'clock that afternoon. The people whom he saw thought he was feeling broken up about leaving; he had to hold back all feeling, they thought; it was that made his face so set and queer and his manner so abrupt and grim.

He had lunch with Harriett. She too thought the breaking up, the going away, had been almost too much for him. She hated to have him go, and yet, for his sake, she would be glad to have it over.

At two o'clock he had finished the things he had to do. He had promised to look in on a few of his friends and say good-by. But when he waited on the corner for the car that would take him down town he knew in his heart that he was not going to take that car. He knew, though up to the very last he tried not to know, that he was going to walk along that street a block and a half farther and turn in at the house Stuart Williams had built. He knew he was not going to leave Freeport without doing that. And when he stood there and let the car go by he faced what he had in his heart known he was going to do ever since reading Ruth's letter, turned and started toward Mrs. Williams', walking very fast, as if to get there before he could turn back. He fairly ran up the steps and pushed the bell in great haste—having to get it pushed before he could refuse to push it.

CHAPTER TWENTY-NINE

When he could not get away, after the maid had let him in and he had given his name and was waiting in the formal little reception room, he was not only more frightened than he had ever been in his life, but frightened in a way he had never known anything about before. He sat far forward on the stiff little French chair, fairly afraid to let his feet press on the rug. He did not look around him; he did not believe he would be able to move when he had to move; he knew he would not be able to speak. He was appalled at the consciousness of what he had done, of where he was. He would joyfully have given anything he had in the world just to be out doors, just not to have been there at all. There was what seemed a long wait and the only way he got through it was by telling himself that Mrs. Williams would not see him. Of course she wouldn't see him!

There was a step on the stairs; he told himself that it was the maid, coming to say Mrs. Williams could not see him. But when he knew there was someone in the doorway he looked up and then, miraculously, he was on his feet and standing there bowing to Mrs. Williams.

He thought she looked startled upon actually

seeing him, as if she had not believed it was really he. There was a hesitating moment when she stood in the doorway, a moment of looking a little as if trying to overcome a feeling of being suddenly sick. Then she stepped forward and, though pale, had her usual manner of complete self-possession. "You wished to see me?" she asked in an even tone faintly tinged with polite incredulity.

"Yes," he said, and was so relieved at his voice sounding pretty much all right that he drew a longer breath.

She looked hesitatingly at a chair, then sat down; he resumed his seat on the edge of the stiff little chair.

She sat there waiting for him to speak; she still had that look of polite incredulity. She sat erect, her hands loosely clasped; she appeared perfectly poised, unperturbed, but when she made a movement for her handkerchief he saw that her hand was shaking.

"I know I've got my nerve to come here, Mrs. Williams," he blurted out.

She smiled faintly, and he saw that as she did so her lip twitched.

"I'm leaving for the West this afternoon. I'm going out there to live—to work." That he had said quite easily. It was a little more effort to add: "And I wanted to see you before I went."

She simply sat there waiting, but there was still that little twitching of her lip.

"Mrs. Williams," he began quietly, "I don't know whether or not you know that I've been with my sister Ruth this summer."

When she heard that name spoken there was a barely perceptible drawing back, as when something is flicked before one's eyes. Then her lips set more firmly. Ted looked down and smoothed out the soft hat he was holding, which he had clutched out of shape. Then he looked up and said, voice low: "Ruth has come to mean a great deal to me, Mrs. Williams."

And still she did not speak, but sat very straight and there were two small red spots now in her pale cheeks.

"And so," he murmured, after a moment, "that's why I came to you."

"I think," she said in a low, incisive, but unsteady voice, "that I do not quite follow."

He looked at her in a very simple, earnest way. "You don't?" he asked. There was a pause and then he said, "I saw you at the theatre last night."

"Indeed?" she murmured with a faint note of irony.

But she did not deflect him from that simple earnestness. "And when I went home I thought about you." He paused and then added, gently, "Most all night, I thought about you."

And still she only sat there looking at him and as if holding herself very tight. She had tried to smile at that last and the little disdainful smile had stiffened on her lips, making them look pulled out of shape and set that way.

"I said to myself," Ted went on, " 'What's *she* getting out of it?' " His voice came up on that; he said it rather roughly.

Her face flamed. "If *this* is what you have come here to say—" she began in a low angry voice. "If this is what you have intruded into my house for—*you*—!" She made a movement as if about to rise.

Ted threw out his hand with a little gesture of wanting to explain. "Maybe I shouldn't have put it that way. I hope I didn't seem rude. I only meant," he said gently, "that as I watched you you didn't look as though you were happy."

"And what if I'm not?" she cried, as if stung by that. "What if I'm not? Does that give you any right to come here and tell me so?"

He shook his head, as if troubled at again putting things badly. "I really came," he said, in a low earnest voice, "because it seemed to me it must be that you did not understand. It occurred to me that perhaps no one had ever tried to make you understand. I came because it seemed fairer—to everybody."

Something new leaped into her eyes. "I presume it was suggested to you?" she asked sharply.

"No, Mrs. Williams, it was not suggested to me." As she continued to look at him with suspicion he colored a little and said quietly: "You will have to believe that, because I give you my word that it is true.''

She met the direct look of his clear hazel eyes and the suspicion died out of her own. But new feeling quickly flamed up. "And hasn't it occurred to you," she asked quiveringly, "that you are rather a—well, to be very mild indeed, rather a presumptuous young man to come to me, to come into my house, with *this?*" There was a big rush of feeling as she choked: "Nobody's spoken to me like this in all these years!"

"That's just the trouble," said Ted quickly, as if they were really getting at it now. "That's just the trouble."

"What do you mean?" she asked sharply.

"Why—just that. Nobody has talked to you about it. Everybody has been afraid to, and so you've just been let alone with it. Things get worse, get all twisted up, get themselves into a tight twist that won't come out when we're shut up with them." His face looked older as he said, "I know that myself." He meditated upon that an instant; then, quickly coming back to her, looked up and added gently: "So it seemed to me that maybe you hadn't had a' fair show just because everybody has been afraid of you and let you alone."

Her two trembling hands were pulling at her handkerchief. Her eyes were very bright. "And you aren't afraid of me?" she asked with a little laugh that seemed trying to be mocking but was right on the edge of tears.

He shook his head. "That is," he qualified it with a slight smile, "not much—now." Then he said, as if dropping what they were talking about and giving her a confidence: "While I was waiting for you I was so scared that I wished I could drop dead."

His smile in saying it was so boyish that she too dropped the manner of what they were talking about and faintly smiled back at him. It seemed to help her gain possession of herself and she returned to the other with a crisp, "And so, as I understand it, you thought you'd just drop in and set everything right?"

He flushed and looked at her a little reproachfully. Then he said, simply, "It seemed worth trying." He took a letter from his pocket. "I got this from my sister this morning. The girl who has been working for her has gone away. Her mother came and took her away. She had 'heard.' They're always 'hearing.' This has happened time after time."

"Now just let me understand it," she began in that faintly mocking way, though her voice was shaking. "You propose that I do something to make the—the servant problem easier for your sister. Is that it? I am to do something, you haven't yet said what, to facilitate the domestic arrangements of the woman who is living with my

husband. That's it, isn't it?'' she asked with
seeming concern.

He reddened, but her scoffing seemed to give him
courage, as if he had something not to be scoffed
at and could produce it. ''It can be made to sound
ridiculous, can't it?'' he concurred. ''But—'' he
broke off and his eyes went very serious. ''You
never knew Ruth very well, did you, Mrs. Williams?'' he asked quietly.

The flush spread over her face. ''We were not
intimate friends,'' was her dry answer, but in that
voice not steady.

He again colored, but that steady light was not
driven from his eyes. ''Ruth's had a terrible
time, Mrs. Williams,'' he said in a quiet voice of
strong feeling. ''And if you had known her very
well—knew just what it is Ruth is like—it seems
to me you would have to feel sorry for her.''

She seemed about to speak again in that mocking way, but looking at his face—the fine seriousness, the tender concern—she kept silence.

''And just what is it you propose that I do?''
she asked after a moment, as if trying to appear
faintly amused.

Very seriously he looked up at her. ''It would
help—even at this late day—if you would get a
divorce.''

She gasped; whether she had been prepared for
it or not she was manifestly unprepared for the
simple way he said it. For a moment she stared

at him. Then she laughed. "You are a most amazing young man!" she said quiveringly.

As he did not speak, but only looked at her in that simple direct way, she went on, with rising feeling, "You come here, to *me,* into my house, proposing that—in order to make things easier for your sister in living with my husband—I get a divorce!"

He did not flinch. "It might do more than make things easier for my sister," he said quietly.

"What do you mean?" she demanded sharply.

"It might make things easier for you."

"And what do you mean by *that?*" she asked in that quick sharp way.

"It might make things easier," he said, "just to feel that, even at this late day, you've done the decent thing."

She stood up. "Do you know, young man, that you've said things to me that are outrageous to have said?" She was trembling so it seemed hard to speak. "I've let you go on just because I was stupified by your presumption—staggered, and rather amused at your childish audacity. But you've gone a little too far! How *dare* you talk to me like this?" she demanded with passion.

He had moved toward the door. He looked at her, then looked away. His control was all broken down now. "I'm sorry to have it end like this," he muttered.

She laughed a little, but she was shaken with the

sobs she was plainly making a big effort to hold back. "I'm so sorry," he said with such real feeling that the tears brimmed from her eyes.

He stood there awkwardly. Somehow her house seemed very lonely, comfortless. And now that her composure was broken down, the way she looked made him very sorry for her.

"I don't want you to think," he said gently, "that I don't see how bad it has been for you."

She tried to laugh. "You don't think your sister was very—fair to me, do you?" she asked chokingly, looking at him in a way more appealing than aggressive.

"I suppose not," he said. "No, I suppose not." He stood there considering that. "But I guess," he went on diffidently, "I don't just know myself— but it seems there come times when being fair gets sort of—lost sight of."

The tears were running down her face and she was not trying to check them.

He stood there another minute and then timidly held out his hand. "Good-by, Mrs. Williams," he said gently.

She took his hand with a queer, choking little laugh and held it very tight for a minute, as if to steady herself.

His own eyes had dimmed. Then he smiled—a smile that seemed to want to go ahead and take any offence or hurt from what he was about to say. "Maybe, Mrs. Williams, that you will come to feel like being fairer to Ruth than Ruth was to you.'' His smile widened and he looked very boyish as he finished, ''And that would be *one* way of getting back, you know!''

CHAPTER THIRTY

Freeport had a revival of interest in Mrs. Stuart Williams that fall. They talked so much of her in the first years that discussion had pretty well spent itself, and latterly it had only been rarely—to a stranger, or when something came up to bring it to them freshly—that they did more than occasionally repeat the expressions which that first feeling had created. There was no new thing to say of their feeling about her. No one had become intimate with her in those years, and that itself somehow kept the picture. She was unique, and fascinated them in the way she was one of them and yet apart. The mystery enveloping her made it mean more than it could have meant through disclosures from her. It kept it more poignant to speculate about a concealed suffering than it could have continued to be through discussing confidences. But even speculation as to what was beneath that unperturbed surface had rather talked itself out, certainly had lost its keen edge of interest with the passing of the years.

That fall, however, they began to speak of a change in her. They said first that she did not look well; then they began to talk about her manner being different. She had always kept so calm,

and now there were times when she appeared
nervous. She had had throughout a certain cold
serenity. Now she was sometimes irritable, disclosing a fretfulness close under the untroubled
surface. She looked older, they said; her brows
knit and there were lines about mouth and eyes.
She seemed less sure of herself. It made interest
in her a fresh thing. They wondered if she were
not at last breaking, spoke with a careful show of
regret, concern, but whetted anticipations gave
eagerness to voices of sympathy. They wondered
if Ruth Holland's having come home in the Spring,
the feeling of her being in the town, could have
been too much of a strain, preying upon the deserted wife and causing her later to break. There
were greedy wonderings as to whether she could
possibly have seen Ruth Holland, whether anything had happened that they did not know about.

Late one December afternoon Mrs. Williams
came home from a church bazaar and curtly telephoned that she would not be back for the evening.
She spoke of a headache. And her head did ache.
It ached, she bitterly reflected, from being looked
at, from knowing they were taking observations
for subsequent speculation. She had been in
charge of a table at the bazaar; a number of little
things had gone wrong and she got out of patience
with one of her assistants. Other people got irritated upon occasions of that sort—and that was all
there was to it. But she was not at liberty to

show annoyance. She knew at the time that they were whispering around about it, connecting it with the thing about her that it seemed never really went out of their minds. The sense of that had made her really angry and she had said sharp things she knew she would be sorry for because they would just be turned over as part of the thing that was everlastingly being turned over. She was not free; they were always watching her; even after all these years always thinking that everything had something to do with *that*.

Mrs. Hughes, her housekeeper and cook, had followed her upstairs. At the door of her room she turned impatiently. She had known by the way the woman hung around downstairs that she wanted to say something to her and she had petulantly not given her the chance. She did not want anything said to her. She wanted to be let alone.

"Well?" she inquired ungraciously.

Mrs. Hughes was a small trim woman who had a look of modestly trying not to be obtrusive about her many virtues. She had now that manner of one who could be depended upon to assume responsibilities a less worthy person would pass by.

"I thought perhaps you should know, Mrs. Williams," she said with faintly rebuking patience, "that Lily has gone to bed."

"Oh, she's really sick then, is she?" asked Mrs. Williams, unbending a little.

"She says so," replied Mrs. Hughes.

The tone caused her to look at the woman in surprise. "Well, I presume she is then," she answered sharply.

Lily was the second girl. Two servants were not needed for the actual work as the household consisted only of Mrs. Williams and an aged aunt who had lived with her since she had been alone, but the house itself did not seem adapted to a one servant menage. There had been two before, and in that, as in other things, she had gone right on in the same way. Mrs. Hughes had been with her for several years but Lily had been there only three or four months. She had been a strange addition to the household; she laughed a good deal and tripped about at her work and sang. But she had not sung so much of late and in the last few days had plainly not been well.

"If she's really sick, we'll have to have a doctor for her," Mrs. Williams said, her hand on the knob she was about to turn.

"She says she doesn't want a doctor," answered Mrs. Hughes, and again her tone made Mrs. Williams look at her in impatient inquiry.

"Well, I'll go up after while and see her myself," she said, opening the door of her room. "Meanwhile you look after her, please. And oh, Mrs. Hughes," she called back, "I shan't want any dinner. I had a heavy tea at the bazaar," she added hurriedly, and as if resentful of having to make any explanation.

Alone, she took off her hat, pushed back her hair as if it oppressed her, then sank into a low, luxurious chair, and, eyes closed, pressed her fingers over her temples as if to command quiet within. But after a moment she impatiently got up and went over to her dressing-table and sat looking into the mirror.

The thing that had started her afternoon wrong was that a friend of her girlhood, whom she had not seen for about thirteen years, had appeared unexpectedly at her table, startling her and then laughing at her confusion. She had not known that Stella Cutting was in town; to be confronted that way with some one out of the past had been unnerving, and then she had been furious with herself for not being able more easily to regain composure. People around her had seen; later she saw them looking at her strangely, covertly interested when she spoke in that sharp way to Mildred Woodbury because she had tossed things about. She had been disturbed, for one thing, at finding Mildred Woodbury at her table.

She was looking in the glass now because Stella Cutting had been one of her bridesmaids. She was not able to put down a miserable desire to try to see just what changes Stella had found.

The dissatisfaction in her face deepened with her scrutiny of it. Doubtless Stella was that very minute talking of how pitifully Marion Averley had changed; how her color used to be clear and even, features firmly molded, eyes bright. She herself remembered how she had looked the night Stella Cutting was her bridesmaid. And now her color was muddy and there were crow's feet about her eyes and deep lines from her nostrils to the corners of her mouth.

Stella Cutting looked older herself, very considerably older. But it was a different way of looking older. She had grown stout and her face was too full. But she did not look *pulled at* like this. As she talked of her children hers was the face of a woman normally, contentedly growing older. The woman sitting before the mirror bitterly turned away now from that reflection of dissatisfaction with emptiness.

It was that boy had done it! she thought with a new rise of resentment. She had been able to go along very evenly until he impertinently came into her house and rudely and stupidly broke through the things she had carefully builded up around herself. Ever since he had plunged into things even she herself had been careful not to break into, there had been this inner turmoil that was giving her the look of an old woman. If Stella Cutting had come just a few months earlier she could not have had so much to say about how terribly Marion Averley had changed.

Why was she so absurd as to let herself be upset? she angrily asked of herself, beginning to unfasten the dress she was wearing that she might get into something loose and try to relax. A hook caught in some lace and in her vexation at not being able at once to unfasten it she gave it a jerk that tore the lace. She bit her lips and could have cried. Those were the things she did these days! —since that boy came and blunderingly broke into guarded places.

She sat in a low, deep chair before the open fire that burned in the sitting-room adjoining her bedroom. It was the room that had been her husband's. After he went away she took it for an upstairs sitting-room—a part of her program of unconcern. As she sank down into the gracious chair she told herself that she would rest for that evening, not think about things. But not to think about things was impossible that night. Stella Cutting had brought old things near and made them newly real: her girlhood, her falling in love with Stuart Williams, her wedding. Those reminiscences caught her and swept her on to other things. She thought of her marriage; thought of things that, ever since that boy came and made her know how insecure she really was in the defences she had put up for herself, it had been a struggle to keep away from.

She had not done much thinking—probing—as to why it was her marriage had failed. That was another one of the things her pride shut her out from. When it failed she turned from it, clothed in pride, never naked before the truth. There was something relaxing in just letting down the barriers, barriers which had recently been so shaken that she was fretted with trying to hold them up.

She wondered why Stella Cutting's marriage had succeeded and hers had failed. The old answer that her marriage had failed because her husband was unfaithful to her—answer that used always to leave her newly fortified, did not satisfy tonight. She pushed on through that. There was a curious emotional satisfaction in thus disobeying herself by rushing into the denied places of self-examination. She was stirred by what she was doing.

Her long holding back from this very thing was part of that same instinct for restraint, what she had been pleased to think of as fastidiousness, that had always held her back in love. It was alien to her to let herself go; she had an instinct that held her away from certain things—from the things themselves and from free thinking about them. What she was doing now charged her with excitement.

She was wondering about herself and the man who was still legally her husband. She was thinking of how different they were in the things of love; how he gave and wanted giving, while her instinct had always been to hold herself a little apart. There was something that displeased her in abandonment to feeling. She did not like herself when she fully gave. There had been something in her, some holding back, that passionate love out-raged. Intense demonstration was indelicate to her; she was that way, she had not been able to help it. She loved in what she thought of as her own fastidious way. Passion violated something in her. Falling in love had made her happy, but with her love had never been able to sweep down the reserves, and so things which love should have made beautiful had remained for her ugly facts of life that she had an instinct to hold herself away from. What she felt she did not like herself for feeling. And so their marriage had been less union than manœuvering.

She supposed she had, to be very blunt, starved Stuart's love. For he wanted much love, a full and intense love life. He was passionate and demonstrative. He gave and wanted, perhaps needed, much giving. He did not understand that constant holding back. For him the beauty of love was in the expression of it. She supposed, in this curious self-indulgence of facing things to-night, that it had been he who was normal; she had memories of many times when she had puzzled and disappointed and hurt him.

And so when Gertrude Freemont—an old school friend of hers, a warm-natured Southern girl—came to visit her, Stuart turned away from things grudging and often chill to Gertrude's playfulness and sunniness and warmth. There was a curious shock to her tonight when she found herself actually thinking that perhaps it was not much to be wondered at. He was like that. She had not made him over to be like her.

At first he had found Gertrude enlivening, and from a flirtation it went to one of those passages of passion between a man and a woman, a thing that flames up and then dies away, in a measure a matter of circumstance. That was the way he tried to explain it to her when, just as Gertrude was leaving, she came to know—even in this present abandonment to thinking she went hurriedly past the shock of that terrible sordid night of "finding out." Stuart had weakly and appealingly said that he hadn't been able to help it, that he was sorry—that it was all over.

But with it their marriage was all over. She told him so then—told him quite calmly, it would seem serenely; went on telling him so through those first days of his unhappiness and persistence. She was always quite unperturbed in telling him so. Politely, almost pleasantly, she would tell him that she would never be his wife again.

She never was. She had known very certainly from the first that she never would be. Tonight she probed into that too—why she had been so sure, why she had never wavered. It was a more inner thing than just jealousy, resentment, hurt, revenge—though all those things were there too. But those were things that might have broken down, and this was not a thing that would break down. It was more particularly temperamental than any of those things. It was that thing in her which had always held her back from giving. She *had* given—and then her giving had been outraged! Even now she burned in the thought of that. He had called out a thing in her that she had all along—just because she was as she was—resented having had called out. And then he had flouted it. Even after all those years there was tonight that old prickling of her scalp in thinking of it. The things she might have said—of its being her own friend, in her own house—she did not much dwell upon, even to herself. It was a more inner injury than that. Something in her that was curiously against her had been called to life by him —and then he had outraged what she had all along resented his finding in her. To give at all had been so tremendous a thing—then to have it lightly held! It outraged something that was simply outside the sphere of things forgivable.

And that outraged thing had its own satisfaction. What he had called to life in her and then, as it seemed, left there unwanted, what he had made in her that was not herself—then left her with, became something else, something that made her life. From the first until now—or at any rate until two months ago when that boy came and forced her to look at herself—the thing in her that had been outraged became something that took the place of love, that was as the other pole of love, something that yielded a satisfaction of its own, a satisfaction intense as the things of love are intense, but cold, ordered, certain. It was the power to hurt; the power to bring pain by simply doing nothing. It was not tempestuously done; it had none of the uncertainty of passionate feeling; it had the satisfaction of power without effort, of disturbing and remaining undisturbed, of hurting and giving no sign. It was the revenge of what was deeply herself for calling her out from herself, for not wanting what was found in her that was not herself.

Stuart wanted her again; terribly wanted her, more than ever wanted her. He loved and so could be hurt. He needed love and so could be given pain. He thought she would give in; she knew that she would not. There was power in that knowledge. And so she watched him suffer and herself gained new poise. She did not consider how it was a sorry thing to fill her life with. When, that night that was like being struck by lightning, she came to know that the man to whom she had given—*she*—had turned from her to another woman it was as if she was then and there sealed in. She would never let herself leave again. Outraged pride blocked every path out from self. She was shut in with her power to inflict pain. That was all she had. And then that boy came and made her look at herself and know that she was poor! That was why Stella Cutting could be talking of how Marion Averley had "broken."

They were talking about it, of course; about her and Ruth Holland and her husband. *Her* husband, she thought insistently, but without getting the accustomed satisfaction from the thought. Miserably she wondered just what they were saying; she flinched in the thought of their talk about her hurt, her loneliness. And then she felt a little as if she could cry. She had wondered if she had anybody's real pity.

That thought of their talking of it opened it to her, drew her to it. She thought of Ruth Holland, gave up the worn pretense of disinterest and let herself go in thinking of her.

The first feeling she had had when she suspected that her husband was drawn to that girl, Ruth Holland, was one of chagrin, a further hurt to pride. For her power to give pain would be cut off. Once she saw the girl's face light as Stuart went up to her for a dance. She knew then that the man who had that girl's love could not be hurt in the way she had been hurting. At first she was not so much jealous as strangely desolated. And then as time went on and in those little ways that can make things known to those made acute through unhappiness she came to know that her husband cared for this girl and had her love, anger at having been again stripped, again left there outraged, made her seize upon the only power left, that more sordid, more commonplace kind of power. She could no longer hurt by withholding herself; she could only hurt by standing in the way. Rage at the humiliation of being reduced to that fastened her to it with a hold not to be let go. All else was taken from her and she was left with just that. Somehow she reduced herself to it; she became of the quality of it.

Pride, or rather self-valuation, incapacity for self-depreciation, had never let her be honest with herself. As there were barriers shutting the world out from her hurt and humiliation, so too were there barriers shutting herself out. She did not acknowledge pain, loneliness, for that meant admission that she could not have what she would have. She thought of it as withdrawal, dignified withdrawal from one not fit. She had always tried to feel that her only humiliation was in having given to one not worth her—one lesser.

But in this reckless and curiously exciting mood of honesty tonight she got some idea of how great the real hurt had been. She knew now that when she came to know—to feel in a way that was knowing—that her husband loved Ruth Holland she suffered something much more than hurt to pride. It was pride that would not let her look at herself and see how she was hurt. And pride would not let her say one word, make one effort. It was simply not in her to bring herself to *try* to have love given her. And so she was left with the sordid satisfaction of the hurt she dealt in just being.

That became her reason for existence—the ugly reason for her barren existence. She lived alone with it for so long that she came to be of it. Her spirit seemed empty of all else. It had kept her from everything; it had kept her from herself.

But now tonight she could strangely get to herself, and now she knew that far from Ruth Holland not mattering her whole being had from the first been steeped in hatred of her. Her jealousy had been of a freezing quality; it had even frozen her power to know' about herself. When, after one little thing and then another had let her know there was love between her husband and this girl, to go to places where Ruth Holland was would make her numb—that was the way it was with her. Once in going somewhere—a part of that hideous doing things together which she kept up because it was one way of showing she was there, would continue to be there—she and Stuart drove past the Hollands', and this girl was out in the yard, romping with her dog, tusseling with him like a little girl. She looked up, flushed, tumbled, panting, saw them, tried to straighten her hair, laughed in confusion and retreated. Stuart had raised his hat to her, trying to look nothing more than discreetly amused. But a little later after she—his wife—had been looking from the other window as if not at all concerned she turned her head and saw his face in the mirror on the opposite side of the carriage. He had forgotten her; she was taking him unawares. Up to that time she had not been sure—at least not sure of its meaning much. But when she saw that tender little smile playing about his mouth she knew it was true that her power to hurt him had reduced itself to being in his way. That she should be reduced to that made her feeling about it as ugly as the thing itself.

She did not sleep that night—after seeing Ruth Holland romping with her dog. She had cried—and was furious that she should cry, that it could make her cry. And furious at herself because of the feeling she had—a strange stir of passion, a wave of that feeling which had seemed to her unlovely even when it was desired and that it was unbearably humiliating to feel unwanted. It was in this girl he wanted those things now; that girl who could let herself go, whom life rioted in, who doubtless could abandon herself to love as she could in romping with her dog. It tortured her to think of the girl's flushed, glowing face—panting there, hair tumbled. She cringed in the thought of how perhaps what she had given was measured by what this girl could give.

As time went on she knew that her husband was more happy than he had ever been before—and increasingly unhappy. Her torture in the thought of his happiness made her wrest the last drop of satisfaction she could from the knowledge that she could continue the unhappiness. Sometimes he would come home and she would know he had been with this girl, know it as if he had shouted it at her—it fairly breathed from him. To feel that happiness near would have maddened her had she not been able to feel that her very being there dealt unhappiness. It was a wretched thing to live with. Beauty had not come into her life; it would not come where that was.

And then she came to know that they were being cornered. She—knowing—saw misery as well as love in the girl's eyes—a hunted look. Her husband grew terribly nervous, irritable, like one trapped. It was hurting his business; it was breaking down his health. Not until afterward did she know that there was also a disease breaking down his health. She did not know what difference it might have made had she known that. By that time she had sunk pretty deep into lust for hurting, into hating.

She saw that this love was going to wreck his life. His happiness was going to break him. If the world came to know it would be known that her husband did not want her, that he wanted some-one else. She smarted under that—and so fortified herself the stronger in an appearance of unconcern. She could better bear exposure of his uncaringness for her than let him suspect that he could hurt her. And they would be hurt! If it became known it would wreck life for them both. The town would know then about Ruth Holland— that wanton who looked so spiritual! They would know then what the girl they had made so much of really was! She would not any longer have to listen to that talk of Ruth Holland as so sweet, so fine!

And so she waited; sure that it would come, would come without her having given any sign, without her having been moved from her refuge of unconcern—she who had given and not been wanted! That week before Edith Lawrence's wedding she knew that it was coming, that something was happening. Stuart looked like a creature driven into a corner. And he looked sick; he seemed to have lost hold on himself. Once as she was passing the door of his room it blew a little open and she saw him sitting on the bed, face buried in his hands. After she passed the door she halted—but went on. She heard him moving around in the night; once she heard him groan. Instinctively she had sat up in bed, but had lain down again—remembering, remembering that he was groaning because he did not want her, because she was in the way of the woman he wanted.

She saw in those days, that week before Edith Lawrence's wedding, that he was trying to say something to her and could not, that he was wretched in his fruitless attempts to say it. He would come where she was, sit there white, miserable, dogged, then go away after having said only some trivial thing. Once—she was always quite cool, unperturbed, through those attempts of his—he had passionately cried out, "You're pretty superior, aren't you, Marion? Pretty damned serene!" It was a cry of desperation, a cry from unbearable pain, but she gave no sign. Like steel round her heart was that feeling that he was paying now.

After that outburst he did not try to talk to her; that was the last night he was at home. He came home at noon next day and said he was going away on a business trip. She heard him packing in his room. She knew—felt sure—that it was something more than a business trip. She felt sure that he was leaving. And then she wanted to go to him and say something, whether reproaches or entreaties she did not know; listened to him moving around in there, wanted to go and say something and could not; could only sit there listening, hearing every smallest sound. She heard him speak a surly word to a servant in the hall. He never spoke that way to the servants. When he shut the front door she knew that he would not open it again. She got to the window and saw him before he passed from sight—carrying his bag, head bent, stooped. He was broken, and he was going away. She knew it.

Even tonight she could not let herself think much about that afternoon, the portentous emptiness, the strangeness of the house; going into his room to see what he had taken, in there being tied up as with panic, sinking down on his bed and unable to move for a long time.

She had forced herself to go to Edith Lawrence's wedding. And she knew by Ruth Holland's face that it was true something was happening, knew it by the girl's face as she walked down the aisle after attending her friend at the altar, knew it by her much laughter, by what was not in the laughter. Once during the evening she saw Edith put her arm around Ruth Holland and at the girl's face then she knew with certainty, did not need the letter that came from Stuart next day. She had the picture of Ruth Holland now as she was that last night, in that filmy dress of pale yellow that made her look so delicate. She was helped through that evening by the thought that if she was going to be publicly humiliated Ruth Holland would be publicly disgraced. She would have heard the last about that fine, delicate quality—about sweetness and luminousness! They would know, finally, that she was not those things she looked.

And after it happened the fact that they did know it helped her to go on. She went right on, almost as if nothing had happened. She would not let herself go away because then they would say she went away because she could not bear it, because she did not want them to see. She must stay and show them that there was nothing to see.

Forcing herself to do that so occupied her as to help her with things within. She could not let herself feel for feeling would show on the surface. Even before herself she had kept up that manner of unconcern and had come to be influenced by her own front.

And so the years went by and her life had been made by that going on in apparent unconcern, and by that inner feeling that she was hurting them by just being in life. It was not a lovely reason for being in life; she had not known what a poor thing it was until that boy came and forced her to look at herself and consider how little she had.

She rose and stood looking into the mirror above the fireplace. It seemed to her that she could tell by her face that the desire to do harm had been her reason for living.

Several hours had gone by while she sat there given over to old things. She wished she had a book, something absorbing, something to take her away from that other thinking that was lying in wait for her—those thoughts about what there was for her to live with in the years still to be lived. The magazine she had picked up could not get any hold on her; that was why, though she had made it clear she did not want to be disturbed, there was relief in her voice as she answered the tap at her door.

She frowned a little though at sight of Mrs. Hughes standing there deferential but visibly excited. She had that look of trying not to intrude her worthiness as she said: ''Excuse me, Mrs. Williams, for disturbing you, but there is something I thought you ought to know.'' In answer to the not very cordial look of inquiry she went on, ''It's about Lily; she says she won't have a doctor, but—she needs one.''

There was something in her manner, something excited and yet grim, that Mrs. Williams did not understand. But then she did not much trouble herself to understand Mrs. Hughes, she was always appearing to see some hidden significance in things. ''I'll go up and see her,'' she said.

After the visit she came down to telephone for her doctor. She saw that the girl was really ill, and she had concluded from her strange manner that she was feverish. Lily protested that she wanted to be let alone, that she would be all right in a day or two; but she looked too ill for those protestations to be respected.

She telephoned for her own doctor only to learn that he was out of town. Upon calling another physician's house she was told that he had the grip and could not go out. She then sat for some minutes in front of the 'phone before she looked up a number in the book and called Dr. Deane Franklin. When she rose after doing that she felt as if her knees were likely to give way. The thought of his coming into her house, coming just when she had been living through old things, was unnerving. But she was really worried about the girl and knew no one else to call whom she could trust.

When he came she was grateful to him for his professional manner which seemed to take no account of personal things, to have no personal memory. "I'd like to see you when you come down, doctor," she said as Mrs. Hughes was taking him to the maid's room on the third floor.

She was waiting for him at the door of her upstairs sitting-room. He stepped in and then stood hesitatingly there. He too had a queer grim look, she thought.

"And what is the trouble?" she asked.

He gave her a strange sideways glance and snapped shut a pocket of the bag he carried. Then he said, brusquely: "It's a miscarriage."

She felt the blood surging into her face. She had stepped a little back from him. "Why—I don't see how that's possible," she faltered.

He smiled a little and she had a feeling that he took a satisfaction in saying to her, grimly, "Oh, it's possible, all right."

She colored anew. She resented his manner and that made her collect herself and ask with dignity what was the best thing to do.

"I presume we'd better take her to the hospital," he said in that short way. "She's been— horribly treated. She's going to need attention— and doubtless it would be disagreeable to have her here."

That too she suspected him of finding a satisfaction in saying. She made a curt inquiry as to whether the girl would be all right there for the night. He said yes and left saying he would be back in the morning.

She escaped Mrs. Hughes—whom now she understood. She did not go up again to see Lily; she could not do that then. She was angry with herself for being unnerved. She told herself that at any other time she would have been able to deal sensibly with such a situation. But coming just when things were all opened up like that—old feeling fresh—and coming from Deane Franklin! She would be quite impersonal, rational, in the morning. But for a long time she could not go to sleep. Something had intruded into her guarded places. And the things of life from which she had withdrawn were here—in her house. It affected her physically, almost made her sick—this proximity of the things she had shut out of her life. It was invasion.

And she thought about Lily. She tried not to, but could not help wondering about her. She wondered how this had happened—what the girl was feeling. Was there someone she loved? She lay there thinking of how, just recently, this girl who lived in her house had been going through those things. It made her know that the things of life were all the time around one. There was something singularly disturbing in the thought.

Next morning she went up to see Lily. She told herself it was only common decency to do that, her responsibility to a person in her house.

As she opened the door Lily turned her head and looked at her. When she saw who it was her eyes went sullen, defiant. But pain was in them too, and with all the rest something wistful. As she looked at the girl lying there—in trouble, in pain, she could see Lily, just a little while before, laughing and singing at her work. Something she had not felt in years, that she had felt but little in her whole life, stirred in her heart.

"Well, Lily," she said, uncertainly but not unkindly.

The girl's eyes were down, her face turned a little away. But she could see that her chin was quivering.

"I'm sorry you are ill," Mrs. Williams murmured, and then gave a little start at the sound of her own voice.

The girl turned her head and stole a look. A moment later there were tears on her lashes.

"We'll have to get you well," said Mrs. Williams in a practical, cheerful voice. And then she abruptly left the room. Her heart was beating too fast.

Mrs. Hughes lay in wait for her as she came downstairs. "May I speak to you, Mrs. Williams?" she asked in a manner at once deferential and firm.

"She's to be taken away, isn't she?" she inquired in a hard voice.

For a moment Mrs. Williams did not speak. She looked at the woman before her, all tightened up with outraged virtue. And then she heard herself saying: "No, I think it will be better for Lily to remain at home." After she had heard herself say it she had that feeling that her knees were about to give way.

For an instant Mrs. Hughes' lips shut tight. Then, "Do you know what's the matter with her?" she demanded in that sharp, hard voice.

"Yes," replied Mrs. Williams, "I know."

"And you're going to keep such a person in your house?"

"Yes."

"Then you can't expect *me* to stay in your house!" flashed the woman who was outraged.

"As you like, Mrs. Hughes," was the answer.

Mrs. Hughes moved a little away, plainly discomfited.

"I should be sorry to have you go," Mrs. Williams continued courteously, "but of course that is for you to decide."

"I'm a respectable woman," she muttered. "You can't expect *me* to wait on a person like that!"

"You needn't wait on her, then," was the reply. "Until the nurse comes, I will wait on her myself." And again she turned abruptly away.

Once more her heart was beating too fast.

When the doctor came and began about the arrangement he had been able to make at the hospital, she quietly told him that, if it would be as well, she would rather keep Lily at home. His startled look made her flush. His manner with her was less brusque as he said good-by. She smiled a little over that last puzzled glance he stole at her.

Then she went back to Lily's room. She straightened her bed for her, telling her that in a little while the nurse would be there to make her really comfortable. She bathed the girl's hot face and hands. She got her a cold drink. As she put her hand behind her head to raise her a little for that, the girl murmured brokenly: "You're so kind!"

She went out and sat in an adjoining room, to be within call. And as she sat there a feeling of strange peace stole through her. It was as if she had been set free, as if something that had chained her for years had fallen away. When in her talk with Mrs. Hughes she became that other woman, the woman on the other side, on compassion's side, something just fell from her. When that poor girl murmured, "You're so kind!" she suddenly knew that she must have something more from life than that satisfaction of harming those who had hurt her. When she washed the girl's face she knew what she could not unknow. She had served.

She could not find the old satisfaction in working harm. The soft, warm thing that filled her heart with that cry, "You're so kind!" had killed forever the old cruel satisfaction in being in the way.

She felt very quiet in this wonderful new liberation. She began shaping life as something more than a standing in the way of others. It made life seem a different thing just to think of it as something other than that. And suddenly she knew that she did not hate Ruth Holland any more; that she did not even hate the man who had been her husband. Hating had worn itself out; it fell from her, a thing outlived. It was wonderful to have it gone. For a long time she sat there very quiet in the wonder of that peace of knowing that she was free—freed of the long hideous servitude of hating, freed of wanting to harm. It made life new and sweet. She wanted something from life. She must have more of that gentle sweetness that warmed her heart when Lily murmured, "You're so kind!"

CHAPTER THIRTY-ONE

Ruth Holland stood at the window looking out at Colorado in January. The wide valley was buried under snow. It was late afternoon and the sun was passing behind the western mountains. From the window where she stood she could not see the western mountains, but the sunset colors had been thrown over to the eastern range, some fifty miles away. When she first came there, five years before, it had seemed strange to find the east lighted at sunset, more luminous than the west. The eastern range was a mighty one. Now there was snow down to its feet and there was no warmth in the colors that lighted it. They only seemed to reveal that the mountains were frozen. It would not have seemed possible for red—those mountains had been named Sangre de Cristo because they went red at sunset—to be so dazzling cold. The lighted snow brought out the contour of the mountains. They were wonderfully beautiful so, but the woman looking out at them was not thinking of them as beautiful. She was thinking of them as monuments of coldness. To her it was as if they had locked that valley in to merciless cold.

But it was not the sunset colors that really

marked coming night for her. All through that
winter something else had marked night, something she tried to keep from looking out at, but
which she was not able to hold away from. She
was looking at it now, looking off into the adjoining field where the sheep were huddling for the
night.

They had begun their huddling some time before. With the first dimming of the light, the
first wave of new cold that meant coming night, a
few of them would get together; others would
gather around them, then more and more. Now
there was the struggle not to be left on the outside.
The outer ones were pushing toward the center;
they knew by other nights that this night would be
frigid, that they could only keep alive by that
warmth they could get from one another. Yet
there were always some that must make that outer
rim of the big circle, must be left there to the un-
broken cold. She watched them; it had become
a terrible thing for her to see, but she could not
keep from looking. Many of those unprotected
sheep had died that bitter winter; others would die
before spring came. It was a cruel country, a
country of cold.

That was their flock of sheep. They had been
driven there the summer before from the lambing
grounds in the mountains. The day they got there
the lambs were exhausted from the long journey.
One of them had dropped before the house and

died right there beside the field it had come the
long way to gain. Her efforts to revive it were
useless; the little thing was worn out. They were
all of them close to worn out. And now they had
the winter to fight; night after night she watched
them huddling there, the big pitiful mass of them
out in the bitter cold. It was the way of the country to leave them so; the only way, the sheep men
said, that sheep could be made to pay. They esti-
mated that the loss by freezing was small com-
pared with what would be the cost of shelter for
droves that ran into thousands, into tens of thousands.

Ruth would wake at night and think of them
huddled out there, would lie thinking of them as
she drew the covers around herself, think of them
when the wind drove against the house, and often,
as tonight, when it was every instant growing
colder, she wondered if what was before them filled
them with terror. Sometimes she could not keep
away and went nearer and looked at them; they
were unbearably pitiful to her, their necks
wrapped around each other's necks, trying to get
from one another the only warmth there was for
them, so helpless, so patient, they, play-loving
creatures, gentle things, bearing these lives that
men might finally use them for clothing and for
food. There were times when the pathos of them
was a thing she could not bear. They seemed to
represent the whole cruelty of life, made real to

her the terrible suffering of the world that winter of the war.

She watched the sheep until the quick dusk had fallen, and then stood thinking of them huddled over there in the frigid darkness. When she found that her face was wet and realized that she had sobbed aloud she turned from the window to the stove, drew a chair up close to it and put her feet on the fender. It was so bitterly cold that the room was warm only near the stove; over there by the window she had grown chilled. And as the heat enveloped her ankles she thought of the legs of those poor frightened things that had been the last comers and not able to get to the inside of the circle—that living outer rim which was left all exposed to the frigid January night in that high mountain valley. She could feel the cold cutting against their legs, could see their trembling and their vain, frantic efforts to get within the solidly packed mass. She was crying, and she said to herself, her fingers clenched down into her palm, *"Stop that! Stop that!"* She did not know what might not happen to her if she were unable to stop such thinking as that.

To try and force herself away from it she got up and lighted a lamp. She looked about on her desk for a magazine she had put there. She would make herself read something while waiting for Stuart. He had had to drive into town. He would be almost frozen when he got back from that two-mile drive. She paused in her search for the magazine and went into the kitchen to make sure that the fire there was going well. Then she put some potatoes in to bake; baked potatoes were hot things—they would be good after that drive. The heat from the oven poured out to her, and it swept her again to the thought of the living huddled mass out there in the frigid darkness. The wind beat against the house; it was beating against them. She bit her lip hard and again she said to herself—"*No!*"

She made some other preparations for supper. She had those things to do herself now. The Chinaman Ted had brought home with him in the fall had left in December. He had appeared before her ready for leaving and had calmly said, "Cold here, missis. And too all alone. Me go where more others are." She had said nothing at all in reply to him, in protest, too held by what he had said—"Cold here, and too all alone!" She had stood at the window and watched him going up the road toward town, going where "more others" were.

She went back now into their main room; it was both living and dining room these days, for since the extreme cold had fastened on them they had abandoned their two little upstairs bedrooms and taken for sleeping the room which in summer was used as living-room. That could be heated a little by leaving the door open, and it had seemed out of the question to go to bed in those upstairs rooms where the cold had been left untouched. Since they had been doing their own work all extra things had had to be cut down; an upstairs fire would mean more work, and it seemed there was already more work than Ruth could get done and have time for anything else. She was tired all the time these days; she would think during the day of the good time she was going to have with a book that evening, and then night would find her so tired she could scarcely keep awake, and she would huddle there before the fire, dreading the cold of the night.

Life had reduced itself to necessities; things had to be ruthlessly rearranged for meeting conditions. She loved her own room to sleep in. She needed it. But she had given that up because it was too cold, because she could not do any more work. There was something that made her cringe in the thought of their sharing a bed, not because of love of being together, but because of the necessity of fighting the cold. And it made crowded quarters downstairs. She began "picking up" the room now. Things were piled up on the sewing machine, on the reading table. It seemed impossible to keep them put away. She tried hard to keep the room an attractive place to sit in, but it was in disorder, uninviting, most of the time. Often, after doing the kitchen work, she would clean it all up with the idea of making it attractive to sit in, then would be too utterly tired to enjoy it. She lagged in putting things away now; she would stand holding them helplessly, not knowing where to put them; she got sick of it and just threw some of them into a closet, anything to get them out of sight for the time. She knew that was not the way to do, that it would make it harder another time. She felt like crying. It seemed things had got ahead of her, that she was swamped by them, and somehow she did not have the spirit, or the strength, to get a new start, make a new plan.

Finally she had the room looking a little less slovenly, not so sordid, and was about to sit down with her magazine. But the lamp was flickering, and then she remembered that she had not filled it that day. She picked the lamp up and slowly, drooping, started for the kitchen. She gave the can an angry little tilt and the oil overflowed on the table. She was biting her lips as she went about looking for a cloth to wipe it up. She heard sleigh bells and knew Stuart was coming. Hastily she washed the oil from her hands, she always hated herself when her hands smelled of kerosene, and began getting things ready for supper.

Stuart came hurrying and stamping in after putting the horse away, quickly banging the door shut and standing there pounding his feet and rubbing his stiffened hands.

"Fearfully cold?" she inquired, hurriedly getting out the box of codfish she was going to cream for their supper.

"Cold!" he scoffed, as if in scorn for the inadequacy of the word. After a minute he came up to the stove. "I was afraid," he said, holding his right hand in his left, "that it had got these fingers."

He took off his big bear-skin coat. A package he had taken from the pocket of it he threw over on the kitchen table. "Don't throw the bacon there, Stuart," hurriedly advised Ruth, busy with the cream sauce she was making, "I've just spilled oil there."

"Heavens!" he said irritably, shoving the bacon farther back.

His tone made Ruth's hand tremble. "If you think I'm so careless you might fill the lamps yourself," she said tremulously.

"Who said you were careless?" he muttered. He went in the other room and after a minute called out, as one trying to be pleasant, "What we going to have for supper?"

"Creamed codfish," she told him.

"For a little change!" he said, under his breath.

"I don't think that's very kind, Stuart," she called back, quiveringly. "It's not so simple a matter to have 'changes' here now."

"Oh, I know it," he said, wearily.

She brought the things in and they began the

meal in silence. She had not taken time to lay the table properly. Things were not so placed as to make them attractive. Stuart tasted a piece of bread and then hastily put it aside, not concealing a grimace of distaste. "What's the matter?" Ruth asked sharply.

"I don't seem to care much for bread and oil," he said in a voice it was plainly an effort to make light.

Ruth's eyes filled. She picked up the plate of bread and took it to the kitchen. Stuart rose and went after her. "I'll get some more bread, Ruth," he said kindly. "Guess you're tired to-night, aren't you?"

She turned away from him and took a drink of water. Then she made a big effort for control and went to the dining-room. She asked some questions about town and they talked in a perfunctory way until supper was over.

He had brought papers and a couple of letters from town. Ruth was out in the kitchen doing the dishes when she heard a queer exclamation from him. "What is it, Stuart?" it made her ask quickly, going to the dining-room door with the cup she was wiping.

He gave her a strange look; and then suddenly he laughed. "What *is* it?" the laugh made her repeat in quick, sharp voice.

"Well, you'll never guess!" he said.

She frowned and stood there waiting.

"Marion's going to get a divorce." He looked at her as if he did not believe what he said.

Ruth put her hand out to the casement of the door. "She *is?*" she said dully.

He held up a legal looking paper. "Official notice," he said. Then suddenly he threw the thing over on the table and with a short hard laugh pulled his chair around to the fire. Ruth stood a moment looking at it lying there. Then she turned and went back to the dishes. When she returned to the living-room the paper still lay there on the table. She had some darning to do and she got out her things and sat down, chair turned to one side, not facing the legal looking document.

After a little while Stuart, who had been figuring in a memorandum book, yawned and said he guessed he'd go to bed. He shook down the fire, then got up and picked up the paper from the table, folded it and took it over to the big desk in the corner where his business things were. "Well, Ruth," he remarked, "this would have meant a good deal to us ten or twelve years ago, wouldn't it?"

She nodded, her head bent over the sock she was darning.

"Oh, well," he said, after a pause, "maybe it will help some even yet."

. She made no answer.

"I suppose Marion wants to get married," he

went on meditatively, after a moment adding bitterly, "Her wanting it is the only thing that would ever make her do it."

He went down cellar for coal, and after he had filled the stove began undressing before it. When ready for bed he sat there a little before the fire, as if taking in all the heat he could for the night. Ruth had finished her darning and was putting the things away. "Coming to bed?" he asked of her.

"Not right away," she said, her voice restrained.

"Better not try to sit up late, Ruth," he said kindly. "You need plenty of sleep. I notice you're often pretty tired at night."

She did not reply, putting things in the machine drawer. Her back was to him. "Well, Ruth," he said, in a voice genial but slightly ironic, "we can get married now."

She went on doing things and still did not speak.

"Better late than never," he said pleasantly, yawning.

He stood up, ready for going into the bedroom, but still hating to leave the fire, standing there with his back to it. "When shall we get married, Ruth?" he went on, in a slightly amused voice.

"Oh, I don't know, Stuart," she replied shortly from the kitchen.

"Have to plan it out," he said sleepily, yawning once more. Then he laughed, as if the idea more and more amused him. After that he murmured, in the voice of one mildly curious about a thing, "I wonder if Marion *is* going to get married?"

Ruth wanted to take a bath before she went to bed. Taking a bath was no easy matter under their circumstances. It was so much work and usually she was so tired that she would sometimes let it go longer than she would have supposed she would ever let bathing go. She was determined not to let it go tonight. She had the water on heating; she went down for the tub, went upstairs into her frigid room for the fresh things to put on in the morning. The room was so cold that there was a sort of horror about it. She went over to the window; the snow made the valley bright. Dimly she could see a massed thing— the huddled sheep. With a hard little laugh for the sob that shook her she hurried out of the room.

She took her bath before the fire in the living-room. Stuart had piled on one chair the clothes that he had taken off and would put on in the morning. She placed on another the things for herself. And suddenly she looked at those two chairs and the thing that she had been trying not to think about—that now they two could be married—seemed to sear her whole soul with mockery. She was rubbing some lotion on her red, chapped hands, hands defaced by work and cold.

She had a picture of her hands as they used to be—back there in those years when to have been free to marry Stuart would have made life radiant. She sat a long time before the fire, not wanting to go to bed. She particularly wanted to go to bed alone that night. There seemed something shameful in that night sharing a bed as a matter of expediency. Stuart was snoring a little. She sat there, her face buried in her hands. The wind was beating against the house. It was beating against the sheep out there, too—it had a clean sweep against that outer rim of living things. She cried for a little while; and then, so utterly tired that it did not matter much, she went in the other room and crept into bed.

CHAPTER THIRTY-TWO

But at last the cold had let go of them. It was April, the snow had gone and the air promised that even to that valley spring would come. Ruth, out feeding the chickens, felt that spring nearness. She raised her face gratefully to the breeze. It had seemed almost unbelievable that the wind would ever again bring anything but blighting cold.

As she stood there, held by that first feel of spring, an automobile came along, slowed, and Stuart went running out of the house to meet it. It was his friend Stoddard, a real-estate man there. He had become friends with this man in the last few months. He had had little in friendships with men and this had brightened him amazingly. He had a new interest in business things, new hopes. It had seemed to make him younger, keener. He and Mr. Stoddard had a plan for going into Montana where the latter was interested in a land developing company, and going into business together. Stuart was alive with interest in it; it promised new things for him, a new chance. They would live in a town, and it would be business life, which he cared for as he had never come to care for ranching. He was be-

ginning to talk to Ruth about moving, of selling
off their stock and some of their things. He was
eager to make the change.

She had gone in the house as the machine
stopped, having seen that there were people in
the car with Mr. Stoddard and not feeling pre-
sentably dressed. She went upstairs to do the
work and as she glanced down from the upper
window she saw Stuart in laughing conversation
with a girl in the automobile. Something about
it arrested her. He was standing to the far side
of the machine so she could see his face. There
was something in it she had not seen for a long
time—that interest in women, an unmistakable
pleasure in talking with an attractive girl. She
stood there, a little back from the window, watching them. There was nothing at all wrong about
it; nothing to resent, simply a little gay bantering with a girl. It was natural to him; it had
been once, it could be again. His laugh came up
to her. So he could still laugh like that; she had
not heard him for a long time. He turned and
started hurriedly for the house, the car waiting
for him. He was smiling, his step was buoyant.
"Ruth," he called up to her, and his voice too
had the old buoyancy, "I'm going into town with
Stoddard. We want to go over some things.
He'll bring me back before night."

"All right, Stuart," she called back pleasantly.
She watched the car out of sight. Stuart, sit-

ting in the front seat with his friend, had turned and was gayly talking with the women behind. When she first knew him, when she was still a little girl and used to see him around with his own set, he had been like that.

She did not want to stay in the house. That house had shut her in all winter. The road stretched invitingly away. About a mile down it there was a creek, willows grew there. Perhaps there she would find some real spring. Anyway she had an impulse to get out to the moving water. She had seemed locked in, everything had seemed locked in for so long.

As she was getting her coat she put into the pocket a letter she had received the day before from Deane Franklin. After she had sat a little while by the running water she took the letter out to reread, but did not at first open it. She was wishing Deane were sitting there with her. She would like to talk to him.

This letter was a gloomy one. It seemed that Deane too was locked in. Soon after Ted came back from Freeport in the fall she had got it out of him about the Franklins. She had sensed at once that there was something about Deane he did not want to tell her, and before he left for his own place she had it from him that the Franklins had indeed separated, and that the gossip of Freeport was that it was because of Mrs. Franklin's resentment of her. And that was one of the things had seemed to make it possible for the winter somehow to *take* her; that was the thing had seemed to close the last door to her spirit, the last of those doors that had been thrown wide open when she left Annie's home in Freeport the spring before.

She had tried to write to Deane. She felt that she should write to him, but she had a feeling of powerlessness. Finally, only a little while before, she had brought herself to do it. She knew it was a poor letter, a halting, constrained thing, but it seemed the best she could do, and so finally, after a great deal of uncertainty, she sent it.

His reply made her feel that he realized how it had been, why she had been so long in writing, why the letter had been the stilted thing it was. It gave her a feeling that her friend had not withdrawn from her because of what she had brought down upon him, that that open channel between him and her was there as it had ever been. And though his letter did not make her happy, it loosened something in her to be able to feel that the way between her and Deane was not closed.

"Don't distress yourself, Ruth," she now re-read, "or have it upon your spirit, where too much has lain heavy all these years. You want to know the truth, and the truth is that Amy did resent my feeling about you—about you and your situation—and that put us apart. But you see it was not in us to stay together, or we could not have been thus put apart. Love can't do it all, Ruth—not for long; I mean love that hasn't roots down in the spirit can't. And where there isn't that spiritual underneath, without a hinterland, love is pretty insecure.

"I could have held on to it a while longer, I suppose, by cutting clear loose from the thing really me. And I suppose I would have done it if I could—I did in fact make attempts at it—but that me-ness, I'm afraid, is most infernal strong in my miserable make-up. And somehow the withdrawal of one's self seems a lot to pay for even the happiness of love. There are some of us can't seem able to do it.

"So it's not you, Ruth; it's that it was like that, and that it came out through the controversy about you. Cast from your mind any feeling adding the wrecking of my happiness to your list of crimes.

"But, Ruth, I'm *not* happy. I couldn't get along in happiness, and I don't get along without it. It's a paralyzing thing not to have happiness—or to lose it, rather. Does it ever seem to you that life is a pretty paralyzing thing? That little by little—a little here and a little there—it *gets* us? We get harness-broke, you see. Seems to have gone that way with most of the people I know. Seems to be that way with me. Don't let it do it to you!

"Somehow I don't believe it will. I think that you, Ruth, would be a fine little prison-breaker. Might stand some show of being one myself if I were anywhere but in this town. There's something about it that has *got* me, Ruth. If it hadn't —I'd be getting out of it now.

"But of course I'm a pretty poor sort, not worth making a fight for, or it wouldn't be like this. And—for that matter—what's the difference? Lives aren't counting for much these days —men who *are* the right sort going down by the thousands, by the hundred of thousands, so what —for heaven's sake—does it matter about me?

"I wish I could see you!

"I'm glad for you about the divorce. I believe the case comes up this April term, so it may be all over by the time you get this letter. Pretty late in coming, and I suppose it must seem a good deal of a mockery—getting it now—but maybe it will help some for the future, make you feel more comfortable, and I'm awfully glad.

"Funny about it, isn't it? I wonder what made her do it! I was called there this winter, maid sick—miscarriage—and Mrs. Williams puzzled me. Didn't turn the girl out, awfully decent to her. I would have supposed she would have been quite the other way. And now this. Queer, don't you think?

"Write to me sometimes, Ruth. Sometimes write to me what you're thinking about. Maybe it will stir me up. Write to me to take a brace and get out of this town! If you went for me hard enough, called me all the insulting names you could think of, and told me a living dead man was the most cowardly and most disgusting object cluttering up the earth, you might get a rise out of me. You're the one could do it, if it can be done.

"One thing I *do* know—writing this has made me want like blazes to see you!

"DEANE."

Ruth sat there in the arm of a low willow, her hands resting upon Deane's letter, her eyes closed, the faint breath of coming spring upon her face. She was tired and very sad. She was thinking of Deane's life, of her own life, of the way one seemed mocked. She wished that Deane were there; she could talk to him and she would like to talk. His letter moved something in her, something that had long seemed locked in stirred a little. Her feeling about life had seemed a thing frozen within her. Now the feeling that there was still this' open channel between her and Deane was as a thawing, an outlet.

She thought of her last talk with Deane, of their walk together that day, almost a year before, when he came to see her at Annie's, the very day she was starting back West. She had felt anything but locked in that day. There was that triumphant sense of openness to life, the joy of new interest in it, of zest for it. And then she came back West, to Stuart, and somehow the radiance went, courage ebbed, it came to seem that life was all fixed, almost as if life, in the real sense, was over. That sense of having failed, having been inadequate to her own feeling, struck her down to a wretched powerlessness. And so routine, hard work, bitter cold, loneliness, that sense of the cruelty of life which the sternness of the country gave—those things had been able to take her; it was because something had gone dead in her.

She thought of that spiritual hinterland Deane talked about. She thought of her and Stuart. She grew very sad in the thinking. She wondered if it was her fault. However it was, it was true they no longer found the live things in one another. She had not been able to communicate to him the feeling with which she came back from Annie's. It was a lesser thing for trying to talk of it to him. She did not reach him; she knew that he only thought her a little absurd. After that she did not try to talk to him of what she felt. Life lessened; things were as they were; they too were as they were. It came to seem just a matter of following out what had been begun. And then that news of the divorce had come to mock her.

But she must do something for Deane. Deane must not go like that. She had brought pencil and

writing tablet with her, thinking that perhaps out
of doors, away from the house where she had
seemed locked in all winter, she could write to him.
She thought of things to say, things that should be
said, but she did not seem to have any power to
charge them with life.   How could the dead rouse
the dead?   She sat there thinking of her and
Deane, of how they had always been able to reach
one another.   And finally she began:

"Dear Deane,
"You must find your way back to life."

She did not go on.   She sat staring at what she
had written.   She read it over; she said it aloud.
It surged in upon her, into shut places.   She sat
looking at it, frightened at what it was doing.   Sat
looking at it after it was all blurred by tears—
looking down at the words she herself had written
—"You must find your way back to life."

CHAPTER THIRTY-THREE

Ruth was very quiet through the next week. Stuart was preoccupied with the plans he was making for going to Montana; when he talked with her it was of that, of arrangements to be made for it, and his own absorption apparently kept him from taking note of her being more quiet than usual, or different. It was all working out very well. He had found a renter for the ranch, the prospects for the venture in Montana were good. They were to move within a month. And one night in late April when he came home from town he handed Ruth a long envelope, with a laughing, "Better late than never." Then he was soon deep in some papers.

Ruth was sorting a box of things; there were many things to be gone through preparatory to moving. She had put the paper announcing his divorce aside without comment; but she loitered over what she was doing. She was watching Stuart, thinking about him.

She was thinking with satisfaction that he looked well. He had thrown off the trouble that had brought about their departure from Freeport twelve years before. He was growing rather stout; his fair hair had gone somewhat gray and his face was lined, he had not the look of a young man. But he looked strong, alert. His new hopes had given him vigor, a new buoyancy. She sat there thinking of the years she had lived with him, of the wonder and the happiness she had known through him, of the hard things they had faced together. Her voice was gentle as she replied to his inquiry about what day of the month it was.

"I think," he said, "that we can get off by the fifteenth, don't you, Ruth?"

"Perhaps." Her voice shook a little, but he was following his own thoughts and did not notice. After a little he came and sat across the table from her. "And, Ruth, about this getting married business—" He broke off with a laugh. "Seems absurd, doesn't it?"

She nodded, fumbling with the things in the box, her head bent over them.

"Well, I was thinking we'd better stop somewhere along the way and attend to it. Can't do it here—don't want to there."

She lifted her hands from the box and laid them on the table that was between him and her. She looked over at him and said, quietly, in a voice that shook only a little: "I do not want to get married, Stuart."

He was filling his pipe and stopped abruptly, spilling the tobacco on the table. "What did you say?" he asked in the voice of one sure he must have heard wrong.

"I said," she repeated, "that I did not want to get married."

He stared at her, his face screwed up. Then it relaxed a little. "Oh, yes—yes, I know how you feel. It seems so absurd—after all this time—after all there has been. But we must attend to it, Ruth. It's right that we should—now that we can. God knows we wanted to bad enough—long ago. And it will make us feel better about going into a new place. We can face people better." He gathered up the tobacco he had spilled and put it in his pipe.

For a moment she did not speak. Then, "That wasn't what I meant, Stuart," she said, falteringly.

"Well, then, what in the world *do* you mean?" he asked impatiently.

She did not at once say what she meant. Her eyes held him, they were so strangely steady. "Just why would we be getting married, Stuart?" she asked simply.

At first he could only stare at her, appeared to be waiting for her to throw light on what she had asked. When she did not do that he moved impatiently, as if resentful of being quizzed this way. "Why—why, because we can now. Because it's the thing to do. Because it will be expected of us," he concluded, with gathering impatience for this unnecessary explanation.

A faint smile traced itself about Ruth's mouth,

It made her face very sad as she said: "I do not seem to be anxious to marry for any of those reasons, Stuart."

"Ruth, what are you driving at?" he demanded, thoroughly vexed at the way she had bewildered him.

"This is what I am driving at, Stuart," she began, a little more spiritedly. But then she stopped, as if dumb before it. She looked over at him as if hoping her eyes would tell it for her. But as he continued in that look of waiting, impatient bewilderment she sighed and turned a little away. "Don't you think, Stuart," she asked, her voice low, "that the future is rather too important a thing to be given up to ratifying the past?"

He pushed his chair back in impatience that was mounting to anger. "Just what do you mean?" he asked, stiffly.

She picked up the long envelope lying on the table between them. She held it in her hand a moment without speaking. For as she touched it she had a sense of what it would have meant to have held it in her hand twelve years before, over on the other side of their life together, a new sense of the irony and the pity of not having had it then —and having it now. She laid it down between them. "To me," she said, "this sets me free.

"Free to choose," she went on, as he only stared at her. There was a moment of looking at him out of eyes so full of feeling that they held back the feeling that had flushed his face. "And my choice," she said, with a strange steadiness, "is that I now go my way alone."

He spoke then; but it was only to stammer: "Why,—*Ruth!*" Helplessly he repeated: "*Ruth!*".

"But you see? You do see?" she cried. "If it had *not* been so much—so beautiful! Just because it *was* what it was—" She choked and could not go on.

He came around and sat down beside her. The seriousness of his face, something she had touched in him, made it finer than it had been in those last years of routine. It was more as it used to be. His voice too seemed out of old days as he said: "Ruth, I don't know yet what you mean—why you're saying this?"

"I think you do, Stuart," she said simply. "Or I think you will, if you'll let yourself. It's simply that this—" she touched the envelope on the table before her—"that this finds us over on the other side of marriage. And this is what I mean!" she flamed. "I mean that the marriage between us was too real to go through the mockery this would make possible now!" She turned away because she was close to tears.

He sat there in silence. Then, "Have I done anything, Ruth?" he asked in the hesitating way of one at sea.

She shook her head without turning back to him.

"You apparently have got the impression," he went on, a faint touch of resentment creeping into his voice at having to make the declaration, "that I don't care any more. That—that isn't so," he said awkwardly and with a little rise of resentment.

Ruth had turned a little more toward him, but was looking down at her hands, working with them as if struggling for better control. "I have no—complaint on that score," she said very low.

"Things change," he went on, with a more open manner of defence. "The first kind of love doesn't last forever. It doesn't with anyone," he finished, rather sullenly.

"I know that, Stuart," she said quietly. "I know enough to know that. But I know this as well. I know that sometimes that first kind of love leaves a living thing to live by. I know that it does—sometimes. And I know that with us—it hasn't."

As if stung by that he got up and began walking angrily about the room. "You're talking nonsense! Why wouldn't we get married, I'd like to know, after all this time together? We *will* get married—that's all there is to it! A nice spectacle we would make of ourselves if we didn't! Have you thought of that?" he demanded. "Have you thought of what people would say?"

Again her lips traced that faint smile that

showed the sadness of her face. "There was a time, Stuart," she said wearily, "when we were not governed by what people would say."

He frowned, but went on more mildly: "You've got the thing all twisted up, Ruth. You do that sometimes. You often have a queer way of looking at a thing; not the usual way—a—well, a sort of twisted way."

She got up. One hand was at her throat as if feeling some impediment there; the knuckles of her clenched hand were tapping the table. "A queer way of looking at things," she said in quick, sharp voice that was like the tapping of her knuckles. "Not the usual way. A—sort of twisted way. Perhaps. Perhaps that's true. Perhaps that was the way I had of looking at things twelve years ago—when I left them all behind and went with you. Perhaps that was what made me do it—that queer, twisted way of looking at things! But this much is true, Stuart, and this you have got to know is true. I went with you because I was as I was. I'm going my way alone now because I am as I am. And what you don't see is this,—that the thing that made me go with you then is the thing that makes me go my way alone now."

For a moment they stood there facing each other, her eyes forcing home what she had said. But she was trembling and suddenly, weakly, she sat down.

"Well, I simply can't understand it!" he cried petulantly and flung open the door and stood looking out.

"Look here, Ruth," he turned sharply to her after a little, "have you thought of the position this puts *me* in? Have you thought of the position you would put *me* in?" he contended hotly. "Do you know what people would say about me? You ought to know what they'd say! They'd say *I* was the one!—they'd say *I* didn't want to do it!"

There was a little catch something like a laugh as she replied: "Of course. They'll say men don't marry women of that sort, won't they?"

"Oh, you can't do this, Ruth," he went on quickly. "You see, it can't be done. I tell you it wouldn't be right! It just wouldn't be *right*— in any sense. Why can't you see that? Can't you see that we've got to vindicate the whole thing? That we've got to show them that it *does* last! That's the vindication for it," he finished stoutly, "that it's the kind of a love that doesn't die!

"And I'd like to know where under the sun you'd go!" he demanded hotly, irritated at the slight smile his last words had brought.

"What I will do, Stuart, after leaving you, is for me to determine, isn't it?"

"A nice way to treat me!" he cried, and threw himself down on the couch, elbows on his knees and his face buried in his hands. "After all these years—after all there has been—that's a *nice* way —" he choked.

She was quick to go over and sit beside him; she leaned a little against him, her hand on his arm, just as she had sat many times when he needed her, when she brought him comfort. The thought of all those times rose in her and brought tears to her eyes that had been burning dry a moment before. She felt the feeling this had whipped to life in him and was moved by it, and by an underlying feeling of the sadness of change. For his expostulations spoke of just that—change. She knew this for the last hurt she could help him through, that she must help him through this hurt brought him by this last thing she could do for him. Something about things being like that moved her deeply. She saw it all so clearly, and so sadly. It was not grief this brought him; this was not the frenzy or the anguish in the thought of losing her that there would have been in those other years. It was shock, rather—disturbance, and the forcing home to him that sense of change. He would have gone on without much taking stock, because, as he had said, it was the thing to do. Habit, a sense of fitness, rather than deep personal need, would have made him go on. And now it was his sense that it was gone, his resentment against that, his momentary feeling of being left desolate. She looked at his bowed head through tears. Gently she laid her hand on it. She thought of him as he stood before the automobile the other day lighting up in the gay talk with that girl. She knew, with a sudden wrench in her heart she knew it, that he would not be long desolate. She understood him too well for that. She knew that, hard as she seemed in that hour, she was doing for Stuart in leaving him the greatest thing she could now do for him. A tear fell to her hand in her clear knowing of that. There was deep sadness in knowing that, after all there had been, to leave the way cleared of herself was doing a greater thing than anything else she could do for him.

A sob shook her and he raised his face upon which there were tears and clutched her two wrists with his hands. "Ruth," he whispered, "it will come back. I feel that this has—has brought it back."

The look of old feeling had transformed his face. After barren days it was sweet to her. It tempted her, tempted her to shut her eyes to what she knew and sink into the sweetness of believing herself loving and loved again. Perhaps, for a little time, they could do it. To be deeply swayed by this common feeling, to go together in an emotion, was like dear days gone. But it was her very fidelity to those days gone that made her draw just a little away, and, tears running down her face, shake her head. She knew too well, and she had the courage of her knowing. This was something that had seeped up from old feeling; it had no life of its own. What they were sharing now was grief over a dead thing that had been theirs together. That grief, that sharing, left them tender. This was their moment—their moment for leaving it. They must leave it before it lay there between them both dead and unmourned, clogging life for them. She whispered to him: "Just because of all it has meant—let's leave it while we can leave it like this!"

CHAPTER THIRTY-FOUR

The man who worked for them had gone ahead in the spring wagon with her trunk. She was waiting for Ted to hitch the other horse to the buggy and drive her in to the train. She was all ready and stood there looking about the house she was leaving. There were things in that room which they had had since their first years together —that couch, this chair, had come to them in Arizona in the days when they loved each other with a passion that made everything else in the world a pale thing before their love. She stood picking out things that they had had when love was flaming strong in them and it seemed they two fought together against the whole world. And as she stood there alone in their place in common that she was about to leave she was made sick by a sense of failure—that desolate sense of failure she had tried all along to beat down. That love had been theirs—and this was what it had come to. That wonder had been—and it ended in the misery of this leavetaking. She turned sharply around, opened the door and stood there in the doorway, her back to the place she was quitting, her pale stern face turned to the mountains—to that eastern range which she was going to cross. She tried to draw something from them, draw strength for the final conflict which she knew she would have with Ted while they drove in to town. She looked toward the barn-yard to see if he was most ready, and could not but smile a little at his grim, resolute face as he was checking up the horse. She could see so well that he was going to make the best of his time while driving her in to the train. And it seemed she had nothing left in her for combat; she would be glad to see the train that was to take her away.

Three days before Stuart had gone suddenly to Denver. He went with his friend Stoddard, regarding some of their arrangements for Montana. He had found only at the last minute that he would have to go, had hurriedly driven out from town to get his things and tell her he was going. He had been in the house only a few minutes and was all excitement about the unexpected trip. It was two days after their talk. After their moment of being swept together by the feeling of things gone he had, as if having to get a footing on every-day ground, ended the talk with saying: "I'll tell you, Ruth, you need a little change. We'll have to work it out." The next day they were both subdued, more gentle with each other than they had been of late, but they did not refer to the night before. After he had hurriedly kissed her good-by when leaving for Denver he had turned back and said, "And don't you worry—

about things, Ruth. We'll get everything fixed up
—and a little change—'' He had hurried down to
the machine without finishing it.

She had gone to the window and watched him
disappear. He was sitting erect, alert, talking
animatedly with his friend. She watched him as
far as she could see him. She knew that she would
not see him again.

And then she hitched up the horse and drove
into town and telephoned Ted, who lived about
fifty miles to the north. She told him that she was
going East and asked him to come down the next
day and see her.

She had known that Ted would not approve,
would not understand, but she had not expected
him to make the fight he had. It had taken every
bit of her will, her force, to meet him. Worn now,
and under the stress of the taking leave, at once
too tired and too emotional, she wished that he
would let it rest. But the grim line of his jaw
told her that he had no such intention. She felt
almost faint as they drove through the gate. She
closed her eyes and did not open them for some
time.

"You see, Ruth," Ted began gently, as if
realizing that she was very worn, "you just don't
realize how crazy the whole thing is. It's ridiculous for you to go to New York—alone! You've
never been there," he said firmly.

"No. That is one reason for going," she answered, rather feebly.

"One reason for going!" he cried. "What'll you do when the train pulls in? Where'll you *go?*"

"I don't know, Ted," she said patiently, "just where I will go. And I rather like that—not knowing where I will go. It's all new, you see. Nothing is mapped out."

"It's a fool thing!" he cried. "Don't you know that something will happen to you?"

She smiled a little, very wearily. "Lots of things have happened to me, Ted, and I've come through them somehow." After a moment she added, with more spirit: "There's just one thing might happen to me that I haven't the courage to face." He looked at her inquiringly. "Nothing happening," she said, with a little smile.

He turned impatiently and slapped the horse with the reins. "You seem to have lost your senses," he said sharply.

He drove along in silence for a little. Ruth looked at him and his face seemed hard. She thought of how close she and Ted had come, how good he had been, how much it had meant. She could not leave him like this. She must make the effort, must gather herself together and try and make Ted see. "Perhaps, Ted," she began tremulously, "you think I have taken leave of my senses because you haven't tried very hard to understand just what it is I feel.'' She smiled wanly as she added, ''You've been so absorbed in your own disapproval, you know.''

''Well, how can I be any other way?'' he demanded. ''Going away like this—for no reason —on a wild goose chase! Isn't Stuart good to you?'' he asked abruptly.

''Yes, Ted,'' she answered, as if she were tired of saying it, ''Stuart is good enough to me.''

''I suppose things aren't—just as they used to be,'' he went on, a little doggedly. ''Heavens!— they aren't with anybody! And what will people say?'' he broke out with new force. ''Think of what people in Freeport will say, Ruth. They'll say the whole thing was a failure, and that it was because you did wrong. They'll say, when the chance finally came, that Stuart didn't want to marry you.'' He colored but brought it out bluntly.

''I suppose they will,'' agreed Ruth.

''And if they knew the truth—or what I know, though heaven knows I'm balled up enough about what the truth really is!—they'd say it just shows again that you are different, not—something wrong,'' he finished bitterly.

She said nothing for a moment. ''And is that what you think, Ted?'' she asked, choking a little.

''I don't understand it, Ruth,'' he said, less ag-

gressively. "I had thought you would be so glad
of the chance to marry. I—" he hesitated but
did not pursue that. He had never told her of
going to see Mrs. Williams, of the effort he had
made for her. "It seemed that now, when your
chance came, you ought to show people that you
do want to do the right thing. It surprises me a
lot, Ruth, that you don't feel that way, and—Oh!
I don't get it at all," he concluded abruptly.

Tears were very close when, after a little, she
answered: "Well, Ted, maybe when you have
less of life left you will understand better what
it is I feel. Perhaps," she went on in answer to
his look inquiry, "when the future has shrunk
down to fewer years you'll see it as more important to get from it what you can."

They drove for a little time in silence. They
had come in sight of the town and she had not
won Ted; she was going away without his sympathy. And she was going away alone, more
alone this time than she had been twelve years before.

She laid her hand on his arm, left it there while
she was speaking. "Ted," she said, "it's like
this. This has gone for me. It's all gone. It
was wonderful—but it's gone. Some people, I
know, could go on with the life love had made
after love was gone. I am not one of those people—that's all. You speak of there being something discreditable in my going away just when

I could marry. To me there would be something discreditable in going on. It would be—" she put her hand over her heart and said it very simply, "it would be unfaithful to something here." She choked a little and he turned away.

"But I don't see how you can bear, Ruth," he said after a moment, made gentle by her confidence, "to feel that it has—failed. I don't see how you can bear—after all you paid for it—to let it come to nothing."

"Don't say that, Ted!" she cried in a voice that told he had touched the sorest place. "Don't say that!" she repeated, a little wildly. "You don't know what you're talking about. *Failed?* A thing that glorified life for years—*failed?*"

Her voice broke, but it was more steadily she went on: "That's the very reason I'm going to New York—simply that it may *not* come to nothing. I'm going away from it for that very reason —that it may not come to nothing! That my life may not come to nothing. What I've had—what I've gone through—lives in me, Ted. It doesn't come to nothing if I—come to something!" She stopped abruptly with a choking little laugh.

Ted looked at her wonderingly; but the hardness had gone out of his look. "But what are you going to do, Ruth?" he asked gently.

"I don't know yet. I've got to find out."

"You must see that I can't help but worry about it," he went on. "Going so far away—to a place absolutely unknown to you—where I'm afraid it will be so much harder than you think.''

She did not answer him, looking off to that eastern range she was going to cross, as if the mountains could help her to hold on to her own feeling against the doubts he was trying to throw around her.

''You see, Ruth,'' he went on, as if feeling his way, not wanting to hurt her, ''what has been may make it hard to go on. You can't tell. You'll never know—never be sure. Old things may come up to spoil new ones for you. That's what I'm so afraid of. That's what it seems you aren't seeing. You would be so much—safer—to stay with Stuart.''

She turned to him with a little laugh, her lashes wet. ''Yes, Ted dear, I suppose I would. But I never did seem to stay where I was safest—did I?''

''Don't worry about me, Ted,'' she said just as they were coming into town. ''I'm going to take some of father's money—yes, yes, I know it isn't a great deal, but enough for a little while, till I get my bearings—and I'm going to make things come alive for me again. I'm not through yet, that's all. I could have stayed with life gone dead; it would have been safer, as you say. But you see I'm not through yet, Ted—I guess that's the secret of it all. I want more life—more things from life. And I'm going to New York just be-

cause it will be so completely new—so completely
beginning new—and because it's the center of so
many living things. And it's such a wonderful
time, Ted. It seems to me the war is going to
make a new world—a whole new way of looking
at things. It's as if a lot of old things, old ideas,
had been melted, and were fluid now, and were
to be shaped anew. That's the way it seems to
me, and that makes me the more eager to get some
things from life that I haven't had. I've been
shut in with my own experience. If I stayed on
here I'd be shut in with my own dead experiences.
I want to go on! I can't stop here—that's all.
And we have to find our way for going on. We
must find our own way, Ted, even," she choked,
"though what we see as the way may seem a wild
goose chase to some one we love. I'll tell you
why I'm going to New York," she flashed with
sudden defiance. "I'm going because I want
to!"

She laughed a little and he laughed with her.
Then she went on more gently: "Because I want
to. Just the thought of it has made life come
alive for me—that's reason enough for going to
the ends of the earth! I'm going to *live* again,
Ted—not just go on with what living has left.
I'm going to find some work to do. Yes I *can!*"
she cried passionately in response to his gesture.
"I suppose to you it seems just looking out for
myself—seems unfaithful to Stuart. Well, it

isn't—that's all I can say, and maybe some day you'll see that it wasn't. It isn't unfaithful to turn from a person you have nothing more to offer, for whom you no longer make life a living thing. It's more faithful to go. You'll see that some time, Ted. But be good to Stuart," she hastily added. "You stay with him till he can get off. I've made all the arrangements with Mrs. Baxter for packing up—sending on the things. It would be hard for him to do that, I know. And once away from here—new interests —life all new again—oh, no, Ted dear," she laughed a little chokingly, "don't worry about Stuart."

"I'm not worrying about Stuart," he muttered. "I'm worrying about you."

She squeezed his arm in affectionate gratitude for the love in the growling words. "Don't *worry* about me, Ted," she implored, "be glad with me! I'm alive again! It's so wonderful to be alive again. There's the future—a great, beautiful unknown. It *is* wonderful, Ted," she said with insistence, as if she would banish his fears— and her own.

They had a few minutes to wait, and Ted ran over to the postoffice to get her mail for her—she was expecting a paper she wanted to read on the train. She tucked what he handed her into her bag and then when she heard the train coming she held on to Ted's arm, held it as if she could not bear let-

ting it go. "It's all right," were her last words
to him, smiling through tears.

She had been trying all along to hold her mind
from the thought that they would pass through
Freeport. Late the next afternoon, when she
knew they were nearing it, she grew restless. It
was then she remembered the paper in her bag—
she had been in no mood for reading, too charged
with her own feeling. She got it out now and
found that with the paper was a letter. It was a
letter from Deane Franklin.

She held it for a little while without opening it.
It seemed so strange to have it just as she was
nearing Freeport.

The letter was dated the week before. It read:

"Dear Ruth:

"I'm leaving Freeport tonight. I'm going to
Europe—to volunteer my services as a doctor.
Parker, whom I knew well at Hopkins, is right in
the midst of it. He can work me in. And the
need for doctors is going to go on for some time,
I fancy; it won't end with the war.

"I'm happy in this decision, Ruth, and I know
you'll be glad for me. It was your letter that got
me—made me see myself and hate myself, made
me know that I had to 'come out of it.' And then
this idea came to me, and I wish I could tell you
how different everything seemed as soon as I saw

some reason for my existence. I'm ashamed of
myself for not having seen it this way before. As
if this were any time for a man who's had my
training to sit around moping!

"Life is bigger than just ourselves. And isn't
it curious how seeing that brings us back to ourselves?

"I'll enclose Parker's address. You can reach
me in care of him. I want to hear from you.

"I can hardly wait to get there!

"DEANE."

She managed to read the letter through with
eyes only a little dimmed. But by the time she
got to Parker's address she could not make it out.
"I knew it!" she kept saying to herself triumphantly.

Deane had been too big not to save himself.
Absorbed in thoughts of him she did not notice
the country through which they were passing.
She was startled by a jolt of the train, by the con-
ductor saying, "Freeport!"

For several minutes the train waited there. She
sat motionless through that time, Deane Franklin's letter clasped tight in her hand. Freeport!
It claimed her:—what had been, what was behind
her; those dead who lived in her, her own past
that lived in her. Freeport. . . . It laid strong
hold on her. She was held there in what had
been. And then a great thing happened. The

train jolted again—moved. It was moving—moving on. *She* was moving—moving on. And she knew then beyond the power of anyone's disapproval to break down that it was right she move on. She had a feeling of the whole flow of her life—and it was still moving—moving on. And because she felt she was moving on that sense of failure slipped from her. In secret she had been fighting that all along. Now she knew that love had not failed because love had transpired into life. What she had paid the great price for was not hers to the end. But what it had made of her was hers! Love could not fail if it left one richer than it had found one. Love had not failed—nothing had failed—and life was wonderful, limitless, a great adventure for which one must have great courage, glad faith. Let come what would come!—she was moving on.

THE END

RETURN TO ➡ CIRCULATION DEPARTMENT
202 Main Library

LOAN PERIOD 1 **HOME USE**	2	3
4	5	6

ALL BOOKS MAY BE RECALLED AFTER 7 DAYS
1-month loans may be renewed by calling 642-3405
1-year loans may be recharged by bringing the books to the Circulation Desk
Renewals and recharges may be made 4 days prior to due date

DUE AS STAMPED BELOW

REC. CIR. DEC 8 83		
SENT ON ILL		
MAR - 5 1997		
U. C. BERKELEY		

UNIVERSITY OF CALIFORNIA, BERKELEY
FORM NO. DD6, 60m, 1/83   BERKELEY, CA 94720

Ⓟs

Lightning Source UK Ltd.
Milton Keynes UK
UKOW06f1305150415

249698UK00007B/129/P